Masculine Shame

Masculine Shame: From Succubus to the Eternal Feminine explores the idea that the image of the succubus, a demonic female creature said to emasculate men and murder mothers and infants, has been created out of the masculine projection of shame and looks at how the transformation of this image can be traced through Western history, mythology, and Judeo-Christian literature.

Divided into three parts areas of discussion include:

- the birth of civilization and the evolution of the succubus
- the image of the succubus in the writings of Freud and Jung
- the succubus as child-killing mother to the restoration of the eternal feminine.

Through a process of detailed cultural and social analysis this book places the image of the succubus at the very heart of psychoanalytic thought, as seen vividly in both Freud's Medusa and Jung's visions of Salome. As such this book will be of great interest to all those in the fields of analytical psychotherapy and psychoanalysis.

Mary Y. Ayers, Ph.D. is the author of *Mother-Infant Attachment and Psychoanalysis: The Eyes of Shame* (Routledge, 2003), winner of the NAAP Gradiva Award (2004). She currently works in private practice in the suburbs of Washington, D.C. where she specializes in analytic work with children and adults.

Masculine Shame

From Succubus to the Eternal Feminine

Mary Y. Ayers

Routledge
Taylor & Francis Group
LONDON AND NEW YORK

First published 2011
by Routledge
27 Church Road, Hove, East Sussex, BN3 2FA

Simultaneously published in the USA and Canada
by Routledge
711 Third Avenue, New York, NY 10017

Routledge is an imprint of the Taylor & Francis Group, an Informa business

Typeset in Times New Roman by RefineCatch Limited, Bungay, Suffolk
Printed and bound in Great Britain by TJ International Ltd, Padstow, Cornwall
Paperback cover design by Andrew Ward

This publication has been produced with paper manufactured to strict environmental standards and with pulp derived from sustainable forests.

British Library Cataloguing in Publication Data
A catalogue record for this book is available from the British Library

Library of Congress Cataloging-in-Publication Data
Ayers, Mary, 1960–
Masculine shame: from succubus to the eternal feminine/Mary Y. Ayers. — 1st ed.
p. cm.
ISBN 978–0–415–39038–5 (hardback) — ISBN 978–0–415–39039–2 (pbk.) 1. Demonology. 2. Parapsychology. 3. Subconsciousness. 4. Freud, Sigmund, 1856–1939. 5. Jung, C. G. (Carl Gustav), 1875–1961. I. Title.
BF1531.A94 2010
150.19'5—dc22

2010028857

ISBN: 978–0–415–39038–5 (hbk)
ISBN: 978–0–415–39039–2 (pbk)

To the Eternal Feminine: may her restoration through this look into her eyes of shame bring about the harmonious balance of male and female forces

and

This book is dedicated to the memory of the late Roger Lyons, the man who helped me learn to think

Contents

Figures

Those Thy lovely forms
in the Three Worlds,
And those Thy furious forms,
Save us in all of them.
(Devi-Mahatmya)

May the eye not be turned to the outside
Lest it simultaneously drive out the images.
(Sister Elsbet Stagel of the Toss
Monastery, fourteenth century)

It is better to light one candle than curse the darkness
(Adage)

...But whate'er shall I be
Nor I, nor any man that but man is,
With nothing shall be pleased, till he be eased
With being nothing...
(Shakespeare, *Richard III*, V5: 38)

Preface

> Midway along the journey of life
> I woke to find myself in a dark wood
> For I had wandered off from the straight path.
> (Dante, *Inferno*, Canto 1)

"If one understands shame, one understands humanity." As I was incubating my ideas for a book that analyzed masculine shame through the image of the eye, this seemingly simple sentence obsessively pressed itself into my mind. I didn't understand the thought, and so it opened up several questions. What can be understood about humanity through an understanding of shame? Does humanity mean humankind, male and female, or does humanity mean the qualities of being good which can inform human action? Does the affect of shame encompass this kind of breadth and depth in the human psyche? This edition on shame is my reflection on these questions.

Differentiating masculine shame from feminine shame was a distinction that had been completely overlooked in my first book (Ayers, 2003), and the source from which my current writing extends, mainly because by examining shame through its quintessential developmental and archetypal image – the human eye – I was scrutinizing shame like a tree in the forest. So of course I missed the forest through the trees. This oversight was brought to my attention by one of the anonymous reviewers (to whom I am truly indebted), who commented that one of its obvious omissions was gender differences. Eager to get the book done, I added a few cursory paragraphs (2003: 76–77).

But I did not escape the matter; left with an insistent, gnawing feeling, the importance of the distinction continued to grow daily in my mind. Little did I know then that my further attempts to address this omission would result in another book on shame, or that I would discover a ubiquitous dynamic that undermines yet dominates relationships among men and women. My research led me into the "forest" of shame, a place of patriarchal dominance deep in the collective unconscious where men as well as women live in absolute shame. This book, then, forms an attempt to translate the unknown darkness in this forest, an articulation of shame's archetypal pattern in order to create a new way of communicating about it in the field of depth psychology.

Thus far, I have learned that masculine shame is not male specifically (just as feminine shame is not limited to females), but is, rather, a type of shame that belongs to the masculine engendered collective psychic reality called patriarchy and its consequent gender images of male and female. The core disturbance in this type of shame entails elimination through annihilation because the good maternal aspects of the feminine principle become absent in an early and deep psychic place. This developmental derailment naturally resonates with the repression of the maternal feminine on the collective, archetypal level. The dynamics resulting from this lie at the heart of why humankind is presently threatened with losing its humanity and true empathy, as well as the ability to love and relate. What maternal feminine absence combines to create for all of us is an untenable and dangerous psychic and social situation. On a personal level, we lose our ability to be and become, to give real value, meaning and direction to our existence. On a collective level, we compromise our convictions and act without conscience. Patriarchy may provide the structure for civilization, but the very soul of our humanity is eroding while we stay petrified; staring into the eyes of Medusa, we fall headlong towards forces that have the potential to destroy both natural and civilized life on our planet today. The reverberations of shame – that endanger sanity and soul, the self, the world, and human life on our planet earth – are indeed profound.

A woman must encounter her nothingness – survive her non-existence – in order to transcend her shame and experience the power of being that gives her the confidence to take responsibility and truly love (Ayers, 2003); in this book, the focus is on a man's need to actualize the shame hidden in his patriarchal concepts of masculinity in order to acquire authentic power within the depth of his own being through a relationship to the maternal feminine – not external power over, or the kind of bullying, militaristic power to take away, destroy, terrorize or victimize that dominates our world today. Perhaps with a power balance and equality restored, the seeds can be sown for compassion, peace, partnership, creative and active hope, and a love that can generate a greater humanity that extends all the way to our care and protection of the earth itself. This is the essence of the idea which will be explained in the pages to come.

Maternal femininity is the carrier for shame, and so the oppression of women provides the archetypal fuel, so to speak, for shame's annihilating capacity to create non-existence. The story of shame deep in the forest commences during a time when, in the then civilized world, the Goddess was steadily being displaced by warlike male gods, and culture was beginning to be dominated by the idea of a warrior monarch triumphing in the humiliation and slaughter of the enemy. This great but devastating change first arose around the fifth millennium B.C., when "high" civilization came to be characterized by the concerns for an institutionalized patriarchy, which in turn created a division of labor, a socially stratified organization, large-scale warfare, economic exploitation, and political relations. Psychologically speaking, this collective situation contributes towards the formation of consciousness and of an ego that we designate "patriarchal," meaning the emphasis on the development of masculinity and its characteristic traits and values.

Symbols grow out of changing communal situations and experience, and are reflected in myth. The emerging image during this phase of patriarchal development – and one of the means by which collective cultural forces ultimately deposed the Goddess and subjugated women – is the archetypal image of the succubus. It is one of the most crudely dehumanizing images of woman; the succubus is the despoiler of all human decency, a blood-sucking, evil demon who seduces a man in order to possess his phallic power, and murders infants and mothers. This archetypal, cultural symbol of the maternal feminine is essentially a program for the unfolding of being; in essence, then, this image facilitates the creation of a succubus world. Spawned in the human imagination deep in the collective unconscious and sustained as plausible by the patriarchy, the succubus legitimized male control of society and justified the oppression of women. She is the means by which the patriarchy has maintained power for the last seven thousand years. And it is precisely for this reason that the succubus is so embedded in our world as a repository for shame. This image, and the idea that the burden of shame should be heaped upon the maternal feminine, has had a compelling hold on the psyches of so many people for thousands of years.

When I set out writing, the density in this forest of shame was intense, pulling me in a profusion of directions. My thoughts threatened to expand beyond the workable as the manifold implications of the succubus suggested themselves. I discovered that while the focus of this book is primarily masculine shame, this image of woman pulled me into some very powerful subjects; mainly feminist thought, and then the more esoteric and slippery subject of evil. And this is all in the context of shame's relationship to psychic development, separation from the mother, the self and the social order. So as not to lose my original point of departure, I grounded myself in where I had left off:

> What stalemate on a global scale are we hoping to understand [through psychology's pursuit of an understanding of shame]. I believe that we seek a solution to the widespread experiences of maternal deprivation, rejection, hatred, and destruction in the world today – universal issues in countless human circumstances that attack life itself. Historically, the emergence of the Terrible Mother coincided with the dominance of masculine values over feminine ones. Perhaps deep within the collective unconscious humankind has remained petrified in this shameful moment. We now wish to acknowledge our shame and yearn for the light of consciousness which only it can engender. On a collective level, this means the restoration of the Great Mother's fertile and creative qualities that can inspire us towards humanness, in addition to progress.
>
> (Ayers, 2003: 222)

As before, I am exploring the most primitive aspects of shame in the core of the self (not ordinary shame, but what I call absolute shame) through an investigation of the eye as its consummate organ of development. Here shame originates in a failure of maternal containment through impingement and absence – the mother's unreflecting eyes (Ayers, 2003). As an archetypal image, shame is constellated by the Evil Eyes in the face of the Terrible Mother. Archetypes are *a priori* conditioning factors that form the substructure for all forms of mental functioning, and there seems little doubt that facial features became the vehicle for depicting the destructive, incinerating, and annihilating aspects of the Great Mother that is tied to an actual human experience of shame. This book, however, is specifically about the eyes in masculine shame. This emphasis punctuates the succubus as a particularly important dimension of a mother's psyche (hence, the different relationship she will have with her male infant), as well as a facet of the Evil Eye, which has a castrating effect upon the patriarchy which incited its creation. This lens reveals that the image of the succubus is a container for masculine shame. In other words, the succubus symbolizes mankind's most fundamental source of powerlessness, fear, disrespect, and loss of self – all the places he feels the deepest kind of shame.

The emphasis on masculine shame requires some change in vocabulary from my previous work. The feminine shame that creates a sense of non-existence is best described as a psychotic anxiety in the core of the self during the holding phase of human development. The female infant becomes a mirror for her mother of the same sex, and annihilation is triggered by the lack of reflection in mother's eyes. If this type of distortion in mirroring occurs, merger with mother's psychic content continues long past the symbiotic phase, or first six months of life. Mother's own absence and need for reflection is connected to the collective fact that women have been shaped, defined, and understood their own selves according to distorting patriarchal dictates. This makes it hard for them to even know their own reality – to exist as human beings in their own right – and so they seek reflection through the eyes of others. If she has been brought up to devalue her femininity, the mother will socialize her daughter to become subordinate to men. Underdevelopment and negation of self are mirrored to a mother's daughter, and the cycle of non-existence continues.

Shame generated in the earliest days of life for a male infant is best described as a central affect in the psychotic core of a narcissistic condition. This is based on the writings of the founders of psychoanalysis, and the fact that the boy is expected to separate and disidentify with his mother. Here, absolute shame constellates more as a violent narcissistic rupture from mother in the area of omnipotence due to a denial of dependency needs. This is the second stage of development, and a time when the baby begins to separate both physically and emotionally from his mother. Even at this early point of differentiation, the male infant is learning that he must completely relinquish his original identification with his mother of the opposite sex, accomplished through a repression of his feminine traits as much as possible. This naturally causes their accumulation in the unconscious, and every man has his own internal succubus within him for this very reason. Moreover, he must eventually prove himself to be a man through tests of endurance, strength, or accomplishments. The temptations for a man must be seductive and overpowering to his manhood, which is why shame at this level of experience will become apparent around a man's Oedipal issues – but more on this later.

Absolute shame generated in the core of the female self results in a world of staring, petrifying eyes always watching, making movement impossible. For a male (and the succubus aspect of woman), the result is blindness and shamelessness. He keeps moving, evading, by blinding his eyes in one form or another and, like Oedipus or Narcissus, alienating himself from his self in a process necessary to the projection of shame onto woman. Man holds onto his psychic traits of intellectuality, transcendent spirit, and autonomous will at the expense of the contrary, female traits of feeling, sensuality and submission to the very humanity that we all must suffer.

In order to face feminine shame, an individual must come to terms with her nonexistence. In order to face masculine shame, one must examine his presence. These distinctions lead to the difference in the way shame is described. A woman in shame expresses feelings of a bad self to the point of not being real, or of not existing. She is acculturated into her submissive sex role through images like Eve or Pandora. In the case where the succubus dominates psychologically, the woman can become shameless and attempts to possess power by dominating a man (this is supported by the time-honored conviction that a woman possesses power only by influencing her husband's). Whichever way feminine shame manifests, nonexistence lays at the core. If a man feels shame, he feels disrespected, powerless, or is secretly threatened with being a wimp. In the core of the self, absolute masculine shame is the underside of narcissistic power and a feeling worse than death. Men are acculturated into a macho sex role through images such as God the Father (infinitely superior to subservient humanity), King, Lord, Master, and Judge who exercises authority over the inferior female who exists to serve the Father.

And the cure? To recreate and reacquire the instinct that recognizes the mother on whom our very existence relies. We need to transcend sexuality in order to discover the spirituality in merely tending our Mother Earth. In other words, we need to humanize our shame. At a deep personal and collective psychic level, shame is psychotic. Intrapsychically, shame is the main affect in the psychotic core of narcissistic power; culturally we are petrified in a collective psychosis terrorism (the petrifaction in shame), the quintessence of mankind's fears of weakness which have become the ultimate spectacle for a tired jaded populace, and global warming – just to name two forms it takes. Therefore, in the same way that absolute shame can be psychoanalytically processed on a personal level, with the goal of internalizing a more legitimate self image through the restoration of the good internal mother, misogyny and its central affect of shame can be more consciously integrated and transcended through an analogous process – the changing of stereotypical images of male and female, or the generation of different role models to internalize a different self-concept through the restoration of the qualities of the Mother Goddess. A life-giving, compassionate and merciful Great Mother is psychologically more reassuring, may produce less social tension and anxiety, and therefore be a calming influence in our world of terror. We may realize that peaceful resolutions are not only possible, but better than violent ones. Then we can work together to focus on the real threat, and what should unite us in concern, for it is a form of destruction which equalizes us all – the very extinction of civilization on earth (the planet will survive).

There are, of course, infinite ways of looking at, and reflecting upon, our current catastrophic world situation. I am not proposing any final, all wrapped up, inclusive and perfect view of reality; all we humans can ever have are interpretations. Nor do I believe that we can really remedy mankind's tragic flaws. I only hope that my attempt to restore vision through the eyes of shame can move us towards freedom from the limits of our current culture and, more importantly, from ourselves, in order to recover the goodness in past times through the symbolic form of the maternal feminine. As long as shame remains an unrecognized outcast of our individual and social lives, driven away by patriarchal power and feminine submission, we'll continue to live in a distortion of male and female images that are contributing to our ultimate plunge towards destruction.

What happens when we begin to crack the prevailing reality system to discover new layers of shame? Can we rectify our errors and revitalize our past? Can we know our shame in order to unlock our humanity?

Acknowledgements

The writing of this book has been a long and painful journey; I have never felt more alone in my life. And so it probably would never have been undertaken if not for the National Association for the Advancement of Psychoanalysis awarding my previous book. I deeply appreciate the recognition, a long overdue response from me because at the luncheon I became overwhelmed and speechless. It was also at that time that my publisher, Kate Hawes, offered congratulations and asked "Do you have any more ideas?" I want to thank NAAP and all the judges who voted in my favor for opening a way to write again. And a thousand more thanks to all the authors referenced in this book – and the many more not mentioned – for giving the thoughts coming into my head validity when they threatened to expand beyond the workable. And last but not least, thanks must go to Brian Weber, who discovered Cezanne's painting entitled *The Eternal Feminine* hanging in an out of the way corner of The Getty and shared it with me. The moment I laid eyes on it I knew that it must appear on the cover of this book.

Permission acknowledgement

Page 1
'Divine Mornings', poem by Susan Gold, writer, hypnotherapist, and high school mythology teacher. Used with kind permission.

Part I

The birth of civilization and the evolution of the succubus

At the dawn of time, there was an age of gold when man was at one with nature, when the eternal harmonies and laws of nature were more clearly expressed in man himself than they have ever been expressed since. Even today, we regard those moments in which our being is at one with the whole of nature as instants of perfect bliss.

(von Schubert, 1808)

He once let her breathe deep
into an ear of his apple orchard,
and she could feel his sky's chest sigh.

Lilith knows where God's eyes can be found;
she has kissed them.

Divine Mornings
And when she wakes
to find the earth's sheets wet with dew,
she knows he still dreams of her.

(Gold, 1998: 127)

He whose vision cannot cover
History's three thousand years,
Must in outer darkness hover,
Live within the day's frontiers.

(Goethe, Westostlicher Diwan)

Chapter 1

The succubus, the evil eye and shame

Shame is the hidden affect that inspires oppression. Woman, once the site of fertility and birth, is oppressed and recast in the image of the succubus. Although strikingly little has been written about her given her 7,000-year history, the succubus is a universal image that appears throughout world history in mainstream and marginal cultures, acquiring a multiplicity of faces and coming to be known under many names. She is the dark feminine inspiration for the femme fatale, castrator, dominatrix, vixen bogey, witch, enchantress, blood sucker, seductress, villainess, scarlet woman, beguiling abomination, preening temptress, predator, demon bride, impure female, Hell's rose, or black widow. More recent names might be bimbo, eye candy, career bitch or feminist. She appears throughout the world in many animal forms, such as a serpent, dog, screeching owl, or donkey, and she inhabits the soul as any creeping creature. Some might know her best by her proper biblical names of Lilith, the first wife of Adam and even worse than Eve because she is demonic from the moment of her creation; the seductive Salome, the temptress who danced for Herod in return for the head of John the Baptist on a silver platter; the beautiful but cunning Delilah, the Philistine woman of the Old Testament who betrayed Samson by having his hair shorn as he slept, thus depriving him of his strength; or Princess Jezebel, who painted her face and waited to be pushed out a window for taking the blood of an innocent man. Some of her mythic names are Circe, the witch in Homer's Odyssey who turned men into swine; Clytemnestra, the screaming bitch who called for an axe so that she could murder the war hero Agamemnon; the infanticidal Medea, who murdered her husband out of rage and revenge; Pandora, the Kallon Kakon or beautiful evil, the lovely curse that men had to pay for getting fire; Rusalka, the Slavic female ghost who seduced men with her eyes that shined with green fire; or Yuki-Ona (Snow Woman), the beautiful woman of Japanese folklore whose skin was transparent, and only her face and pubic hair stood out against the snow. Her eyes would strike terror into mortals, whom she would transform into frost-coated corpses, or lead them astray to die of exposure (shame). And then there are her historical names, the duplicitous seductress Mata Hari or the well known Cleopatra, the Queen of Egypt who captivates our imagination and lives on throughout the ages in myth and legend, novel and poem, paintings and operas, Shakespearean play and Hollywood film.

No matter what the age or culture, the succubus drains the life-force from weak-willed men, encapsulating everything that is morbid, nihilistic, and abortive. The epitome of depraved sexuality, she wastes potential fertility by causing men to ejaculate in their sleep – or else she steals their emissions to inseminate herself in order to produce more demons in revenge for the loss of her own children. In her seductive form, she is a very beautiful but most feared evil woman who through her gaze threatens man's power by taking over his mind and penis. Despite her beguiling beauty, the power of the succubus appears to reside in her fascinating Evil Eyes. The word fascination is a particularly important one when it comes to the succubus, for it has been defined as that power "derived from a pact with the devil, who, when the so-called fascinator looks at another with evil intent, or praises by means known to himself, infects with evil the person at whom he looks" (Elworthy, 1958). A man's mind is attacked when struck by the gaze of the succubus, and, thus weakened, he is led by hell's delusion to take her to his bed. Full of sadistic, voracious malice, her brilliant and cruel orgasm embodies the castration of a man. Figure 1.1 is an engraving by Gustave Dore for *The Succubus* in Balzac's *Les Contes Drolatiques*. It vividly depicts the eyes that can disempower a man and bring him to his knees. Its caption reads "I saw her with a bizarre plumage on her head, having a supernatural color and eyes more flaming than I can tell of, from which came a flame from Hell" (Huxley, 1990: 28).

The succubus as Terrible Mother is the all-inclusive symbol of the devouring aspect of the unconscious. All dangerous affects and impulses, all evils that come from the unconscious of man and overwhelm the ego, are her progeny. Folklore has it that she counts among her offspring the Devil of Christian literature, which makes the seven deadly sins – the root of all evil – her granddaughters (Russell, 1984: 77). The granddaughters' names are pride, envy, wrath, lust, greed, gluttony and sloth.

During the Great Witch Hunt of the sixteenth and seventeenth centuries, writers renamed Lilith "queen of the succubi" (Williams & Williams, 1978: 4), and so her story, which forms the core of Part I of this book, will be shared in some detail in order to illuminate the archetype with which we are dealing. In order to resurrect the central ideas of the myth of Lilith, I will be wandering around like Isis piecing together dismembered pieces of Osiris. Yet I hope that this process, in combination with the historical review tracing Lilith's manifestations in the next chapter, will show exactly how the succubus is a castrating dimension of the Terrible Mother, who, with her Evil Eyes, generates annihilating shame.

Queen of the succubi

For the first two millennia of recorded history, nature and society reflected a more holistic view of the world. Somewhere in the first millennia B.C., however, this communal world view of humanity broke down, and the alienations of civilization began to reshape history. It is during this time (700 B.C.) that Lilith, Adam's

Figure 1.1 Engraving by Gustave Dore for *The Succubus* in Balzac's *Les Contes Drolatiques*. Scanned from a copy of *The Eye: The Seer and the Seen*, by Francis Huxley. Used with permission of Thames and Hudson.

rebellious first wife who demands equality, first appears in the Old Testament Book of Isaiah (34:14) as the "night hag." Isaiah reads:

> And wild beasts shall meet with hyenas,
> The satyr shall cry to his fellow;
> yea, there shall the night hag alight,
> and find for herself a resting place.

This verse is part of a biblical chapter about the Lord's rage at all nations, and the image of Lilith as a night hag is situated between the following two verses. In Isaiah 34:8–12, we read about the Lord's vengeance, when he intends to turn the entire land into pitch night and day so that it

> shall not be quenched;
> its smoke shall go up for ever.
> From generation to generation it shall lie waste…
> the owl and the raven shall dwell in it.
> He shall stretch the line of confusion over it,
> and the plummet of chaos over its nobles.
> They shall name it No Kingdom There,
> and all its princes shall be nothing.

In Isaiah 34:15, reference to Lilith is repeated in the image of an owl:

> There shall the owl nest and lay
> and hatch and gather her young in
> her shadow;
> yea, there shall kites be gathered,
> each one with her mate.

Later, when God comes to save the people, "the eyes of the blind shall be opened, and the ears of the deaf unstopped; then shall the lame man leap like a hart, and the tongue of the dumb sing for joy" (Isaiah 35:5–6).

For the nomadic Hebrews of the desert, Lilith "was the voice howling over the mounds of dead and vanished civilizations; she was the female force living in the desolation of male vanities" (Thompson, 1978: 46). Eyes, smoke, ashes, chaos, confusion, blindness, lameness and a place called No Kingdom There where princes are nothing – images that evoke the incinerating power of absolute shame (Ayers, 2003). Shame always lurks in the places of darkness, ash and waste. God, consumed by rage, dominates the land by threatening to obliterate it and make men powerless, and it is at this point that Lilith makes her first appearance. Could this vengeance the Lord is acting upon be due to his shame over the limits of his own power and goodness, an evil aspect of God's own nature? In his book entitled *God: A Biography*, Jack Miles (1996) makes an interesting observation about God: he states that when God created woman he suffered considerable anxiety. God is narcissistically fretting over the perceived flaw in his supposedly perfect creation of Adam – the fact that he is alone, either as male or as androgyny. God is compelled to attempt its correction through the creation of a woman. God says "It is not good for a man to be alone; I will make a fitting helper for him." Thus, says Miles, "it is understood desire, admitted need, that shames" (p. 37). In needing woman (as both sexual object and mother) the perfection of God's sovereignty is compromised. And why are not Adam and Eve, in their shameful desire for each other, an image of God who created them in his own image? "Is it this – their presentation to him of himself as not exercising mastery but as experiencing need – that enrages him? And is he, his rage spent, ashamed of his own desire and moved to cover his shame by covering theirs?" (p. 37).

What, then, does God's dissociated shame have to do with the creation of the succubus, that desirable female created by God? God is dependent and cannot be without woman, and so he projects this need into man which inspires woman's creation (in the same way he later projects his humanity into man through Jesus, who had to be given birth through woman). In other words, the patriarchal God, that same perfect, omnipotent God that eradicated the Great Mother, can't create the world without a woman because of his need-driven desire. He does not create perfection in a single stroke, but, like any human being, struggles towards perfection time and time again. In order to rid God of his shame, another creation story emerges (one that we later learn precedes Eve) introducing the image of Lilith. Desirousness, that unruly emotion which is the hallmark of the man's attraction to the succubus, is now evil, and it is this sin that incites the generation of absolute shame in the masculine psyche.

Lilith's story is told in a sixth century A.D. Judaic book entitled *The Alphabet of Ben Sira*, which has been kept alive to this day.

> When the Almighty – may his name be praised – created the first, solitary man, He said: It is not good for man to be alone. And He fashioned for man a woman from the earth, like him (Adam), and called her Lilith. Soon, they began to quarrel with each other. She said to him: I will not lie underneath, and he said: I will not lie underneath but above, for you are meant to lie underneath and I to lie above. She said to him: We are both equal, because we are both (created) from the earth. But they didn't listen to each other. When Lilith saw this, she pronounced God's avowed name and flew into the air. Adam stood in prayer before his Creator and said: Lord of the World! The woman you have given me has gone away from me. Immediately, the Almighty – may His name be praised – sent three angels after her, to bring her back. The Almighty – may His name be praised – said to him (Adam): If she decides to return, it is good, but if not, then she must take it upon herself to ensure that a hundred of her children die each day. They went to her and found her in the middle of the sea, in the raging water in which one day the Egyptians would drown. And they told her the word of God. But she refused to return. They said to her: We must drown you in the sea. She said to them: Leave me! I was created for no other purpose than to harm children, eight days (after birth) for boys and twenty for girls...
>
> (1858: 23)

According to this passage, Lilith is Adam's first wife, a shameless, sterile avenging witch who leaves her husband after a bitter quarrel and denies her own motherhood in pursuit of supremacy. At his elation at having a mate, Adam tries to do what he has seen the animals doing, and so puts her on the ground and tries to mount her. Adam attempts to compel her obedience by force, but Lilith, full of her own wildness and instinctual power, is no object to be placed under control. In her rage she utters the magic name of God, rises up into the air, and flees. In her departure a great theme of division between male and female is being announced, and it is one that will echo throughout history all the way to the present. Lilith is not a loyal companion; as demon-wife, her power is derived from the shame that a man feels when he has been unable to command his wife's exclusive loyalty.

The source of Lilith's omnipotence is speaking God's name, for to know the secret name of something is to know how to gain power over it. The unity of God is expressed in the tetragram YHWH. In one version of the Zohar, Lilith tears his divine name apart.

> She it is who separates the two H's from each other and prevents the entry of the W between them. When Lilith stands between the one H and the other, then the Almighty, may His name be praised, cannot join them together.
>
> (quoted in Hurwitz, 1999: 148)

Lilith has the will to speak God's name, and this gives her the power to not accept His patriarchal authority and flee from Adam. As a result of her stand God divides his unity and dissociates from his female side. In order for God to maintain his omnipotence, mind and heart, thinking and emotion, reason and imagination are no longer united in a harmonious fashion. Captured in this idea is the essence of God's dysfunctional relationship not only to woman, but to the whole of Israel. In the following biblical passages, the Master of all the powers in the universe reveals his feelings of impotence as He rages at Israel – metaphorically his wanton wife (Frymer-Kensky, 1992: 144): "I will then uncover her shame in the very sight of her lovers" (Hosea 2:10); and "I myself will lift up your skirts over your face and your shame shall be seen; I have seen your abominations, your adulteries and neighings, your lewd harlotries … How long will it be before you are made clean?" (Jeremiah 13:26–27).

Lilith was a complete failure, and so now God needs to create another woman, a completely subordinate being who complies with Adam's wishes without hesitation. Adam's second wife is the more well-known and docile Eve – but even she is to become another tempting bitch by talking Adam into eating an apple from the forbidden Tree of the Knowledge of Good and Evil. It is no accident that the unknowing Adam meets with the mate who is to become the agent for his expulsion from the garden. Their moment of shame marks the beginning of Western history. Unity with God is lost and existence is more intensely polarized. The word separation becomes very important. Adam and Eve move out of a blissful world of oneness towards a world of limitation and death, of good and evil, light and dark, male and female. The price of sexuality and individuation is death: long before Freud put forth his interpretations, Eros and Thanatos were inseparably linked in our cultural myths.

Also inseparably linked is shame with the image of this eye. In the post-Edenic psyche, shame depicted as an eye lies at the core of our inescapable human predicament. In their move toward knowledge, Adam and Eve reduce humankind to hiding in shame. Figure 1.2 entitled *Garden of Paradise* depicts the single-eyed fountain of life witnessing the creation of Adam and Eve, a time when harmony and connection are imagined to have been possible. In the pupil of this eye a little child dances. This painting also depicts the world of order and reason being created out of dark, chthonic depths – the patriarchal world built upon the foundations of the dark matriarchal.

Lilith and Eve are two women central to the Judeo-Christian patriarchy (and the first religions to completely banish the Great Mother). Both were sexual temptresses who assert their will against God, and suffer the misogyny of the Church Fathers for being in some way irresistible. Both are models for the relations between men and women (and internally the structure of ego and consciousness) who present two stories that set the tone of how women will be viewed. When patriarchy arises through the negation of the Great Mother as a figure of autonomy and power, as repeatedly has been said, a splitting of the whole into good and bad, male and female, occurs, and in this dichotomy, women are forced to identify with either Lilith or Eve.

These two wives of Adam lead us to the idea of a shame spectrum of women, one not much better than the other. Eve appears as completely subordinate, and has no problem assuming the position Adam expects, while Lilith refuses the

Figure 1.2 Garden of Paradise, c. 1500, oil on panel, by Hieronymus Bosch, Netherlandish, c. 1450/60–1516. Photography copyright © The Art Institute of Chicago.

lower position, claiming that they were both made from the earth at the same time. With the move from Eve to Lilith, shameful nakedness becomes shameless sexuality. The maternal physical features of corpulence, wide child bearing hips, pendulous breasts and enormous stomach disappear in the face of sexiness, the sleek, young maiden with voluptuous breasts, curvaceous torso, slight waist and slender, long legs.

At one end of the spectrum we find Eve, the non-existent woman who lives engulfed in shame for causing the downfall of all humanity. Eve does not mother us all with her cosmic reproductive power; she is a seductive little housewife who does a number on Adam and sends the world to hell. Eve accepts expulsion from the Garden of Eden in order to redeem herself in God's eyes. Eve's beauty is a manifestation of God's omnipotence: She is made from Adam, although even this subservience did not allow her to escape tarnishing. That Eve carries all the shame of the world, to the point of her non-being, is clear.

On the other end of the spectrum we have Lilith, the alluring and seductive figure of fatal enchantment, created by God at the same time as Adam. It is on the basis of her simultaneous creation that she demands equality. Denied and enraged by her unequal treatment, she dominates a man and kills children. She is a woman shamelessly identified with a masculine power, or will, which leads to power over. She is the cold, lying, ruthless, heartless, manipulative, back-biting female who won't obey the rules. Lilith's beauty and her possession of it is a manifestation of God's impotence. This preening for power is described in the following passage from Jewish literature (Stone, 1984):

> Women are evil . . . because they have no power or strength to stand up against man, they use wiles and try to ensnare him by their charms; and man, whom women cannot subdue by strength, she subdues by guile . . . they lay plots in their hearts against men: by the way they adorn themselves they first lead their minds astray, and by a look they instill the poison . . . for a woman cannot overcome a man by force.

On an intrapsychic level, the succubus can be encountered any time a woman reaches for power out of her own non-existence (shame), or an aspect of the masculine psyche that gets activated and disconnects from the feminine whenever he feels made small, inferior or disrespected (shamed). She is the cruel, vain, and dark side of woman's nature, and, on the collective level, a castrating aspect of the Terrible Mother with the Evil Eyes. This element gets played out between men and women. For example, she can emerge when a manipulative female uses sexuality in an attempt to have power over a man, or when a man, identified with power, requires an armpiece to decorate him for his own enjoyment. The following vignette depicts this dynamic well: a woman meets a man and, pressing for marriage, is engaged 20 days following her own sobriety. She is a sexy, voluptuous woman with large breast implants and impeccably manicured fake nails. When the couple first got engaged they argued about children; she wanted to have one, but he already had two from his first marriage and didn't want any more. Once married, Vicki covertly helped herself to $40,000 of her husband's money that he had saved for his children's college tuition and spent it instead on artificial insemination. When she was no longer able to hide her pregnancy, she boldly told her husband what she had done. Two years later (after she had the baby who was under his care) she reveals that her story was a lie; the truth is that she had been having an affair with his business partner with whom she conceived the child.

And what might the unconscious have to say about such an act? One patient dreamt the following during a time when she was struggling to face her feelings in order to attain some sense of existence, or succumb to her temptations to return to a life of public relations and white collar crime:

> I am facing a huge mountain of ice. I know that I must climb the mountain to conquer the summit. Once there, I will be making a pact with the devil to solve my money problems.

Her feelings are frozen in ice. Because she has disregarded them, they begin to grow in the cold regions. An evil twist takes hold of her unconscious processes. Avoiding her helplessness through a conquering will entails a pact with the devil, the loss of her own soul – powerlessness is always the occasion for a pact with the devil (and the devil won, for shortly after this dream the patient terminated treatment). The shamelessness of the succubus is a loss of soul. Such a woman is an empty receptacle, internalizing the projections that cut off the flow of her own being. She becomes a projection screen for men, her absence of shame magnetically attracting a man's shame to fill up her hollowness.

The succubus and the shame she contains is the psychic heritage of all humankind, for shame is the affect which makes us human. She derives her powers from mankind's fatal flaw – unbounded omnipotence. On a human level, she is a devouring aspect of woman who does not know portions; she is herself pursued by an insatiable appetite, craving adulation, dominating to possess power as a substitute for soul. If the cravings go, nearly all she calls self will go with them, and then she is threatened with being engulfed by emptiness and helplessness. Instead, she stays wild with suppressed fury and vengeance, full of narcissistic envy in her fixation on the surface and the look of things. She is unprincipled, has no values, self-respect or pride, stands for nothing, and therefore goes for whatever suits her. This vacancy locks up and freezes all of her real powers of self. In woman, the succubus is a lost soul. And for a man, she becomes his worst nightmare. Her hunger is really her need for recognition, to be seen as good. But her inability to touch her own shame may never allow her the sense of existence she so desperately needs.

The imagery of the collective unconscious is enduring. Or, as Faulkner puts it, "the past is never dead; it is not even past". A new incarnation of the succubus is developing in a modern kind of female killer, the suicide bombers of Al Qaeda or the "black widows" of Chechnya. The presence of these killers concretizes the relationship between the succubus and masculine shame. Having lost husbands and sons, these women want to live only long enough to take revenge. Arab men who see foreign occupation as a form of emasculation (one Muslim was quoted as saying that the occupation was "part of a plan to steal our souls – to castrate us") recruit and train these women for battle (Dickey, 2005: 32). The women are told that after martyring themselves they can be redeemed in paradise by becoming "the purest and most beautiful form of angel at the highest level possible in heaven" (p. 34). In other words, their suicidal sacrifice will provide the recognition that they need, and purge them of their evils to become good. Meanwhile, men who martyr themselves will attain the succubus – 72 *houris* – virginal beings with black eyes and alabaster skin that will attend to all of their sexual desires in paradise (p. 31). Emasculation will be transformed into power.

No matter what form she takes, the succubus, shaped by historical concerns, comes to represent something central to our culture, a symbol of our current "Age of Chaos" (Thompson, 1981). She continues to shape the perceptions of masculinity and femininity to this day. This primordial image, common to all humanity, is an inexhaustible subject that begs for interpretation; for the purpose of my present analysis, however, the succubus conveys something important about masculine shame. Patriarchy has proposed the succubus woman as a symbol for its own shame, a scheming, wicked woman with a lust for phallic power and vengeance. The image of the succubus cannot be looked at as a single image, as a female alone; she derives her power through the devil (her husband) to wreak revenge on a man, a mother and an infant.

Chapter 2

The historic unfolding of the image of the succubus

The movement into the future always involves the revisioning of the past.
(Thompson, 1981: 208)

The Earth began its existence as a separate body in space about 4,500 million years, or four and a half aeons ago. Little is known about the origin of life on our planet, and still less about its early evolution. The earliest traces of human life, however, show that the creature which has today changed the entire face of the habitable earth came up out of Africa only a little better equipped than his cousin, the ape. Mental capacities and physical adaptability enabled humans to develop culture and embellish the natural world in which they lived. During the Ice Age, the impact that humans could make upon the Earth, a virgin planet abounding in so many forms of life, is hardly greater than that of a squirrel collecting nuts. For many thousands of years after evolution, humankind's way of life and culture remained in union with the cycles and seasons of the earth. People were hunters and gatherers, just some of the many other animals that picked food from the natural abundance provided by the earth.

Legend has it that during this time people worshiped the Great Mother Goddess. Cro-magnon people left evidence that the Goddess religion flowered and became progressively more advanced in Europe and the Near East during Paleolithic times (35000–9000 B.C.E.), and extended well into Neolithic times, up until the fifth millennium B.C.E. Although there is no written record, myths, or stories (and therefore no history as usually defined by civilization), Aurignacian sculpted female images are distributed throughout a region which stretches from Siberia to Southern France (Levy, 1948: 54), and sanctuaries reveal a gynocentric artistic tradition with a rich array of symbolism from nature.

The image of woman at this time is clear and direct through artifacts that attest to the awe and wonder at the sacred and beautiful mystery of life. Woman was a formidable creature in every way, incarnating a long list of feminine wonders. The Goddess' body, the planet Earth, symbolized the nurturing and regenerating powers incarnate in the female body. The male phallus was deeply embedded in the body of the Great Mother, as with the backside of the Venus of Lespugue with phallic neck and breasts shaped like the glans penis (Figure 2.1 and Figure 4.3 in

Ayers, 2003: 114). The phallus belonged to the Goddess simply because of its life-giving properties and the nature of reproduction. Neumann/Mannheim (1974) describes the maternal feminine as that which

> tends to hold fast to everything that springs from it and to surround it like an eternal substance. Everything born of it belongs to it and remains subject to it, and even if the individual becomes independent, the Archetypal Feminine relativizes this independence into a nonessential variant of her own perpetual being.
>
> (1974: 76)

The entire system of the Paleolithic cosmology explicated by the prehistorian Andre Leroi-Gourhan (1967) is the pairing and balancing of male and female forces. Fertility cults centered on the figure of the Great Mother and her son, who affirmed and strengthened the active female elements. Explicit images of human

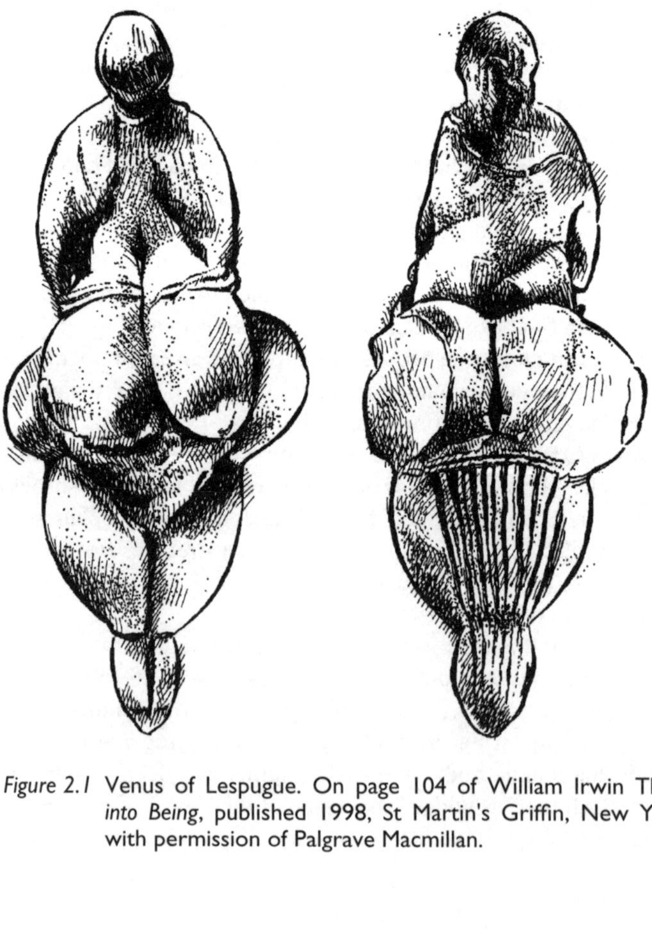

Figure 2.1 Venus of Lespugue. On page 104 of William Irwin Thompson, *Coming into Being*, published 1998, St Martin's Griffin, New York. Reproduced with permission of Palgrave Macmillan.

males are almost non-existent and very sketchy when they do appear. The creative powers of nature, rather than the powers to destroy, were given the highest value, and neither male nor female was subordinate to the other. This balance of the sexes in a harmonious division of labor, the hunters and gatherers, is celebrated in the juxtaposed male and female signs on the walls of caves. The egalitarian society that valued the feminine was one where power was doubled, for they knew that it increased whenever they cooperated with one other. Existence was integrated within the life of the group; everything an individual did and the way he went about doing it remained an expression of the collective, which was considered more significant in the life of the individual than his own personal needs. The transpersonal shaped experience and the numinous in nature supported and engendered consciousness. Death was not feared; it was simply a continuation of life in another state of being.

The birth of civilization

The story of the birth of civilization begins more than ten thousand years ago with two radical steps towards man's creation of an artificial environment – the agricultural revolution, which then led to the urban one. With gathering, women unconsciously took nature into culture: in striking the stalk of wild wheat with her sickle she helped to scatter the wild-blown seeds; in carrying the grasses home she increased the proportion of grains with large heads that stuck to the stalk. Their gathering began to produce more and more food, and the storage of it required a new kind of sedentary life. The domestication of wild plants and animals was the single most important breakthrough in the material technology of our species.

The period of 8000–6000 B.C. saw the rise of domestic architecture and permanent villages. This shift from the seasonal round to permanent settlement was inspired by religious as well as economic or environmental reasons. The new techniques also spread rapidly, and the success of agriculture necessitated its physical expansion which led to a rapid increase in population. Small villages comprising perhaps two to three hundred people developed where man's mental powers could flourish and bear the fruits of human civilization.

Meanwhile, male hunting required greater distances and longer-lived seasonal camps. Storage in the granaries produced wealth, and this would require male presence to protect it. In other words, wealth and possessions engendered the need for defense; the subculture of the hunt became male competition and aggression as men came to understand that they need not stop at defense, but could not include hunting for other people's wealth. Population pressures also forced them to exploit other lands in order to create larger communities. And yet as Thompson puts it, "every culture which has ever created a class to protect itself has ended up having to protect itself from the protectors" (1981: 133–134).

For hundreds of thousands of years the culture of women and women's mysteries was the dominant ideology of humanity. The distance and tension between the female and the male patterns of life became increasingly pronounced. With the accumulation of property, of herds, fields, irrigation systems, walls and temples, there was no going back: the supremacy of the male over the female had begun. By the fifth millennium B.C.E. there is evidence of invasions causing large-scale destruction and dislocation (Eisler, 1987: 43). From about 4300 to 2800 B.C.E., the ancient world was battered by wave after wave of barbarian invasion. The warriors conquered the people and brought with them their powerful priests, as well as their fierce and angry male gods of war. The land was being changed by a culture that developed and devoted themselves to the art of war. It is in this psychological climate that humanity opted for violence and rigid order over egalitarianism.

The transition from matriarchal to patriarchal was accomplished through violent aggression, brutal massacres and the conquering of territories (and this is how institutionalized violence became the shadow of the Neolithic revolution). The enantiodromia created by the discovery of cereals by women is that it created warfare for men who discovered a new way to be powerful. In a self-reinforcing process, conquering increased the size of the settlements, and as a consequence greater technological and organizational efficiency was demanded. A warlike tendency of conquering, cruelty, killing and might developed as civilization evolved. Civilization and warfare spelled the end of the Great Mother, and by 4000 B.C. the world became decidedly masculine. A striking fact is that in matriarchal times humankind lived as food-gatherers for tens of thousands of years, but it took only three thousand years, from around 6000 B.C. to the later part of the third millennium, for the institution of patriarchal values to occur (Huxley, 1966: 205).

Ancient cultures were urban, male, literate, agricultural and militaristic. Village settlements changed into organized, hierarchical cities run by classes of knights and priests. The culture of custom and authority gives way to a culture of power. Monumental buildings were erected, and a socially shared system of writing developed. Rivalry among economic elites for control over scarce resources led to increased centralization of the state and to militarism. The form of the city itself is an expression of the power of the rational mind to repel chaos, manifesting the triumph of mind over matter, male over female. There is a shift from the religious and magical authority of the Goddess to masculine military power, the way of death that becomes a way of life. The male body's greater physical strength became the basis for social oppression, organized warfare, or the concentration of physical property in the hands of the strongest man. In the face of all the technological wonders of male civilization, woman's ways appeared simple and primitive.

A conflict between the sexes arises with woman's accidental discovery of gathering and gardening that led to the shift from the Neolithic matrilineal order to the civilized, patriarchal one. The archetypal foundation for civilization appears to be the displacement of the maternal feminine: "whether he is challenging Mother Nature in flying away from her in rockets, or in changing her on earth through genetic engineering, man has not given up in the attempt to take away the mystery of life from the Great Mother and the conservative feminine religion" (Thompson, 1981: 163). Women became private property in the new trading and raiding society: "Mesolithic society may have seen the domestication of animals, and Neolithic society may have seen the domestication of plants, but the age after the Neolithic sees the domestication of women by men" (p. 155).

Humanity has shifted from the simplicity of the custom-bound life of the intimate matrilineal village to the law-ruled life of the complex patrilineal state. The both monotheistic and polytheistic mother goddess was displaced by a single and all powerful father god. Through a subtle but consistent erasing process, the goddess was demythologized so that the numinosity that once belonged to her imbues other deities. Technologies of destruction are given the highest priority. Golden figurines are melted down and fashioned into chariots. Their precious stones are embedded in the hilts of shields and swords. Patrons of agricultural enterprises became patrons of war, and then the warrior gods drive the Goddess people out. The Goddess is murdered and from her raped body the new state is constructed. The earth is a possession to be plundered by mankind for the benefit of civilization. The instrument which rendered man able to change his relationship to the earth is the plow, new technology that performs like a great phallus, taking gardening away from women and turning it into agriculture.

The period of warfare placed a heavy burden on the development of human culture. Transformations, being imperceptible in culture, do not take place in history; revolutions take place through myth, and it is due to this that they render the invisible visible (Thompson, 1981). Civilization itself is merely an externalization of consciousness, a fact which makes this transition not only a cultural evolution but also an evolution in consciousness. Egohood dawned with civilization in the same way it emerges in the development of the infant in its frustrations and separation from mother. And as humanity moved forward in a process of increasing individuation we paid a high price for that ego: repression and a great divorce between the ego and the soul. In the shift from village life to civilization there was psychological shift in archetypes.

In the revolution to patriarchal civilization woman becomes victim, and the Great Mother is diabolized through her eyes. First depicted without facial features, she eventually becomes the Terrible Mother with the Evil Eyes, or even just eyes (Ayers, 2003: 110–118). Mankind attempts to conquer her too. One example is Hathor, an Egyptian Winged Cow of Creation who is now sent out in the form of a large all-seeing eye by the sun god to spy on the human race. Fiercely aroused, she becomes savage and begins to destroy humanity. Hathor's malevolence takes the form of the Evil Eye, when she is solely a destructive figure (Husain, 2003: 135). Inanna, the most beloved of Mother Goddesses whose eyes of love adorned her temple (see Figure 2.2), was transformed into a goddess of war whose glance could kill. In the following passage from the Ninmesarra Hymn, Enheduanna depicts Inanna as a strong and ferocious warrior whose rage was contained in her eyes. This rage was then co-opted by mankind to ensure victories:

Figure 2.2 Frieze of Inanna's Eye Temple. Courtesy of the Oriental Institute of the University of Chicago.

> That you totally destroy rebellious lands – be it known!
> That you roar at the land – be it known!
> That you kill – be it known!
> That like a dog you eat the corpses – be it known!
> That your glance is terrible – be it known!
> That your glance flashes – be it known!
> At those who do not obey – be it known!
> That you attain victories – be it known!
> (quoted in Frymer-Kensky, 1992: 65)

The Terrible Mothers' Evil Eyes appeared on the helmets of warriors as badges of honor (which is intimately linked to shame, for the face is a synonym for both shame and honor) (see Figure 2.3), and/or was used to strike fear into their enemies, the ones with whom they came face-to-face. The face of Medusa, the Gorgon who shamed and castrated men upon eye contact, was used on shields and helmets to possess the power of this vengeful being. Acts of violence, war and aggression formed an effort to subvert and subsume her power.

Patriarchy dug in with pure military power to stay for a long time to come. Even today, defense departments still use the powers of the Terrible Mother for military might. The largest and most powerful high explosive ever built by the U.S. has been named the "Mother Of All Bombs" (after which the Russians announced a larger one which they named "The Father Of All Bombs"). The MOAB is a lethal cocktail of explosives weighing "9.5 tons of sheer hell" with a blast radius of 150 square yards, or nine city blocks. It is the mother of all bombs because it will cause the mother of all damage. It has also been called a man-made earthquake. In 1991, Saddam Hussein conquered Kuwait and postured with threats to deliver the "Mother of All Battles" (Umm Al Ma'arik). This turned into among other things the "Mother of All Retreats," "The Mother of All Blowouts," "The Mother of all Marine Operations" and the "Mother of all Briefings."

Figure 2.3 Thracian gold ceremonial helmet from Romania. (Getian princely helmet, discovered at Coţofeneşti (Vărbilău commune, Prahova county, Romania), 4th – 3rd centuries BC), copyright © National History Museum of Romania, Bucharest, photo: eng. Marius Amarie.

And yet there can be no conquering of the Terrible Mother. A basic psychoanalytic tenet is that repression always creates pathological potential. So, like any psychic content that is repressed and only grows more powerful, the Great Mother will remain extremely and progressively terrible so long as patriarchy oppresses the maternal feminine. The dark side of the mother, a place of massive collective repression, only grows in negativity as she is silenced and banished from expression. The unconscious gets projected onto the feminine, and, thus ensnared, man becomes victim. The masculine entered culture by splitting off the Great Mother, relegating her to the depths of the unconscious. This throws the sexes, heretofore in a balanced relationship, into opposition. "Man cut the umbilical cord to the Great Mother with a sword, and the sword has been hanging over his head ever since" (Thompson, 1981: 156).

In the shift from one mentality to another, humanity begins to become separated from nature, divide subject and object, split value from analysis, and knowledge from myth. And women, as a result of these material conditions, are systematically subordinated in a pattern that is to recur over and over again throughout history. Intellect replaces heart. Reason replaces feeling. Throughout this conversion process the image of the succubus – that mask for men's shame – has played a pivotal role. It is through her that a deliberate reversal of reality as it has formerly been perceived is effected: the Great Goddess is transformed into a symbol of pure evil, and woman is blamed for all the misfortunes of humanity (or the weaknesses of men).

I want now to quote from Eisler who in her writings on this omnipotent militaristic takeover and dominance of the patriarchy depicts precisely the place where cultural shame enters and petrifies in our history:

> But concealed within this purportedly grand and glorious beginning was the flaw that has widened into the most dangerous of chasms in our time. After millennia of upward movement in our technological, social, and cultural evolution, an ominous split was now underway. Like the deep cracks left by violent movements of the earth in that time, the breach between our technological and social evolution on the one hand and our cultural evolution on the other would steadily widen. The technological and social movement toward greater complexity of structure and function resumed. But the possibilities for cultural development were now to be stunted – rigidly caged in a dominator society.
>
> (1987: 56)

Eisler is writing of the moment where the communal world view of humanity started to break down, and the alienations of civilization with a "codified hero system" (Becker, 1973: 7) begins to reshape history. Shame is the affect that is concealed and threatens to erupt in the chasm that splits the advances of civilization from culture, law from custom, military power from religious authority, the individual warrior from the cohesion of the collective. The maternal feminine has been, however, "rigidly caged" or petrified by the domination of women who are seen as intrinsically hostile to the aims of civilized life. It is in this crack that shame takes its hold, the dark, blinded maternal feminine out of which attempts at an ordered social and political life are made. Today, the cry of shame threatens to split the crevice in the earth even wider.

History speaks to the fact that the idea of woman began to change when humankind entered what is called high civilization. Symbols of femininity are eventually reversed under the patriarchy; once revered as sacred, awe-inspiring and fertile, the idea that the female element is now evil is forcibly expressed in the earliest written material of Western culture. This is the phenomena that will be explored for the remainder of this chapter, and it will be shown that the shadow of the succubus has fallen on women from its first conception to the present day, and that the underside of this potent image is the affect of shame.

The succubus takes hold

This phenomena is demonstrated well by witchcraft (the conception of the witch and her practices), which originally belonged to a social and cultural world that supported the Great Mother. The witch was originally not an evil being, but performed useful, constructive and healing acts through magic. As religious thought was revolutionized, the witch was demythologized. Demonic forms were imposed upon her image through her eyes, which turned her into an unmitigated, evil woman.

So like the evil eye that she used, the witch became the explanation for every kind of misfortune. How did this happen? What brought about this dramatic change? Abusch (2002) looks at the literature on witchcraft beliefs and practices in ancient Mesopotamia through his translation of engraved tablets that form what is called the *Maqlû*, an Akkadian magical series of eight tablets of incantations that achieved their long text form by the first millennium. Combing through it stanza by stanza, he has discovered that it contains many inconsistencies and redundancies which he attributes to historical developments which attest to changes.

He starts by making a connection between witchcraft and the anger of a personal god (a new idea at the time) and uses these two forces to serve as a prism through which to observe the society and intellectual thought of the time. A battle was waged between these two independent entities, the witch and the divine god. Consider the following passages from *Maqlu*, and pay particular attention to the shaming (or castrating) power contained in the eye of the witch:

> The witch saw me and came after me,
> With her spittle, she cut off (commercial) traffic,
> With her witchcraft, she cut off (my) trading,
> She drove away my god and goddess from my person
> (III 13–16)

> Because a witch has bewitched me,
> A deceitful woman has accused me,
> Has (thereby) caused my god and goddess to be estranged from me (and)
> I have become sickening in the sight of anyone who beholds me,
> I am therefore unable to rest day or night.
> (I 4–8)

> (Because) I have been made unclean (smeared) by witchcraft,
> I stand before you,
> (Because) I have been cursed in the presence of god and man,
> I come before you
> (Because) I am sickening in the sight of anyone who beholds me,
> I bow down before you.
> (II 86–88)
> (quoted in Abusch, 2002: 29–30)

Abusch includes a footnote that god refers to the city god, "the anger of god, king, nobleman and prince you have set upon me" (p. 30). The new idea was created that the witch could cause the personal god to be angry, and thus cause divine abandonment.

He speculates that the negative image of the witch was shaped and brought into line with certain beliefs and ideologies evolving at that time. Abusch states:

> Initially … the *asipu*, a main-stream "white magician," was probably not the primary person who fought against witchcraft. But at some point, perhaps in the early second millennium, witchcraft became a concern of the *asipu*, perhaps because the female witch had changed her character but more because of the expanding role of the male *asipu* as a result of increasingly centralization and stratification of state, temple, and economy.
>
> (2002: 28)

Abusch determines that witchcraft as a means of providing explanations of evil and misfortune is a later or secondary addition to the text: "Different forms of textual evidence prove that various traditional texts were rewritten to include witchcraft" (2002: 47). Sentences like "That man: witchcraft has been practiced against him; he has been cursed before god and goddess" mark the entry of a new form of witchcraft that conveys the idea that "the removal (and distancing) of the personal god … is fundamentally the primitive and infantile fear that another – here a woman – may take away a man's power and sense of being" (p. 46). From this statement it is clear that the good witch of Mesopotamian literature has been deliberately transformed into an image of the succubus, that woman who can castrate a man, and thus deprive him of favor with his omnipotent god. In other words, these changes did not simply emerge from the natural, autopoetic mind of a culturally complex system: the image was composed by the more artificial intelligence of the conscious mind.

Historical transformations of culture are reflected in myths and so resemble each other. The figure chosen to play the sexual temptress Lilith in the first Judaic creation story was originally Sumerian, the beneficent Inanna. She was a Goddess revered in the city of Sumer as the Queen of Heaven and Earth, the Goddess of Love. Inanna's awesome facial features loom large over her temple (see Figure 2.2, caption reads "the temple frieze of the House of Inanna (or of Heaven)"), which is full of statues with startling, staring eyes, heavily outlined in black, their pupils set with deep blue lapis lazuli. Lilit, or the dark, sexual side of Inanna, was once addressed in prayer on a four thousand-year-old tablet. This mere mention of her name in connection with sexuality was enough to turn the Goddess Inanna into a she-demon of the succubus variety.

By the third millennium B.C., Inanna succumbs to the many hostile intrusions into her domain by patriarchal sky gods. The unified world view of the Great Goddess shatters, and her powers are undermined by a male god named An. While the surviving record is written from the vantage point of those who would suppress the Goddess, a critical reading of her hymns sheds light on the key issues involved in the patriarchal transformation of Inanna into a succubus. During the period 1950–1700 B.C., Lilith makes her first appearance in a fragment of a Sumerian version of the Gilgamesh Epic (the original is said to be appreciably older, and is believed to date from the fortieth century B.C.) (Hurwitz, 1999: 49). We first meet Inanna rescuing the tree of life, the huluppu tree, from the world flood and planting it in her garden. She wants to make a shining throne and sacred marriage bed from the growing tree, claiming her queenship and womanhood. Yet in order to do this she must first get rid of the unwelcome intruders who live in the tree – the serpent who nests in the tree, the anzu bird whose young live in the branches, and the "dark-maid Lilith" who "built her throne in the trunk." Inanna is powerless in the face of them, and so she calls on her earthly brother Gilgamesh for help. "Gilgamesh is the brazen young hero, full of manliness and equipped with signs of his physical strength – his heavy axe, which weighs 450 pounds, and his great armor, which weighs 60 pounds." Gilgamesh uses the axe, the "cutting weapon of civilization" (or sword that hangs over our heads), to cut down the tree. He defeats the "serpent who could not be charmed," the bird flies with "his" young to the mountain, and a terror-stricken Lilith flees to wild, uninhabitable places. The hero has conquered the succubus. The bird, the snake and Lilith are all forms of the Goddess now outlawed by the patriarchy. The loving and good Mother Goddess is debased and made into the night-demon Lilith. The change to a new male culture is openly celebrated in the Epic of Gilgamesh. In defeating the chaotic lawlessness of nature, Gilgamesh epitomizes the hero, and the story is for all intents and purposes an ode to the phallus. The main point of reference in the story is the social order, the need to dominate and subdue the feminine as the only way to make a safe connection to the female other (a theme for the remainder of this book).

Another name for Inanna was Divine Lady Owl, the roots of the Old Testament (Isaiah) reference to Lilith as a night or screech. Lilith appears in ancient Sumerian bas reliefs from 2000 B.C. with bird feet, flanked by owls and lions (see Figure 2.4). Walker (2000: 216) guesses that Lilith was also embodied in the owl-eyed "Eye Goddess" statuettes of the House of Inanna. The Latin word for "owl," *strix*, evolved into the Italian *strega*, "witch" (p. 6).

The symbol of the owl remained for centuries to come, for even throughout Europe in the witch-crazed Middle Ages, Lilith is represented as the nocturnal, predatory owl. Night flying witches were often depicted with owl wings. In Figure 2.5, she is depicted atop a human skull in an ancient tomb, with the shining sun rising behind her. The sun compels her to return to her hiding place in the forest. The motto written in Middle German behind the owl reads "*Ich Fyrcht Den Tag*," or "I Dread the Day". Tales of Lilith's shaming powers in her form as owl were handed down by word of mouth, and the following story was recorded by Brothers Grimm in the nineteenth century:

> Many hundreds of years ago a horned monster lost its way. It was an owl with sharp talons and two tall, feathery horns, one above each eye. Spotting an open barn door, in a quiet little village located on the edge of a deep, dark forest, the creature flew inside and perched on a rafter to spend the night. Bright and early the next morning the farmer came in to milk the cows. But

Figure 2.4 Sumerian bas reliefs from 2000 B.C. Lilith with bird feet, flanked by owls and lions. Copyright © The Trustees of the British Museum/Art Resource, New York.

catching sight of the monster, he raced out, terrified. He screamed to his neighbors for help. They all came running, armed with pitchforks and scythes. One look at those huge, foreboding eyes, however, froze them in their tracks.

So the farmer sent for the man known as the bravest and strongest in the entire village. "Have courage," the fearless one assured them. "It will not stare at us much longer!" And he pranced into the barn as if he were going to gather the morning eggs, sitting primly in their little nests.

But he saw those eyes big as saucers and just as unwavering, those feathered horns rising under the monster's head like the horns of some demon from the underworld. The rescuer reached no further than the fifth rung of the ladder. He half-slid, half-fell to the ground and sped out of the barn.

Figure 2.5 Lilith in the form of an owl atop a human skull. The motto written in Middle German behind the owl reads "*Ich Fyrcht Den Tag*," or "I Dread the Day". Copyright © The Trustees of the British Museum.

The villagers were in a frenzy. Their best man had just run away. The creature threatened to destroy them all. Finally, the town burgomaster proposed that everyone contribute enough money to pay the owner for his barn and all his hay, corn, and animals inside.

The next morning, where the barn had once stood, nothing but grey ashes remained.

And the owl was no more.

(Grimm & Grimm, 1944: 174)

The succubus in Ancient Greece

We move from the diabolization of the original Lilith and the witch in Ancient Mesopotamia – from creative Great Mother to the Terrible Mother with the Evil Eyes – to the Greek myth of Perseus and Medusa, which picks up on the same theme. The image of Medusa marks the progression from a world dominated by the generative powers of the female to one overseen by the moral authority of the male. According to many classical legends, Medusa was once a most beautiful woman, a Gorgon whose grimace meant the pain of childbirth. She eventually became a seductress who was raped in the Temple of Athena by Poseidon. In revenge, Athena, the goddess born without a mother from the head of Zeus, changed her beautiful face into a monstrous one, the epitome of ugliness and evil. The monster Medusa (whose name meant "queen" or "ruler" in the feminine gender) could turn men to stone with a single glance from her lovely, terrible face.

After Perseus beheads her, Medusa's head is placed on Athena's breastplate. Here Medusa's potential survives in just her face, a form that subordinates its powers to the control of the patriarchal state. Medusa has remained to this day the quintessential succubus, the symbol of male castration and death (see Figure 2.6, Medusa

Figure 2.6 Medusa as *La Syphilis*, from Louis Raemaker's *L'Hecatombe*. Courtesy of Ebling Library for the Health Sciences, Rare Books and Special Collections, University of Wisconsin-Madison.

as *La Syphilis*, from Louis Raemaker's *L'Hecatombe*). She wrenches masculinity away from the male through eye contact – his eyes meeting those of Medusa looking at him. Her castrating powers, in other words, are derived from the onlooker's own desire, and she seduces a man to meet her stare with petrifying results.

It is in the ransacking of matriarchal Greek culture that we are afforded a close look at the derivatives of the succubus. The value system, norms, and the mores of Greek society were totally committed to instituting the domination of women; in fact, the Greeks considered the victory of males over females the very foundation for a civilized existence. The succubus explodes in Plato's philosophy that the authentic soul is incarnated as a male, and only when it succumbs to the body is it reincarnated in the body of a female, and then into the body of some beast resembling the evil character into which it has fallen. The body becomes the site of shame, and patriarchy projects upon the female of the race all its abhorrence, hostility and fear of the bodily powers which tempt and seduce, and from which he wishes to be independent. One can feel this hostile shame in the despised and rejected form of the succubus, the power of woman in the face of which he feels threatened by diminishment. "Woman," says Euripides, "is a more terrible thing than the violence of the raging sea, than the force of torrents, than the sweeping breath of fire." Aeschylus's vision of the feminine is of a disgusting "wet biology." His vision conjures forth images of the furies, archaic beings dripping with dark blood screaming for revenge. In the *Oresteia*, Orestes cries out to Apollo, when, after the matricide, he sees the furies:

> Ah, Lord Apollo, how they grow and multiply,
> Repulsive for the blood drops of their dripping eyes.
> (Aeschylus/Lattimore, 1969: 161)

This is what has become of woman's ties with nature; her very existence has become a testimony to the gods' hatred of mankind. Unfortunately, this is also a supreme articulation of man's alienation from the sources of his own natural essence as a human being.

The succubus in the Judeo-Christian world

Greek attitudes towards women had an enormous impact on the Judeo-Christian religion. The mythic narratives of Western religion set up the structures of consciousness that we inherited from Greek mythology and philosophy (which are based upon ancient Mesopotamian narratives).The fact that the religion of the Goddess was a target for Hebrew oppression, and that the Church Fathers of the Judeo-Christian tradition were misogynists has been written about extensively. Repression of the feminine dimension of the divine in the early church seems to be based on Philo's law of preeminence, which "always pertains to the masculine, and the feminine always comes short of and is less than it" (Engelsman, 1979: 139). What this means is "anything feminine cannot be divine, and anything divine must be masculine" (p. 139). It was upon the last assaults by the Hebrews and Christians of the first centuries after Christ that the religion of the goddess was finally suppressed. Elaine Pagels, for example, states that "by the time the process of sorting the various writings ended virtually all the feminine imagery for God had disappeared from orthodox Christian tradition" (1979: 57).

In Judeo-Christianity, males possess the generative power of nature. Creation takes place through an act of will; material comes into being through a purely mental act. The male as father is an embodiment of this Logos:

> In the beginning when God created the heavens and the earth, the earth was a formless void and darkness covered the face of the deep, while a wind from God swept over the face of the waters. Then God said, "Let there be light"; and there was light.
>
> (Genesis 1:1–4)

A disembodied mind is the source and origin of all being. In other words, mind produces matter. Mankind has lost the feminine contribution to creation.

There are countless infamous passages depicting the succubus woman in the Old and New Testaments. For example, in Ecclesiastes, the first openly misogynistic statement in the Bible appears: "Now I find woman more bitter than death; she is all traps, her hands are fetters and her heart is snares." That the content being projected to create this image of woman is shame is not so clear, but made obvious in the fact that the Levite priests misspelled and mispronounced the name of the Goddess Baal by saying "boseth" which means shame, and referred to her only in the masculine gender (Stone, 1976: 166).

Men of the late Middle Ages and Renaissance elaborated the theme of woman's abominable nature, the temptress who leads man to his downfall in a variety of ways. Through the violent imposition and eventually forced acceptance of the male religions, woman had finally been maneuvered into a role far removed from the ancient status she once held in the lands where the Queen of Heaven reigned. Most alarming was the quality of the absolute in the decrees credited to the omnipotent male deity. As time went on, the long, powerful arm of the Church reached everywhere and with it came the unquestionable "moral" attitudes and shame-riddened subservient role assigned to woman.

The concept of a creative goddess was banned by Christian theologians over two thousand years ago, and by Jewish leaders hundreds of years before that. Once the Judeo-Christian tradition took hold, woman's sphere of influence increasingly shrank. But it took until 1300 A.D. to thoroughly eradicate the image of woman as benign Earth Mother. This final *coup de grâc*e was affected through the persecution of the witch, what Dr. Margaret Murray suggests was simply a continuation of the suppression of the ancient goddess religion (Stone, 1976). The eradication of the maternal feminine was completed in the same way it began – through the image of the witch. Pope Innocent the VIII, with his Bul of 1484, made the demonization of female power official with "a campaign of torture and death began that would take the lives of an estimated 9 million people, 80 percent of whom were women" (Starhawk, 1979: 262).

The witch was an easy scapegoat for communities suffering the pitiless, unending struggle for existence. She could inflict harm by employing her magical powers – her Evil Eye. As the devil's agent and death's handmaiden, she concocted evil which took the large-scale form of wholesale death by famine, plagues, pestilence, tyranny and war. It was a time when no man could prevent his crops from being decimated, prisons were filled with malefactors and debtors, the stench and unaccustomed noise of new industry was inescapable, and no woman could be assured a safe childbirth when infant after infant died for no obvious reason (Williams & Williams, 1978). This could not be God's doing, for such suffering could not be squared with an ultimate purpose of love. Desperate to account for these afflictions in order to have some form of control, the people surmised that something of a supernatural nature was afoot. People turned to religious writings, the Bible and treatises of ancient Greek philosophers. It was under these afflicted conditions and patriarchal influences that European civilization came to be haunted by the idea of the witch. And their solution? Purifying society of evil necessitated killing the witches – and they did this in massive numbers. This phase of history epitomizes the human potential for inhumanity in what is now called the woman's holocaust.

The witch hunts were driven by the strong erotic and misogynistic elements of Medieval Christianity – factors that might well be expected in the sexually repressed, male-dominated society that remains tragically current. The image of the succubus comes across clearly in every paragraph of the *Malleus Maleficarum* (Hammer of Witches, 1486), a book which makes evil and woman synonymous with the word witch. Written by two Dominican Inquisitors to explain why women are more prone to evil, this single book served for two hundred years as a manual for the killing of witches. It is a study in repression and fear of woman, the enigma who is both sexually omnipotent and morally weak. Man had a place to put his highly sexual, shamed self that needed to be denied onto the female – those fertile, powerful creatures who menstruate and give birth. These unmentionable sexual fears lay at the root of witch-hunting terrorism in general, as well as the root of many forms of shame-driven male violence against women today (Gilligan, 1992). The relationship between the witch who could kill with a single glance, absolute shame and the succubus is made clear in the following passage: "all witchcraft is from carnal lust, which is in woman insatiable … wherefore for the sake of fulfilling their lust they consort even with devils" (Kramer & Sprenger, 1971: 127). And even more clearly in relation to shame, another passage states: "We must answer the question why God permits witchcraft to affect the generative powers more than any other human function … It is on account of the shamefulness of … the venereal act … and because the original sin due to the guilt of our first parents is inherited by means of that act." Witches could place "evil impediments on the act of generative power" (p. 52), one of the most alarming of which was causing a man's penis to vanish into thin air, so that he could "see and feel nothing except his smooth body, uninterrupted by any member" (p. 130). The witches' evil deeds, just like the child-killing aspect of the succubus, include killing infants both in the womb and at birth. They are even in the habit of stealing, vampire like, into the homes to drink the blood of children.

The shift from Great to Terrible Mother was complete with the notion that the Evil Eyes of the witch had the power to destroy. Kramer and Sprenger accepted as an established fact that the gaze of certain persons – menstruating women for example – had a natural power capable of doing real harm to others' minds. According to the *Malleus Maleficarum*, witches cause harm "by a mere look or glance from their eyes, and publicly boast that they cannot be punished" (1971: 131). This look is directed against men: "Witches can with the help of the Devil bring harm upon men and their affairs … their reputation, their body, their reason, and their life" (p. 134). The inquisitors were so terrified of the witches' eyes that the accused had to approach them walking backwards to ensure the avoidance of eye contact.

Many of the punishments were public spectacles with the intention of shaming and eradicating any relationship to a mother's goodness, even on a personal level. Primarily women became the victims for the horror of torture, burning at the stake or hanging in the gallows. Consider the following vignette of one execution:

> The crowd of spectators began to stir. Two open, horse-drawn carts started to make their way through the throng … The executioner tested the pincers, large iron tongs, the ends of which had been plunged into the smoking brazier…
>
> Then he walked up to Anna Pappenheimer, seized her linen shift with both hands at the neck, and ripped it open with one powerful tug … The people who could see this part of the execution craned their necks, surged toward the spot … The executioner drew the first of the red-hot pincers … Finally the executioner sliced off Anna Pappenheimer's breasts … the severed breasts were rubbed around Anna's mouth and around the mouths of her two sons…
>
> (Heinemann/Kiraly, 2000: 2)

Those victims who dared to speak out or inquire further would be made to wear any number of enormously heavy iron heads which were called "Masks of Shame" (see Figure 2.7). Those women who violated clothing regulations would be made to wear the "Wooden Ruff," the dressmaker's huge cast iron collar.

The Witch Hunt crossed the ocean and entered the New World, influencing the colonists long established in Massachusetts, by the late seventeenth century. The accusers were mostly men, and they were accusing mostly women. By the turn of the seventeenth century, 20 out of 21 witches were women (Williams & Williams, 1978: 11). Even after the persecution of witches ended in the eighteenth century, women continued to experience a contraction of social and personal liberties. From the Renaissance through to the present, masculine principles dominate and,

Figure 2.7 Mask of Shame. The long tongue and big ears symbolize gossip and nosiness. (Formerly on display in the Medieval Crime and Punishment Museum in Rothenburg, Germany.)

in more recent times, have peaked in the expansion and the rise of capitalism (greed), the industrial revolution (and industrial waste), and the triumphs of science and technology (and nuclear weaponry). And along with this rise, external achievement and the creation of structures dominate over process, science rules over nature, trade and commerce are more important than agriculture and cooking, the public life of business and politics take precedence over family relations and motherhood, worship of money replaces reverence for the earth and, most of all, people are treated more as objects than as subjects (Thompson, 1981). Overall, the highest value is placed on a masculine sense of achievement and power – and yet, it is the kind of power that gets generated out of the driving force of the succubus, a form of conscienceless power due to the dissociation resulting from the projection of absolute shame.

The succubus today

In this chapter, we have focused on the image of the succubus as a deeply religious and cultural symbol that has betrayed women by making them containers for men's shame. Eternal and compelling, the succubus exists today as she has in the past. The feminine, oppressed into non-existence as a carrier for shame, loses her own reality and power. When woman's power is taken from her, it can no longer be direct and open. The feminine compensation for this shift in the natural balance of things is a shift in sexual emphasis from fertility, or reproductive power, to erotic power. This means power over the lover and maternal absence, not empowerment of the child. After all, Eve was told "I will greatly multiply your pain in childbearing; in pain you shall bring forth children, yet your desire shall be for your husband" (Genesis 3:16). Female power is no longer connected to being the mother of sons, but the destroyer of men. The obese Great Mother is succeeded by the *femme fatale*. Gone is the Great Mother as symbol of fertility, with pendulous breasts and rotund buttocks; come is the voluptuous young maiden with round breasts and slender, long legs whose body is merchandised. In the male order of civilization we encounter sexiness, the erotic power of the beautiful woman to lure a powerful man to his own destruction. Today the succubus lives in the dresses of Versace, who selected the head of Medusa as the defining and abiding symbol of the House of Versace. He chose the image of Medusa for the purpose "of seduction . . . a sense of history, classicism. Medusa means seduction . . . a dangerous attraction" (Seal, 2003: 276).

The power of the masculine over the feminine is the power of absolute shame over humankind. Thompson describes "the archangel of evolution" inevitably created out of the deep collective repression of the feminine:

> if the feminine is totally repressed and blood, nature, and the esoteric dimension of the heavens totally wiped out, then a terrible situation is created which will necessitate the appearance of another avatar of evolution, a Lilith of transformation through destruction.
>
> (1981: 241)

But I am rushing ahead to the end of the book. In the next section, we'll look at the succubus from a psychological point of view, as a powerful and pervasive symbol that has permeated the schools of thought that study the human psyche. The image of the succubus comes forth in the writings and lives of the Fathers of Psychoanalysis, Sigmund Freud and Carl Jung. These two men, who decisively influenced twentieth-century thought, were human – all too human – and very much a product of their time. They inadvertently inculcated the succubus into the very heart of depth psychology.

Part II

The image of the succubus in the writings of Freud and Jung

> The man is afraid of being weakened by the woman, infected with her femininity and of then showing himself incapable. The effect that coitus has of discharging tensions and causing flaccidity may be the prototype of what the man fears; and realization of the influence which the woman gains over him through sexual intercourse, the consideration she thereby forces from him, may justify the extension of this fear.
>
> (Freud, 1964c: 198)

> Unconsciousness is the primal sin, evil itself, for the Logos. Therefore, its first reactive act of liberation is matricide.
>
> (Jung, 1954: 96)

> When men first decided they had the power to understand one another in an entirely new way, it should not surprise us that the result could be tragic.
>
> (Kerr, 1993: 15)

> Just as the faults of princes must be expiated by whole nations, the errors of great minds extend their influence over whole generations and even over centuries.
>
> (Schopenhauer quoted by Bailey, 1965: 61)

Chapter 3

The split between Freud and Jung

Woman – obliterated by her religious persecution as a witch, removed as irrational by the new science of the Renaissance, and silenced by the claustrophobic patriarchal grip of the Victorian era. Her oppression has become so complete that the maternal feminine is excised from consciousness. Inevitably, then, the blinding power of the Terrible Mother, coming as it does from the repressed deep in the unconscious, is completely cut off from conscious control – and so becomes annihilating. The waning role of religion in supporting the sexual caste system is extended to the burgeoning profession of psychoanalysis. The ground is fertile for the succubus to take hold again, this time in the theories of psychoanalysis which came to define the psychology of modern man, and the writings and lives of Sigmund Freud and Carl Jung.

This is not to say that Freud and Jung didn't contribute anything to the severely repressed, turn of the century woman. Both men were gifted with an extraordinary grasp of life and ability to see into people. And by listening in a new way, they gave nervous patients a voice they had not had before. They gave new value to inner psychic realities, and from this came a new appreciation for the externally real. Feeling the openness to express different childhood experiences created the possibility of reflecting in a new way on the origins of one's own personality. The nineteenth century saw the rise of the notion of the unconscious and a new experience of the collective unconscious through their work.

Prior to their influence, disturbed women were taken care of as best they could be by their families, but if this care failed, the most atrocious remedies were attempted. Ovariectomies and clitoridectomies were done to rid the female body of the infection hidden within it. More humanely, Freud noticed a whole host of disorders resulting from Victorian women's silence. He called these hysteria after classic Greek theory which postulated the core of female dis-ease to be the uterus (*hustera* in Latin, hence the name hysteria). Hysterical women were under the influence of deeply primitive material that they couldn't repress, and so had to be caused by some sexual or procreative dysfunction (Kerr, 1993: 22).

Despite what they did give to women through their genius, their best intentions, their intensity towards self-reflection, their disciplined application of analytic principles or their understanding of the dynamics of the unconscious, Jung and

Freud, in pursuit of their own power, passions and desires, played right along with the repression of the maternal feminine and the ego of our culture which is founded on the abjection of the mother. What is denied by vision, however, comes back in through the rear door. Engelsman succinctly describes Freud's conception of the return of repressed material:

> First, certain elements of the feminine might evade the initial repression and remain accessible to memory and occasionally emerge into consciousness. These fragments, however, would still be "isolated, like foreign bodies out of connection with the rest." Or, second, since the material that is repressed maintains its upward urge, it will eventually enter consciousness in disguised form. The fact that it cannot return "smoothly and unaltered" testifies to the resistance of the ego which cannot be overcome.
>
> (1979: 121)

The mythic pattern and archetypal structure of the succubus was bound to surface out of Freud and Jung's unconscious, one manifestation being a theoretical exaggeration of psychoanalysis as science during a time when scientific discoveries would guarantee lasting fame. This stance actually served to intensify the repression of the feminine even more, giving the succubus greater thrust in the realm of reason. Even though they asked deep, primordial questions, psychology was to lose its "psyche;" its roots in soul, or the true self, was to slowly fade out of the picture with their increasing rationalizations around the feminine.

Freud and Jung's intellectual position in itself was a mask, a defense against shame. Their defensiveness, however, did not prevent psychoanalysis' eventual development into an art and humanity as well. Art and science are related modes of thought and spring from the same root structures of consciousness: the artist can experience a dim intuition of truth, and the scientist can prove a dim intuition of truth. Psychoanalysis has become not only a clinical method, but a literary, artistic and cultural movement with the potential of being a *weltanschauung*. Only as an art and science can psychoanalysis serve as bridge between the conscious, the unconscious and the whole of life.

Freud and Jung's shame, however, goes much deeper than their choice of paradigm; it has been built into the very structure of their theories, so that despite their initial affinities (their first meeting lasted 13 hours) that resulted in a profitable give and take, their theories have not found real integration. Sexuality and spirituality are pairs of opposites that need integration, yet it is at this point that shame petrifies psychoanalytic progress, and splits the body of psychoanalysis in two.

I believe that Freud and Jung's blindness to their own shame nearly destroyed the "science" they built together, and its reverberations are still felt in the undercurrents of depth psychology today. Just as shame in the form of the succubus reshaped our cultural history as the alienations of civilization set in, the succubus took hold and began her destructive effects as psychoanalytic theory became increasingly restricted to suit the personal and political need of its founders – and to obscure their male vulnerability and shame.

The complex and disturbing history of the break between Freud and Jung is well-known (see Kerr's *A Most Dangerous Method*): "Of all its manifold dimensions, perhaps the most important has also been the hardest to conceptualize: the relation between the personal factor and the theoretical struggle that arose out of it and ultimately supplanted it" (1993: 10). When one looks at what is hardest to conceptualize through the eyes of shame, however, one clearly and simply sees the image of the succubus linking the "personal factor" and "theoretical struggle" to supplant the foundations of psychoanalysis. Just how this is true will be shown in the pages to come.

Historical background

Before turning to a specific analysis of the succubus and her role in Freud and Jung's shame, a little background on their relationship is necessary. Let me make a long story very short: Freud and Jung enjoyed a six-year partnership that decisively altered the course of twentieth-century thought. During this time Freud and Jung were both ambitious young men, tantalized by prospects of future greatness. Psychoanalysis was founded on Freud's theories, but it was the medically established Jung and his mentor, Eugene Bleuler, who put Freud on the scientific map (Kerr, 1993: 8). Pines states that it was Freud's shame over being Jewish that made him fight desperately to get the Christian Swiss involved so that psychoanalysis would not remain identified with Jewishness (1987: 18). Meanwhile, Jung was formulating a psychology that sought to articulate the problems of individuation and wholeness by building upon the foundation of Freudian theory, but when he began to make revisions to Freud's theory of the resolution of the Oedipus Complex, he instigated the final and definitive collapse of their partnership.

Their main theoretical difference is upon the point where a boy must separate from his mother (there is a female version, but it will not be addressed due to my focus on masculine shame). Both Freud and Jung concur that for the sake of the development of masculine consciousness, matricide must be the first act of liberation. Past this point their similarities stop. Freud's Oedipus Complex explains the myth (rather than the other way around), and he concludes that it is only by resisting the regressive pull of the mother that a boy succeeds in strengthening ego, developing a superego, and extricating himself from mother's engulfing grip to eventually fully enter the world of knowledge and power. This is the key to the child's process of individuation; should this not occur, the child remains, according to Freud, in a perpetual state of narcissism.

For Jung, the formation of consciousness and the ego involves not just one initial break from the world of the mother, but repeated breaks in the form of periodic returns to her underworld realm. This is for the purpose of letting go of rational consciousness long enough for renewal, revisioning and discovery. This process of return and separation builds the ego–Self axis, the connecting link between the center of consciousness and the center of the entire psyche (unconscious and conscious). In other words, Freud's paternal law against incest is regularly broken on the symbolic level, and regression to the womb to conquer the mother is part of the hero's journey to rebirth.

Jung turned to myths as purveyors of knowledge that could shed light on the formation of complexes. In *Symbols of Transformation* (1955), the book that precipitated his break with Freud, Jung advances Freud's thinking by turning to antiquity and exploring the archetypal motif of the hero's birth and rebirth in an attempt to link and transform sexuality into spirituality, the meaning, according to Jung, of the hero's descent. By examining massive mythological material from around the world, Jung sought to establish a relationship between the presence of mother–son incest, the rebirth motif and the cyclical rhythms of nature. Freud took issue with using ancient myths to explain the formation of the complex, and thought the motif of self-sacrifice was a projection of a repression of the ego's sacrifice of its vigorous drives – basically a part of the castration complex. Freud could see nothing in the book but engulfment in the mother and resistance to the father.

Freud became very distrustful towards Jung and felt that he had to take back command of psychoanalysis. Freud's determination was reflected in "a look" which Jung speaks of in his memoirs:

> Freud had a dream – I would not think it right to air the problem it involved. I interpreted it as best I could, but added that a great deal more could be said about it if he would supply me with some additional details from his private life. Freud's response to these words was a curious look – a look of utmost suspicion. Then he said, "But I cannot risk my authority!" At that moment he lost it altogether. That sentence burned itself into my memory; and in it the end of our relationship was already foreshadowed. Freud was placing personal authority above truth.
>
> (1965: 158)

After their split, however, Jung did indeed "air the problem it involved," a situation which, if true, would certainly have risked Freud's authority, hence the survival of psychoanalysis. But then, Jung had no room to talk; he also compromised its survival the very same way. Both were seduced by the succubus and fell into different enactments of Oedipal rivalry – but more on this later.

Freud's reaction to Jung, and Jung's reaction to Freud, clearly indicates a place of deep psychic conflict. Yet it is also true that the powers of the succubus run very deeply through the whole of Western culture; she derives her very existence and power from the repression of the mother and the feminine, and she resides at the collision point of the sexual and aggressive instincts. When Freud and Jung began exploring the two drives that make human communal life difficult (to the point that now our very survival is threatened), it was inevitable that they would encounter their internal succubi, and a place where their image of mother is scarcely distinguishable. Yet during their conflict both chose dissociation in the face of her, and both would pursue power even more determinedly. With their shame catalyzed yet repressed, they both forfeit "truth" and activate the underlying structure of beliefs about males and females. Under Freud and Jung's scrutiny, mother continues to be seen as an object of condemnation. With this dynamic in mind, the end of their relationship was just a matter of time. The pursuit of ambition and power inevitably results in less tolerance and more dogma. Freud and Jung's last act of collaboration was "to accept the fact that they were stalemated" (Kerr, 1993: 10). This occurred at the Fourth International Psychoanalytic Congress, September 7–8, 1913, when they spoke not one word to each other: "so it was in silence that one of the most vexed partnerships in the history of ideas ended" (p. 3).

To look only at Freud and Jung's psyches for the source of the problem does not explain why they protect themselves, or that their thinking can span five generations of analysts who have perpetuated the split. Freud and Jung's theories were very much determined by the society in which they lived – hence, plagued with too much of the masculine drive to dominate, degrade and destroy. It is in this impasse that the succubus takes hold and continues to be a driving, splitting force in the field of depth psychology today. At the more manageable level of the personal unconscious, she maintains her hold in the as yet unexplored absolute shame of Freud and Jung. There she takes two forms. Freud conceives of Medusa as the penisless vagina of the mother and proof of her castrating powers that force the resolution of the Oedipal conflict once and for all. Freud also coined the term penis envy, a related concept which captures the image of a mother that wants nothing less than her son's own genitals, and would relish the opportunity to cut off his penis – clearly a place of infantile castration anxiety and primitive shame for Freud.

A blind Salome whose vision is eventually restored visits Jung in two visions during his "confrontation with the unconscious," a process that immediately followed his break with Freud. In this confrontation, we see Jung driven to probe the depths of his own psyche and undergo the death and rebirth experience of the most valued hero that he wrote about extensively in *Symbols* (1955). It appears that the ultimate split from Freud – the loss of the father and a descent into the mother – was so painful that Jung teetered on the edge of insanity for several years. Upon return from his descent, Jung attempted to put as much distance as possible between the split from Freud and his personal memories.

In the pages to come, the images of these succubi will be amplified in order to expose and begin to metabolize Freud and Jung's core shame – an aspect of their scientific genius that has not, as far as I know, been the subject of much in-depth attention. To put it most simply, Freud and Jung personally enacted around the image of the succubus the same two historical male reactions to shame and its projection onto women – oppress and eliminate or dominate and conquer – and in this place the succubus sucked the soul out of psychology. Freud required repudiation of the maternal feminine and acceptance of the universal Oedipus

Complex, while Jung identified with heroic conquering to encounter the feminine in a process of self-transformation. But their projection of shame also led to the destruction of their relationship, the near death of psychoanalysis at the time, and the continuing lack of theoretical integration despite the fact that their theories are simply on opposite sides of the spectrum of human life and death – animal, instinctual sexuality and transcendent spirituality, both dimensions of the maternal feminine as manifest in Lilith, Queen of the Succubi.

In his shame, Freud is threatened with being turned to stone in the face of Medusa, and so, like the hero Perseus who is guided by the hand of the sexless goddess Athena, he eliminates the mother by cutting off her head in a single act of matricide. Jung can return to the underworld and face the incestuous mother because he is identified with Siegfried, the omnipotent hero who conquers – not a cowardly, vulnerable man who dissociates and represses Salome.

Chapter 4

Sigmund Freud's Medusa

Freud was the man whose great contribution was to reveal to us so much about the hidden shame of humankind. His genius opened up whole new territories of the mind, infant and childhood sexuality which exposed the presence and origins of our wildest sexual longings. Our wishes include cannibalizing our enemies, and anal sadistic drives that make eating our own feces enticing; our aggressive and sexual wishes include killing our father (or mothers), and sleeping with our mothers (or fathers). Sexuality, that devious, evil succubus element so repressed in Victorian times, is the unassailable constant, the "unshakable bulwark," of Freud's entire theory.

Freud unmasked humankind's shame over repressed instinctual impulses, and his inspiration may have been that he was a very shame-sensitive person. Pines points out that

> the few references Freud makes to his own visual appearance as seen in mirrors show how much he disliked what he saw. He saw an elderly, ugly man and at times failed to recognize and to own the image as himself.
>
> (1987: 17)

In not realizing the need to look more deeply into the mirror, however, Freud becomes the man who builds the succubus into the structure of his theory on the Oedipus Complex and its resolution – an area in Freud's thinking fraught with dissociated masculine shame. Most everything Freud has to say on this subject is distorted with projection and defensive theorizing – the exquisitely sensitive material re-visioned by Jung. His preoccupation with issues connected to sexuality and castration, a deeply rooted male angst over annihilation and fears of inferiority, made his thinking on the resolution of the Oedipus Complex ludicrous. Transition to the development of the superego calls for an act of matricide, a heroic killing that leads to an elimination of shame. The following detailed examination of the Oedipus Complex and Freud's theory of narcissism will reveal the presence of shame.

Freud's repudiation of the mother

To begin with, psychoanalysis is theoretically prefaced on the need to replace the attachment to the mother with the higher aim of identification with the father. This substitution appears to eradicate the need for the mother altogether. Freud's phallic system validates a person's value to the degree that he succeeds in eliminating the mother and incorporating the father. It is as if Freud evacuates his deepest shame onto the mother, who becomes a contaminated person to be quarantined, isolated and forgotten as much as possible – and that is exactly how a man who fears being weak remains blind to his shame.

Just how missing the mother is in Freud's thinking is exemplified with a passage that appears at the very beginning of *Civilization and Its Discontents* when he is writing about an "oceanic" feeling and its relationship to religion. Correctly understanding that this symbiotic state of oneness stems from the infant's utter dependence on a caring environment, Freud then demonstrates massive repression with an absurd interpretation of just what that nurturing environment is:

> The derivation of religious needs from the infant's helplessness and longing for the father aroused by it seems to me incontrovertible, especially since the feeling is not simply prolonged from childhood days, but is permanently sustained by fear of the superior power of Fate. I cannot think of any need in childhood as strong as the need for the father's protection.
>
> (1964e: 72)

Freud overlooks the obvious. Life begins for the human child in a deep bond with the mother, and all experiences of oneness resonate with this first profound experience. Freud is reluctant to attribute any power to the pre-oedipal mother, and determines that civilization has evolved as a defense against nature – male against female. His continuing unconscious struggle forced Freud into taking stands that he really did not believe in, intellectual positions that were reasonable only on the surface and made the vital importance of the mother non-existent. And that is where his theory of the Oedipus Complex begins.

The Oedipus Complex

Freud defined the Oedipus Complex as that period when the boy is in love with his mother, drawn to her, compelled by desires for her which are fueled by his instincts. Naturally, then, the father becomes the boy's opponent. When the end of the Oedipus Complex is described in detail, Freud tells us that the ego is "smashed to pieces by the threat of castration" (1964d: 257). Through this image, Freud conveys the infantile idea of a fragmentation related to survival and loss of the good mother – the psychotic core of shame (Ayers, 2003). According to Freud, upon realizing the *actual* possibility of castration, and determining to separate from his mother, the child begins to develop a superego. The very point of separation from the mother is psychotic, but this is masked by the Oedipal triad overcoming the pre-oedipal dyad.

Two types of castration anxiety

There are two types of castration anxiety that inspire the erection of a superego. One major source of castration anxiety comes from the father as an implied threat of punishment for his son's interest in the mother/wife. No matter how much this threat is loaded with anxiety, however, it is hard for a boy to avoid the magnetic pull of his sexual connection to his mother, especially given the fact that his first erotic encounter was suckling at her breast. His continued attraction leads him into the deepest area of castration anxiety, one that centers on the prohibition of masturbation. At this level, the primary emasculator is the mother. She threatens castration as the punishment for masturbation, and her penisless genitals – the head of Medusa – provides the final proof and testament that the permanent removal of the penis is a real possibility. Mother's vagina, that dark passageway through which human life is born, is looked upon as dangerous, murky, and ravenous with teeth – an image that captures man's weakness. In Freud's words:

> When the male child's interest turns to his genitals he betrays the fact by manipulating them frequently … More or less plainly, more or less brutally, a threat is pronounced that this part of him which he values so highly will be taken away from him. Usually it is from women that the threat emanates; very often they seek to strengthen their authority by a reference to the father … It is not until a fresh experience comes his way that the child begins to reckon with the possibility of being castrated, and then only hesitatingly and unwillingly … The observation finally breaks down his unbelief in the sight of the female genitals … With this, the loss of his own penis becomes imaginable, and the threat of castration takes its deferred effect … The child turns away from the Oedipus complex.
>
> (1964d: 174)

With the onset of masturbation, the child is aware of another source of pleasure arising in his body which is not connected to his mother's care. The child's display of genital stimulation is not enthusiastically reflected by the gleam in mother's eye. Mother's disapproval becomes one of the first major narcissistic injuries. With this rejection or lack of reflection, good mother becomes terrible mother, and the boy meets the eyes of the succubus in Medusa's gaze.

Medusa

With concepts such as Narcissus and Oedipus, one would tend to see mythology as much on Freud's mind, so the way he starts out his essay "Medusa's Head" (started in 1922, never completed, and published posthumously in 1940) is very strange: "We have not often attempted to interpret individual mythological themes, but an interpretation suggests itself easily in the case of the horrifying decapitated head of Medusa." Freud saw the decapitation of Medusa as an obvious symbol for castration. Decapitation = castration, and the snakes that make up Medusa's hair echo the same. Freud has this to say about Medusa's resting place:

> This symbol of horror is worn upon her dress by the virgin goddess Athena. And right so, for thus she becomes a woman who is unapproachable and repels all sexual desires – since she displays the terrifying genitals of the Mother ... The terror of Medusa is thus a terror of castration that is linked to the sight of something. Numerous analyses have made us familiar with the occasion for this: it occurs when a boy, who has hitherto been unwilling to believe the threat of castration, catches sight of the female genitals ... surrounded by hair, and essentially those of his mother.
>
> (1964g: 273)

And yet Medusa is symbolically incestuous because she seduces the male into surrendering the boundaries of the ego-oriented self to merge with the mother. The turning to stone, stiffening like an erection, however, offers solace and reassures the boy that he is still in possession of his penis. The erect male organ has an apotropaic effect: Freud states that "to display the penis (or any of its surrogates) is to say: 'I am not afraid of you. I defy you. I have a penis. Here, then, is another way of intimidating the Evil Spirit' [Eye]." Medusa is an incarnate Evil Eye, for she can slay by a malign effluence coming from her eyes, and has a face that depicts hatred and terror as the source of evil (Ayers, 2003: 133).

Castration anxiety connected to the father is due to rejection, whereas with the mother it is seduction – the succubus and a psychotic place of maternal loss where Freud is petrified over being "literally smashed to pieces by the threat of castration." Freud theorizes that the boy, panic stricken by the notion that his desire to murder his father and sexually possess his mother will lead to castration, renounces the most assertive impulse he has ever felt (hence, the beginning of a boy's rage). One of the greatest insights of importance in masculine development is the idea that there is no way for a son to develop as a man without undergoing Oedipal erotic defeat, hence, castration. He "identifies with the aggressor" – his father – and participates wholeheartedly in repressing his Oedipal wishes. He no longer wishes to eliminate his father, but to be just like him. The boy sacrifices mirroring by the mother in the hopes of finding similar reflection through satisfactory adult experiences in love and work – the areas Freud marked out as indicative of successful male adaptation to culture. And so it is that castration threat, or the denial of shame, is the means by which the Oedipal conflict with the mother is resolved – and so it is that the mother is repressed and the succubus is catalyzed.

The eyes of shame and Oedipus the King

Freud betrays his unresolved maternal issues in the name he chose for the Oedipus Complex, a tragedy depicting the blind enactment of one's inner, latent, incestuous wishes. The theme of blindness and attacks on sight is as central to the Oedipus story as it is to the core of masculine shame. Oedipus' downfall is brought about by "blind deeds" and a blind search for a ubiquitous truth; Lauis consults the oracle in secret, and ends up banishing Jocasta. This leads to the birth of Oedipus out of deception and seduction – out of the womb of the succubus; Tiresias, the seer made blind for seeing the unacceptable, is consulted and must pronounce an unacceptable truth which he would rather not see and forget. Finally, shamed into telling Oedipus he is his father's murderer, Tiresias says:

> You mock my blindness? Let me tell you this.
> You with your precious eyes,
> You're blind to the corruption of your life,
> to the house you live in, those you live with –
> who are your parents? Do you know? All unknowing
> you are the scourge of your own flesh and blood,
> the dead below the earth and the living here above,
> and the double lash of your mother and father's curse
> will whip you from this land one day, their footfall
> treading you down in terror, darkness shrouding
> your eyes that now can see the light! . . .
> No man will ever be rooted from the earth as brutally as you.
> (Sophocles/Fagles, 1982: 162)

Oedipus the King is also a tale that depicts the dynamics resulting from the kind of failed maternal mirroring that creates shame's earliest form: Oedipus was cast out and abandoned as an infant, deeply craving recognition and identity which motivated his quest (which got derailed into power and authority); Oedipus was born a phallic son with a name meaning "swollen-foot," translated by Freud as meaning "erection" (Kerr, 1993: 258); in masculine shame one attacks seeing while simultaneously being compelled by the drive to see, and Oedipus, in his search for the truth and blinding himself upon its discovery, is plagued by both dimensions; and last, his omnipotence hides a ruthless self-blame. Oedipus' self-blinding is his own castration.

Oedipus epitomizes the relationship between the succubus and a man's shame. The Sphinx, with her ability to lure men to her abode, is an image of the succubus and the element that seals Oedipus' destiny. Interestingly, Lilith, Queen of the Succubi, is depicted as a winged sphinx (or winged lion) (Hurwitz, 1999: 75). The impotent men who could not solve the femme fatale's riddle were devoured on the spot, but Oedipus was as hopelessly drawn to challenge and conquer the Sphinx as Perseus, or Freud, was compelled to cut off Medusa's head. Oedipus, man of supreme power and insight, does not appeal to the gods for help, but uses reflective intelligence alone to answer correctly: It is an answer that will lead to the concretization of his shame and turn him into "the pollution of Thebes:"

> Oedipus, approaching Thebes fresh from the murder of Laius, guessed the answer ... The mortified Sphinx leaped from Mount Phicium and dashed herself to pieces in the valley below. At this the grateful Thebans acclaimed Oedipus King, and he married Jocasta, unaware that she was his mother.
>
> (Graves, 1955: 10)

In answering the riddle, Oedipus made rational man the measure of all things by pronouncing the word "man" – as if the Greek metaphor of man as mind is an answer to all the riddles of life. Oedipus strayed too far from his roots, forgets the power of the gods, and so his life is to end up in a welter of perversity. He may have won the contest, but he didn't kill the Sphinx: she leapt to her own death, creating, in fact, a failed matricide and the intensification of her power in the underworld of the unconscious (Goux, 1993). Oedipus comes to see his shame and is so horrified by the recognition that he killed his father and married his mother that he blinds himself with brooches torn from his dead mother's gown (Jocasta had by this time hung herself). Oedipus, blood splattering his face, cries out:

> I did what I had to. You know I did ... Could these eyes have looked upon my father in the house of Hades? Could these eyes have faced my mother in her agony? I have sinned against them both – a sin no suicide could purge ... Incestuous sin! Bride! Wife! Mother! All of one union! All the most heinous sins that man can know! The most horrible shame – I can no longer speak of it.
>
> (Graves, 1955: 89)

All around the privileged structure of the omnipotent hero there is an emptiness to which Oedipus is unable to bear witness, "the most horrible shame" – so he tears out his eyes. Oedipus gives up all sight and knowledge, and the drama ends with Oedipus bowing to authority. Oedipus is asked to remove his presence which is a "pollution to man's dignity" and he in turn begs to be sent out to a place where "no human voice can greet him."

Freud's shame and Oedipus

In realizing his shame, Oedipus overcomes his self-centered narcissism, accepts responsibility, and relinquishes his title as King and his omnipotent will which could pardon himself. In Sophocles' subsequent tragedy, *Oedipus at Colonus*, the old, blind Oedipus, in realizing the truth about himself, returns to the maternal feminine. According to Sophocles, mother takes ascendancy over ego and consciousness. But Freud never reached Colonus; he remained identified with Oedipus the King (not the shamed outcast who in his death reunites with Mother

Earth). Matricide and its resulting blindness prevented the mystical union with the Great Mother that restored Oedipus' vision. This fact is directly reflected in Freud's own fantasy life. His mother was convinced of her son's great destiny. As a child Freud internalized her reflection by fantasizing military distinction, which later gave way to the ambition of being a cultural hero. Freud dreamed that some day he would be commemorated by a portrait bust in the Aula of the University, and the inscription that he hoped would be thought appropriate to him was the Apollonian line from *Oedipus the King*: "Who solved the riddle of the Sphinx and was a man most mighty." On the occasion of his fiftieth birthday, Freud's supporters presented him with a medallion of himself inscribed with the line as epithet. He felt faint, like the strong among us that "faint away like children when pushed to take the whole meaning of life on themselves, to support it with their own meager creature powers" (Becker, 1973: 20). With this powerful identification in mind, taking the specific form of Freud as cultural hero and discoverer of infant sexuality, let us now look at his theory of narcissism, which contains the shame that atrophied Freud's Oedipus Complex.

Narcissism

Freud's mind seemed drawn to tragedy when he set about understanding the unconscious; Narcissus is another well known Greek myth which Freud relied upon to articulate his scientific formulations in psychoanalytic theory – and his choice again betrays his own shame. Narcissus carries many of the same themes as the Oedipus story, but it is, according to Freud, from a primary, auto-erotic level of development. Nevertheless, just like the story of Oedipus, Narcissus is a myth riddled with images of blindness and vision, failures of eyes and mirrors, looking and reflection which provide rich material on the theme of shame (Ayers, 2003: 89–93). In the interest of brevity, however, I want to focus only on the birth of the hero Narcissus, and the unfolding relationship between himself and his mother.

Liriope is a nymph who was raped and nearly drowned by the river god Cephisus while imprisoned in his waters. When it was time for her to give birth, the beauteous nymph brought forth a son, whom she named Narcissus. Through the naming of her son, Liriope announces her expectations and wish for closeness – Narcissus was to be the birth of a version of herself. Such a mother cannot send back sight of her child, because she can only see herself reflected. Graves (1955: 288) states that Liriope means literally "face of (ope) the lirion," another name for the narcissus flower after which her son was named. Motivated by her own need for mirroring, perhaps stemming from her conception of Narcissus from a rape and her ambivalent feelings towards his birth, she is the first to test the reliability of the blind seer Tiresias (who also played a prominent role in the story of Oedipus). She consults him to ask whether her son is going to live a long life or die young. He predicts that Narcissus will have a long life so long as he does not know himself.

Narcissus was "a child with whom one could have fallen in love even in his cradle" (Ovid, 1955: 83). Even a nymph would love him as a child. Long before Narcissus used his eyes to see his own reflection and fall in love with himself, many others were in love with him. All the youths and maidens sought his love, but "in that slender form was a pride so cold that no youth, no maiden touched his heart." The child must free himself from the admiring reflection of his mother, and at this task Narcissus fails. His life is to end in tragedy because of this inability to grasp the fleeting image he loves so dear: "Hanging there motionless" where "no thought of food or rest can draw him from the spot ... he gazes on that false image with eyes that cannot look their fill and through his own eyes perishes."

According to Freud's second conception of narcissism, its prototype is to be found in intrauterine life (Grunberger/Diamanti, 1979: 1). The infant is born into a complete state of oneness with mother. Although this fusion during the post-partum period facilitates human development, its persistence can lead to various narcissistic pathologies. Narcissus is the quintessential image for a person who has completely withdrawn libido from objects and remains self-contained in a state of primary narcissism, or union with the symbiotic but absent mother because she is seeking her own reflection. The human infant naturally selects his mother's face as the first point of orientation, and looks for his reflection there (Ayers, 2003: 34–60). What did Freud meet in his mother's eyes?

Freud's mother

Freud's actual mother is shrouded in mystery and silence, but if we hold the myths of Oedipus and Narcissus in the back of our minds, and then look at scant clues, we can get at least a sense of Freud's feelings for his mother and his relationship with her. A good lead is provided in a letter dated November 2, 1896 that Freud is writing to his good friend Wilhelm Fliess after his father's death on October 23rd. He says:

> By one of those dark pathways behind the official consciousness the old man's death affected me deeply ... he had a significant effect on my life. By the time he died, his life had long been over, but in [my] inner self the whole past has been reawakened by this event. I now feel as if I had been torn up by the roots.
>
> (Masson, 1985b: 170)

"Torn up by the roots" sounds as desperate an upheaval as "literally smashed to pieces," the image used to describe the resolution of the Oedipus Complex. It is a metaphor that reveals an experience of a shattered part of his self that went deep underground and out of sight (the place of shame) being suddenly and abruptly exposed. This exposure sets everything he had experienced in the last 40 years in motion, including memories buried long ago. "Freud's past, even the past he tried to obliterate eleven years earlier by burning letters, notebooks, diaries, and other writings, had been roused from inactivity to a state of ferment" (Salyard, 1988: 404). The word "roots" implies that something of the early mother–infant relationship has become visible, but tearing up by the roots causes dissociation and detachment, significant derailments in developmental processes. Freud has lost his grounding, has been torn away from reality much as maternal absence can create psychotic anxieties for an infant. Freud moves from petrifaction, to movement, to exposure, to shame.

Then Freud goes on in the letter to relate a "pretty little dream" he had the night of his father's funeral. It is a dream that came to mark a turning point in Freud's inner life which was, in turn, to have important repercussions on his work:

> I found myself in a shop where there was a notice up saying:
> You are requested
> To close the eyes.
>
> (Masson, 1985b: 171)

Freud recognized the setting as the barber shop he went to every day, and says that "on the day of the funeral I was kept waiting, and therefore arrived at the house of mourning rather late." From this reference he proceeds to interpret the dream as "an outlet for the feeling of self-reproach" (p. 171), and feelings of reproach incite shame. A barber shop is a place where a man goes to get his hair cut, a clear reference to castration, for the male removal of hair is an ancient, deeply held idea that is symbolic of emasculation. For example, when a messenger exposes the Egyptian queen Cleopatra to feelings of shame and humiliation by informing her that her lover, Antony, has married another woman, Cleopatra threatens to destroy the messenger's eyes and hair:

> What say you? Hence,
> Horrible villain! or I'll spurn ["kick"] thine eyes
> Like balls before me; I'll unhair thy head...
>
> (Wright, 1940: Act II, 63–64)

Further back in time, however, the shaving of the head played an official part in cults of the Great Mother, and barbers were amongst the Goddess's attendants (Neumann/Mainheim, 1974: 59).

In the dream, eyes are objectified and held at a distance with the noun "the" instead of the pronoun "your." "Close the eyes" carries an injunction that nothing should be seen and could mean any number of things: it was the first instruction Freud would give his patients when commencing treatment, or is what a mother tells her infant as she cradles him to sleep, or is what Jocasta told Oedipus to do upon the opening of his eyes and the dawning realizations. "Close the eyes" could be his father's prohibition (the first form of castration anxiety), when Freud may rather fulfill his wishes for his mother, which are made all the more tempting and seductive by the fact that a dead father is less of a threat than a living one. Patricide is the central event of the Oedipal and his mother is now available, but alas, part of his aggressive wish is foiled by his father's natural death. Maybe what is stirred is his still strong infantile wish to omnipotently kill his father, but then that would also mean his own insignificance as a creature and ultimate death. Perhaps "close the eyes" is a less brutal form of Oedipus' own blinding, for the dream (as well as the "Rome" dreams that follow) anticipate Freud's discovery of the Oedipus Complex.

It is especially significant given our focus on the eyes of shame that upon Freud's father's death eyes move into a prominent position. In fact, Anzieu points out that in all the dreams reported by Freud following the loss of his father, the sense that is given the greatest importance is sight (1986: 207). All in all, his stirred up infantile, narcissistic feelings of shame, connected to the loss of his omnipotence, coincides with his scientific finding called the Oedipus Complex. Freud would come to consider it the central and universal conflict in the human psyche, and pivotal to the most basic structuring of the personality.

Ann Salyard (1988) closely examines a single line that appears later in the letter to Fliess mentioning his eye dream that helps amplify what Freud may have shut his eyes so as not to see on a personal level – his unresolved Oedipus Complex which would be unconsciously relived and repeated. Freud quotes a line from Schiller's poem, "Pegasus yoked to the plough," to describe his experience of himself at that moment. It is, of course, hard to know exactly what this sentence meant to Freud, but as Salyard rightly points out, an elaboration of the meanings of its varied elements can provide a sense of the thoughts and feelings associated with it. After a thorough analysis, she contends that the Pegasus line relates directly to the "whole reawakened past that stirs" and has been "torn up by the roots." Embedded in the phrase is Freud's experience of himself, his father, and his mother – the primal scene. More specifically, it reflects his negative maternal experience and his lack of internal separation from his mother upon his father's death. The way she details her argument will be summarized and integrated with an analysis of Freud's infantile shame constellated by the Oedipus Complex.

Pegasus

Salyard (1988) states that Freud chose the immortal winged horse to describe how he felt in the deepest depths of his "neurosis" following his father's death. Pegasus, a horse symbolic of natural, blind instinct and desire, was born on a remote island, the offspring of Poseidon's rape of none other than Medusa (who lies at the heart of castration anxiety) in Athena's temple. It was because of this despoiling violation that Athena cursed the beautiful Medusa and made her hideous. Pegasus sprang from the neck of Medusa when she was beheaded by Perseus – the narcissistic self beneath Freud's single act of matricide. Pegasus was wild and swift, refusing to let anyone approach him.

In his comment to Fliess, Freud was quoting from the poem entitled "Pegasus in Harness" (Schiller, 1861). In this poem, an impoverished poet takes the great steed to market to sell. A farmer, thinking to tie his wings, makes him the leader of a team to pull a wagon. But no sooner was Pegasus strapped to the wagon when he took off with double speed:

> True the impetuous instinct to,
> Field, fen and bog, he scampers through.
> The frenzy seems to catch the team;
> The driver tugs, the travelers scream.
> O'er ditch, o'er hedge, splash, dash and crash on...
> (Schiller, 1861: 107)

So the farmer tied the winged horse and an ox at a plough together. Pegasus tries desperately but in vain to take flight:

> The unwilling griffin strains his might,
> One last strong struggle yet for flight...
> Until, worn out, the eye grows dim,
> The sinews fail the foundered limb,
> The god steed droops; the strife is past.
> He writhes amidst the mire at last!
> (p. 107)

The "mire at last" as "the eye grows dim" (or closes) and failing sinews points to Freud's shame as Pegasus, true offspring of Medusa. Pegasus might as well be Narcissus gawking at himself in the reflecting pool. Here is the shame he has projected onto the mother who had to be decontaminated and quarantined. This image links his shamed, infant self with his mother Medusa who evokes dread and petrifaction.

Given the one-room living quarters of his parents during infancy and early childhood, it is certainly plausible to think that Freud's early experiences included many sightings of his nude mother, especially the sight of her genitals (and her sightings of his masturbation). There is in fact one widely reported incident of Freud having seen his mother nude when he was four years old (Lerman, 1986: 5). Freud caught sight of Medusa: "It would appear that the Medusa image served as a symbol of Freud's pervasive, complex, frightening, and sexually stimulating experiences connected with his relationship with his mother" (Salyard, 1988: 413). Salyard postulates that the image of Pegasus yoked to the plough suggests intense stimulation of the primal scene as well as maternal seduction (p. 415), the symbiotic mother to whom he remains yoked, an enslavement to dependency. Perhaps Freud had the meaning of Medusa backwards: it is not an image, as he consciously thought, of the castrated genitals of the mother and need for the identification with the father. It is, rather, an image of his unconscious fear of her uncastrated, horrifyingly sexual and seductive power, and his fascinated yet shame-filled attraction.

For her part, there are signs that Freud's mother suffered from "megalomania," meaning a false concept of self-importance. The name she gave to her son means "savior of the world," and, like Liriope, she had a strong desire to confirm his great, portentous destiny. This led her to consult a peasant seer. He predicted that she had given birth to a child who was destined to become an extraordinary man. Like Narcissus, Freud's life was blessed with the prophecies received by his mother. He was born with a caul which was believed to ensure future happiness. And growing up basking in his mother's glowing reflections, he came to possess an attitude of considerable grandiosity. Consider the following passage of a letter Freud wrote to his betrothed, Martha Bernays, in 1885 (also take note of the Sphinx image which echoes Oedipus' solving of the riddle):

> I have just carried out one resolution which one group of people, as yet unborn and fated to misfortune, will feel acutely. Since you can't guess whom I mean I will tell you: they are my biographers. I have destroyed all of my diaries for the past fourteen years, with letters, scientific notes, and the manuscripts of my publications. Only family letters were spared. Yours, my dear one, were never in danger. All my old friendships and associations passed again before my eyes and met their doom ... all my thoughts and feelings about the world in general, and in particular about how it concerned me, have been declared unworthy of survival ... But the stuff simply enveloped me, as the sand does the Sphinx, and soon only my nostrils would show above the mass of paper.... Let the biographers chafe; we won't make it too easy for them. Let each one of them believe he is right in his "Conception of the Development of the Hero:" even now I enjoy the thought of how they will go astray.
>
> (quoted in Jones, 1953: xii)

His famous comment on Adler's death is wickedly sarcastic. Freud said that Adler's death was proof of "how far he had got on. The world really rewarded him richly for his service of contradicting psychoanalysis" (Jones, 1953: 52). And here are more of Freud's seasoned thoughts on human nature coupled with his own reflections on how he ranks:

> I have found little that is "good" about human beings on the whole. In my experience most of them are trash, no matter whether they publicly subscribe to this or that ethical doctrine or none at all ... If we are to talk of ethics, I subscribe to a high ideal from which most of the human beings I have come across depart most lamentably.
>
> (Jones, 1953: 61–62)

Anzieu (1986) references a paper by Besdine, who studied the special kind of relationships that mothers of geniuses-to-be have with their children. "He discovered that Michelangelo, Shakespeare, Goethe, Heine, Balzac, Proust, Sartre, Dostoevsky and, of course, Freud all had mothers who developed veritable

'Jocasta complexes' towards their sons. Such a woman mothers to an extreme degree by not only transferring her incestuous love on to her son, but 'doing so in a deeply symbiotic relationship, thus fulfilling the two vital conditions for the emergence of a genius' (1986: 204). Freud offers the same idea:

> if a man has been his mother's undisputed darling he retains throughout life the triumphant feeling [elsewhere translated as the feeling of a "conqueror"], the confidence in success, which not seldom brings actual success along with it. And Goethe might well have given some such heading to his autobiography as: "My strength has its roots in my relation to my mother."
>
> (1964c: 156)

The love and pride Freud received from his mother included her wish for his success and victory, but Freud struggled with her insistence. He writes:

> Such prophecies must be made very often; there are so many happy and expectant mothers, and so many old peasant women and other old women who, since their mundane power have deserted them, turn their eyes towards the future; and the prophetess is not likely to suffer for her prophecies.
>
> (quoted in Jones, 1953: 5)

Narcissistic coenesthesis is projected upon the mother in order to recreate the unity lost by leaving the womb at birth. This takes place through the face or gaze of the mother, which essentially becomes a substitute for the womb – this, in fact, is why the eyes are symbolic of the womb. Mother's gaze is a source of narcissistic confirmation (Ayers, 2003: 34–60). The Oedipus Complex for Freud was a recapitulation of a symbiotic stage of infancy, and so, by logical extension, a working out of primary narcissism. Fromm, in commenting about the strength sexuality plays in the Oedipus Complex, suggests that Freud missed the dependency aspects of the relationship of a child to his mother in his theoretical formulations because of his own lifelong and unacknowledged dependency on his mother (1959: 15). Is this what happens when mother's face reflects her own need for mirroring, as it did for Narcissus who clung to his own reflection and her absence to him?

Freud's maternal attachment

There is a lack of certainty over the nature and source of Freud's attachment to his mother. On the one hand, Ernest Jones describes a close relationship: "It was strange to a young visitor to hear her refer to the great Master as 'mein goldener Sigi' and evidently there was a close attachment between the two" (1953: 3). Or perhaps Freud experienced this as doting, and so, like Narcissus, inevitably scorned his mother. This idea finds support in the thoughts of others, who said that he appeared to lack genuine affection for his mother. Freud's nephew commented that "even when he kissed his mother on his weekly visits, one felt he did this out of duty" (Freud, 1956: 313). Schur says that

> whatever Freud's early relationship to his mother had been, during her last years it was, at least outwardly, one of cordial filial duty. I had never met her and Freud had spoken of her very little. There was no obvious grief upon her death.
>
> (1972: 423)

If one takes the image of Pegasus being tied to an ox as an expression of Freud's early experience of maternal attachment to the Medusa aspect of his mother, one might say that he could not get free; he was as much held in bondage and subjugation as Narcissus was tied to his own ungraspable image in the pool. Freud was helpless and powerless in a burdensome attachment to his mother. These feelings seem supported by Freud's own words written in a letter to Ferenczi upon his mother's death:

> Above all my warm thanks for your beautiful words about the death of my mother. It has affected me in a peculiar way, this great event. No pain, no grief . . . at the same time a feeling of liberation, of release . . .
>
> (E. Freud, 1960: 164)

While he came to acknowledge his incestuous wishes and fantasies which he cushioned as inevitable due to man's archaic heritage, he never revealed having experienced maternal seduction. Freud's narcissistic confirmations were shared by his Oedipal conflicts. The source of Freud's shame is the mother–lover conflict that forced this sharing of the libidinal cathexis. This atmosphere prematurely destroyed his sense of exclusivity, and he denied his dependency needs. Freud writes:

> Everything connected with the first mother-attachment has in analysis seemed to me so elusive, lost in a past so dim and shadowy, so hard to resuscitate, that it seemed as if it had undergone some specially inexorable repression.
>
> (1964f: 226)

Freud's act of matricide

Salyard believes that when memories of this prehistoric period were stirred up by his father's death, Freud was "overwhelmed by genuine confusion and doubt over who was subject and who was object" (1988: 420) – in other words, a symbiotic form of shame, masked by a considerable degree of narcissism that imaginally shares maternal omnipotence. Both because of his youthful mother and the cultural milieu which forbid sexuality (fertile grounds, then, for an obsession), how easy it would be for desperate feelings of dependency to be co-opted by sexual desire.

Freud kept his focus on the more physically distant, more unattainable mother: he dissociates and projects his shame and neediness. Mother now becomes the succubus he repudiates. During this time of "seething ferment," Freud took a two-week trip to Italy and wrote to Fliess that "in Italy, I am seeking a punch made of Lethe; here and there I get a draft" (Freud quoted in Salyard, 1988: 421). In Greek mythology, Lethe was a river in the underworld. Those about to be reborn would take a drink from its waters which made them forget their experiences in Hell (the realm of the succubus). The drink of Lethe indicates that Freud was seeking to repress all the past that had been awakened at his father's death. Like the blind seer Tiresias quoted by Sophocles as saying "I have known it all, but made myself forget," Freud's wish to forget his past "propelled him to find a legitimate basis on which to disavow the reality of actual events of his past, while not denying the content of his inner world of fantasy and memory" (p. 421).

At this point, Freud must have wondered the same as Oedipus:

> How strange a shadowy memory crossed my mind,
> Just now while you were speaking; it chilled my heart.
>
> (Sophocles, 1951)

Unlike Oedipus, however, Freud ceases to ask questions. In his heart he carries Jocasta, the adoring mother who begs Oedipus not to enquire any further. And unlike Oedipus, who possessed the grace to include himself within the power of the law, Freud adopts infantile omnipotence and remains blind to his shame. Early in his work with hysterical women, Freud had encountered the wounding to the female psyche which he attributed to the reality of father seduction. By the time Freud wrote *Studies on Hysteria* (1893), he had published 13 cases of hysteria, all of which were reported as the result of sexual violation. While Freud was the first to recognize and describe in psychological terms the truly horrific, long-term impacts of sexual abuse, the only thing interesting about it was that it explained hysteria (Kerr, 1993: 37). Just as Freud was able to turn away from believing in the reality of his own past as a source of his disturbance (after all, Freud felt that in a deep reaching psychosis the unconscious memory does not break through so that secretive childhood experiences are not disclosed), he completely shifted his perception of his female patients' realities and real traumas to the nature and significance solely of fantasies arising from the instincts. He dissociates from the suffering female body, and lays the groundwork for the Oedipus Complex.

"Close the eyes"

Freud read the sign and closed his eyes. Caught between his father's injunction and his own desire to look, however, Freud found a compromise solution; he used the power of eyes to capture unquestionable authority in his psychoanalytic work, just as ancient warriors put the eyes of the Terrible Mother on their helmets. According to Fuss and Sanders, Freud placed himself metaphorically in the

"Medusan" position. Consider the following description of the spatial configuration of Freud's office:

> The patient's entry into Freud's office initiates a series of complicated and subtle transactions of power, orchestrated largely by the very precise spatial arrangement of objects and furniture. Freud held initial consultations, between three and four every afternoon, in the study section of his office. Preferring a face-to-face encounter with prospective patients, Freud seated them approximately four feet away from himself, across the divide of a table adjacent to the writing desk. Located in the center of a square room, at the intersection of two axial lines, the patient would appear to occupy the spatial locus of power. As if to confirm the illusion of his centrality, the patient is immediately presented, when seated, with a reflection of his own image, in a small portrait-sized mirror, framed in gold-filigree and hanging, at eye-level, in a facing window. As soon as Freud sits down at his desk, however, interposing himself between patient and mirror, the patient's reflection is blocked by Freud's head. Head substitutes for mirror in a metaphorical staging of the clinical role Freud seeks to assume. "The doctor," Freud pronounces in Papers on Technique, "should be opaque to his patients and, like a mirror, should show them nothing but what is shown to him."
>
> (1996: 267)

Internally, however, the closure of his eyes leads him into a "narcissistic regression of the libido." Petrified by his shame, he loses his capacity to adopt anything new and not connected to his own thoughts. He reduces everything to his own schema rather than seeing the value in other interpretations. He fails to recognize that infantile omnipotence is in fact an illusion, and authority comes to dominate his attitudes about psychoanalysis which is now his narcissistic object choice, and his own relationship with his creation. This is the intrapsychic element behind Freud's inability to accept any criticism, a characteristic Jung describes this way:

> A third impression of those days involves things that became clear to me only much later, things that I thought out fully only after our friendship was gone. When Freud talked of sexuality it was as though he were talking of God – as a man would talk who had undergone a conversion. It was like the Indians talking of the sun with tears in their eyes. I remember one Indian coming up softly behind me while I was looking at the mountain over the pueblo, and saying quite suddenly in my ear, "Don't you think all life is coming from the mountain?" It was just in that way that Freud talked of sexuality. A peculiar emotional quality would come into his face, and the cause of it I was at a loss to understand. Finally I seemed to make it out through the consideration of something else that remained obscure to me then, namely Freud's bitterness. One might say Freud consists of bitterness, every word being loaded with it. His attitude was the bitterness of the person who is entirely misunderstood,

> and his manner always seems to say, "If they don't understand they must be stamped into Hell."
>
> (1925: 20–21)

Jung recalls another incident. Freud turned to him and said with great emotion, "my dear Jung, promise me never to abandon the sexual theory. This is the most essential thing of all. You see, we must make a dogma of it, an unshakable bulwark" (Jung, 1965: 150). And that is exactly what Freud strove to do:

> To be sure, Jung kept bringing up the work of other men in the field, often favorably, while Freud kept knocking them down, largely on the basis that they would not, or could not, accept the libido theory.
>
> (Kerr, 1993: 144)

In a seminar, Jung is talking about Freud's utter blindness towards anything other than repressed sexuality.

> If one remains with a narrow point of view about the dream material, there comes a feeling of dissociation and one feels blind and deaf. When this happens to an isolated man he petrifies.
>
> (Jung, 1925: 22)

It seems that behind Freud's repressed sexuality lies Medusa staring with her petrifying eyes that turn men to stone.

In 1897, in another letter to Wilhelm Fliess, Freud writes a description of his feelings about his dramatic theoretical change:

> Let me tell you straight away the great secret which has been slowly dawning on me in recent months. I no longer believe in my neurotica (theory of neurosis) … It is strange, too, that *no feelings of shame* appeared [italics mine], for which, after all, there could well be occasion. Of course that I shall not tell it in Dan, nor speak of it in Askelon, in the land of the Philistines – but in your eyes and my own, I have more of a feeling of victory than a defeat (which is surely not right) … I vary Hamlet's saying: "To be in readiness:" To be cheerful is everything! I could feel quite discontent. The expectation of eternal fame was so beautiful, as was that of certain wealth, complete independence, travels, and lifting my children above the severe worries which robbed me of my youth.
>
> (Masson, 1985b: 45)

Always looking for the phallic solution, Freud holds to his position of paternal power and authority. But why mention that he had no feelings of shame? The inclusion of this detail alone attracts attention to it. What happens next is astonishing: Freud ironically turns to witchcraft for an understanding of the hysterics' fantasies, linking his "new theory" to the long-standing attitude towards women that create and fuel the dynamics around the succubus:

> What would you say, by the way, if I told you that my brand new theory of the early etiology of hysteria was already well known and had been published a hundred times over, though several centuries ago? ... But why did the devil who took possession of the poor things invariably abuse them sexually and in a loathsome manner? Why are their confessions under torture so like the communications made by my patients in psychological treatment? ... I dream, therefore, of a primeval devil religion whose rites are carried on secretly, and I understand the harsh therapy of the witches' judges.
>
> (1964d: 224–225)

Freud read the *Malleus Maleficarum* and is struck by the similarities between his theory of hysteria and the medieval theory of witches and possession. The inquisitors' cruel ways could be found in the scene of seduction that later engendered hysteria. This phenomenon now becomes "the organic crisis of the organic untruthfulness of woman" (Weininger, 1907: 266). As for the flying witches, the broomstick they straddled could be explained as "the great Lord Penis." Overall – and perhaps because the witch is "straddling the penis" – what Freud seems to be saying is that the torture and murder of the witches are understandable, for the judges were attempting to curtail a heinous cult (Masson, 1985a: 105).

Freud relinquished his seduction theory in favor of fantasy and the vicissitudes of psychic life, and in so doing shifted the emphasis from the actual world of sadness, misery and brutality to an internal setting in which imagined actors performed self-created fantasized dramas for an invisible audience. Many years later, Freud continues to explain his position:

> Before going further into the question of infantile sexuality I must mention an error into which I fell for a while and which might well have had fatal consequences for the whole of my work. Under the influence of the technical procedure which I used at that time, the majority of my patients reproduced from their childhood scenes in which they were sexually seduced by some grown-up person. With female patients the part of the seducer was almost always assigned to their father. I believed these stories, and consequently supposed that I had discovered the roots of the subsequent neurosis in these experiences of sexual seduction in childhood. ... When, however, I was at last obliged to recognize that these scenes of seduction had never taken place, and that they were only phantasies which my patients had made up or which I myself had perhaps forced on them, I was for some time completely at a loss ... neurotic symptoms were not related directly to actual events but to wishful phantasies, and that as far as the neurosis was concerned psychical reality was of more importance than material reality. I do not believe even now that I forced the seduction-phantasies on my patients, that I "suggested" them. I had in fact stumbled for the first time

> upon the Oedipus complex, which was later to assume such overwhelming importance, but which I did not recognize as yet in its disguise as phantasy.
>
> (1964d: 33–34)

A little over a year after his father's death, Freud rejects what is now called the Seduction Theory, and in the weeks following this act proposes the Oedipus Complex (which contained the first hints of his subsequent theory of narcissism). In other words, Freud leaves patriarchal authority intact, and this has important implications for his portrayal of the pre-oedipal mother. It eventually became either the Seduction Theory or the Oedipus Complex. In a letter to Jeffrey Masson dated September 10, 1981, Anna Freud wrote:

> Keeping up the seduction theory would mean to abandon the Oedipus complex, and with it the whole importance of fantasy life, conscious or unconscious fantasy. In fact, I think there would have been no psychoanalysis afterwards.
>
> (Masson, 1985a: 113)

In this split between real and fantasized, it is no wonder that Freud's unconscious shame, an absolute shame deep in his narcissism that sees the threat of castration in everything, casts its shadow on the entire discussion of the Oedipus Complex and its resolution. Freud was right when he said it could not be right that he should have more a feeling of triumph (no disgrace at all) than defeat, a view of himself seen through his mother's admiring reflection for his victory. He would not have felt this way if he had confronted and internalized his deepest shame, his narcissistic defeat at his mother's hand – her inability to give him the exclusive love he needed. His repudiation of the maternal feminine closes off certain lines of creative thinking that prevented a deeper consideration of his interpretation of Medusa.

Freud remains blind to his core shame by identifying with paternal authority, and this petrifaction had significant effects on psychoanalysis. The study of shame, in a preeminent position at the beginning of psychoanalysis, underwent an eclipse that lasted over 60 years (Lansky, 1995). In *Studies on Hysteria*, the book from which psychoanalysis emerged and in which Freud presented his theory on the seductive origins of hysteria, Breuer and Freud (1893–1895) place shame in a central position:

> By means of my psychical work, I have had to overcome a psychical force in the patients which was opposed to the pathogenic ideas becoming conscious (being remembered). From these I recognized the universal characteristic of such ideas. They were all of a distressing nature, calculated to arouse the affects of shame, of self-reproach, and a kind of psychical pain and the feeling of being harmed; they were all of a kind that one would prefer not to have experienced, that one would rather forget. From all this, there arose, as it were, automatically the thought of defense..."
>
> (1893–1895: 268–269)

Freud's emerging structural theory of psychical reality did not depend upon an intersubjective context, internal and external. He preferred to drink Lethe and forget the "kind of psychical pain and the feeling of being harmed." He blinds himself by closing his eyes. When Freud's formulations a few years later began to focus on the concept of desire and intrapsychic fantasy, the original vision of shame as the foremost painful affect of exposure around inferiority disappeared from view. Freud had dissociated his own shame, and, rather than be threatened by depotentiation and humiliation, the "fatal consequences" in the face of which he was petrified, he preserved the authority of the science of psychoanalysis. Freud caught sight of Medusa's huge foreboding eyes and turned to stone.

Freud's forgotten memories belong to a missing period, to the absent mother which is unconsciously played out and replicated in his theories. Not only did Freud act out his shame in his theories, but perhaps in his personal life as well. The idea has been put forth that Freud had an incestuous relationship with his sister-in-law, Minnay Bernays (see Kerr's references to Swales and Stadlen, 1993: 139–140). In the late 1890s he was passionately attracted to his sister-in-law who was a member of his household, and they traveled alone together for the first time in July of 1898. After a thorough analysis of Freud's major psychological works, correspondence, and details of his life, Swales determines that Freud consummated his passions in August and September of 1900. If true, the affair would be a culmination of Freud's special circumstances following the Oedipal upsurge prompted by his father's death. Jung, who reports having been informed of the affair by Minnay herself, had an interview with John Billinsky in 1957 in which he reveals more of Freud's relationship to her:

> And so when Freud told me about the dream in which his wife and her sister played important parts, I asked him to tell me some of his personal associations with the dream. He looked at me and said, "I could tell you more but I can't risk my authority." That of course finished my attempts to deal with his dreams ... He rebelled against that because he would have to deal with problems that were closely related to his theories. If he would have tried to consciously understand the triangle he would have been much better off.
>
> (quoted in Kerr, 1993: 267)

This drama, much like Oedipus' pollution of Thebes, holds a shame, it seems, that no one wants to touch: "But this is a story unto itself, since it involves a great secret that was kept for many, many years and then became a great open secret which, even after it was published, nobody would discuss" (Kerr, 1993: 135).

The feminine in Freud's theories

When Freud's own profoundly disturbing shame and defenses to preserve his patriarchal authority are activated, he projects all over women in order to oppress and eliminate femininity. Freud's mastery through the penis emphasizes a male's lack of commonality with the female; this appears to give him the right to violate femininity as a means of establishing his separateness. The core of narcissism for Freud, in fact, is that women do not have a penis. His theory becomes, essentially, a scientific restatement of the myth of creation, and how Eve was born from Adam. Freud maintains his assertion of difference in his desire to gain prestige and power in his father's eyes. Freud admits to debasing women himself when writing about mother's penisless vagina which can permanently "distort" the male's relationship to women: "This … leads to two reactions, which … permanently determine the boy's relations to women: horror of the mutilated creature or triumphant contempt for her" (1964d: 252).

Contempt is the word that best describes Freud's explanation of the female resolution of the Oedipus Complex. Male superego development is in response to a tremendous fear of castration. Females, however, are "castrated" before the Oedipus conflict and, therefore, are corrupted by never achieving a fully developed superego.

> At this point our material – for some incomprehensible reason – becomes more obscure and full of gaps. The female sex, too, develops an Oedipus complex, a superego and a latency period. May we also attribute a phallic organization and a castration complex to it? The answer is in the affirmative; but these things cannot be the same as they are in boys. Here the feminist demand for equal rights for the sexes does not take us far, for the morphological distinction is bound to find expression in differences of psychical development. "Anatomy is Destiny," to vary a saying of Napoleon's.
>
> … The little girl's clitoris behaves just like a penis to begin with; but, when she makes a comparison with a play fellow of the other sex, she perceives that she has "come off badly" and she feels this as a wrong done to her and as a ground for inferiority … The essential difference thus comes about that the girl accepts castration as an accomplished fact, whereas the boy fears the possibility of its occurrence … The fear of castration thus being excluded in the little girl, a powerful motive also drops out for the setting-up of a superego and for the breaking-off of the infantile organization … The girl's Oedipus complex is much simpler than that of the small bearer of the penis; in my experience, it seldom goes beyond taking of her mother's place and the adopting of a feminine attitude towards the father … In girls the motive for the demolition of the Oedipus complex is lacking. Castration has already had its effect, which was to force the child into the situation of the Oedipus complex. Thus the Oedipus complex escapes the fate which it meets with in boys … I cannot evade the notion (though I hesitate to give it expression) that for women the level of what is ethically normal is different from what it is in men. Their superego is never so inexorable, so impersonal, so independent of its emotional origins as we require it to be in men. Character-traits which critics of every epoch have brought up against women – that they show less justice than men, that they are less ready to submit to the great exigencies of

> life, that they more often influence with their judgments by feelings of affection or hostility – all this would be amply accounted for by the modification in the formation of the superego which we have inferred above. We must not allow ourselves to be deflected from such conclusions by the denials of the feminists, who are anxious to force us to regard the two sexes as completely equal in position and worth...
>
> (1964d: 257–258)

For women, the level of what is ethically normal is different from what it is in men (1964d: 257), and this is despite the fact that Victorian woman was expected to uphold the torch of morality. The lack of superego development for a female also explains her preponderant emotionalism, as well as her inability to develop the powers of reason, judgment, and morality – all qualities which were supposedly more characteristic of men. He also proposes that the girl's cure for the insult to her narcissism – meaning the discovery that she lacks a penis – is to abandon the mother for the father.

Condemning females, however, only makes the dynamics of the succubus more powerfully negative, and it is she who informs Freud's next idea: the only way to appease a woman is by giving her a token penis – and Freud does exactly that:

> Anatomy has recognized the clitoris within the female pudenda as being an organ that is homologous to the penis; and the physiology of the sexual process has been able to add that this small penis ... behaves in fact during childhood like a real and genuine penis.
>
> (1964a: 217)

Here Freud forfeits mastery, yet is so certain of his formulation he says categorically that "probably no male human being is spared the terrifying shock of threatened castration at the sight of the female genitals" (1964g: 197). Yet the only way to triumph over the threat of castration at the sight of the female genitals is to "give" the woman a phallus which then in some way gives the male the courage to be a man? He is placating "the threatening female divinities (who) may be pacified with a gift of a miniature penis and the entitlement to phallic experience" (Kerr, 1993: 117). Freud stuck to the idea of the phallic mother that the little boy wants to believe in.

The feminine in Freud's later life

The Father of Psychoanalysis, not unlike the Church Fathers who preceded him, took revenge on the mother by constructing a theory of a brutal, disciplining and punishing superego, intensifying the level of the aggressive drive with which the boy identifies in Freud's resolution of the Oedipus Complex. And in this enforced absence of maternal care, an infantile part of Freud is completely fragmented and cannot imagine a non-brutal end to the Oedipal. He has a lot of trouble envisioning a loving and benevolent superego, which becomes as harsh and immutable as Yahweh's Divine Law. And again like the Church Fathers, the repudiation of sexuality is the only way to develop one's spiritual sensibilities. Sagan puts it well: "Freud's world of the Oedipus Complex, castration, and the superego is a male world where women exist only as prizes to be awarded to conquerors" (1988: 8–9) – an idea that, as we saw in Part I, had its beginnings in 5000 B.C.

Freud is absolutely right in his theories on the Oedipus Complex and true to himself. He is correct in asserting that this is how things develop for a man. The only point he omits is that because of the archetypal paradigm of the succubus that informs our culture, this is also the way pathology of shame develops. Freud had a genius for self-scrutiny, but acts with his eyes closed when looking at the mother because there can be no vision or recognition of his shame. "In the face of the horror, Freud, like Oedipus, 'blinded himself', acting from impulses and emotions that appeared to arise from an inner sense of obligation 'to close the eyes' in order to 'do one's duty toward the dead'" (Salyard, 1988: 424).

The conclusions that Freud reaches about women and the meaning of femininity are about women as they exist within the fantasy structures of a patriarchal psychic reality. The whole experience of the mother–infant dyad is seen retrospectively as feminine, and the only connection Freud allows to the mother is in seeing the boy with the vulnerability and dependency of an infant. The boy has no choice but to overcome his infancy through his assertion of difference and superiority. Any connection to mother is blocked off through devaluation and denigration, Freud's acts of matricide. He uses massive denial and contempt in a refusal to see past the looming succubus who menaces masculinity; he cannot see woman's virtues or restore his connection to the mother. The wish for the phallic mother may well be a universal experience for all humankind, not for the reason that it awakens unbearable sexual urges, but because the child wants the omnipotent mother. But Freud will fight to the death to defend against a shaming experience with the pre-oedipal mother; this results in an irremedial distortion of his most basic theories. Freud may have recreated a mother–infant world in the methods of psychoanalysis and called his process of a cure "love," but the installment of the Phallos, the Father – the enthronement of the harsh and punishing superego who sits in judgment – results in a loss of compassion, love, nurturance, and seeing, as well as a psychological understanding of the pre-oedipal period and mother–infant attachment.

But Freud the patriarch shared in human weaknesses. One catches a glimpse of Freud's true feelings for the feminine being repressed in his commentary on Leonardo da Vinci's paintings *Bacchus* and *John the Baptist*: "These pictures breathe a mystical air into whose secret one dares not penetrate" (1964b: 117). Further on he writes words that could just as well have been written by Jung, and that demonstrate the feminine place where they really discovered the same principle:

> The figures are still androgynous, but no longer in the sense of the vulture-phantasy. They are beautiful youths of feminine delicacy and with effeminate forms; they do not cast their eyes down [unlike Oedipus], but gaze in mysterious triumph, as if they knew of a great achievement of happiness, about which silence must be kept. The familiar smile of fascination leads one to guess that it is a secret love. It is possible that in these figures Leonardo has denied the unhappiness of his erotic life and has triumphed over it in his art, by representing the wishes of the boy, infatuated with his mother, as fulfilled in this blissful union of the male and female natures.
>
> (pp. 117–118)

Freud knew that he lacked the "oceanic feeling" he attributed to the Father, and with it a feeling for the mother as well as religion. Late in his life, Freud appears to move from a "father-fear theory of culture to a nature-terror one" (Becker, 1973: 97). He peers into the maternal psychic area shrouded in mystery, and feels he made a groundbreaking discovery:

> Our insight into this early, pre-Oedipus phase in girls comes to us as a surprise, like the discovery ... of the Minoan-Mycenean civilization behind the civilization of Greece ... Everything connected with this first mother-attachment has in analysis seemed to me so elusive, lost in a past so dim and shadowy, so hard to resuscitate, that it seemed as if it had undergone some specially inexorable repression.
>
> (1964f: 226)

As the oppressive aspects of sexuality lifted from Freud, he began to perceive that the human species would come to extinction, not, as he had previously written, from conflicts over sexuality (his intellectual bulwark had begun to collapse) – but from uncontrolled destructiveness (the defining feature of the archetype of Lilith, Maid of Desolation). He re-defined the problem of civilization as the instinct of aggression and the attempt of human culture to control it.

Nevertheless, Freud dies with his rational paternal authority intact. He remained bound to his instinct theory. He held onto his mother's most intense beliefs of his authentic talent and single-mindedly strove to engineer his own immortality. There is no doubt that Freud's self-analytic honesty was unique; the truth is, however, that he suffered from "some impairment of self-confidence," (Becker, 1973: 117), and that he "hated helplessness and fought against it, and the emotional feeling of utter helplessness in the face of experience was too much for him to stand. It gave full play to the underside of dependency that he tried to control" – Freud even admitted this to Karl Abraham (p. 115). He completely rid himself of any intellectual dependence on others (except a few men, like Jung, on whom he was at one time extremely dependent) or a spiritual dependency on the illusory comforts of religion. He would not forgo knowledge for love. For this reason, Freud worked the psychoanalytic movement "as a mirror to reflect power back upon himself" (Becker, 1973: 116). Psychoanalysis became his "personal vehicle for heroism, for a transcendence of his vulnerability and human limitations" (Becker, 1973: 109). Jung summarizes Freud's rigid omnipotence this way:

> Freud never asked himself why he was compelled to talk continually of sex, why this idea had taken such possession of him. He remained unaware that his "monotony of interpretation" expressed a flight from himself, or from that other side of him which might perhaps be called mystical ... He was blind toward the paradox and ambiguity of the unconscious, and did not know that everything which arises out of the unconscious has a top and a bottom, an inside and an outside. When we speak of the outside – and that is what Freud did – we are considering only half of the whole, with the result that a counter-reflect arises out of the unconscious.
>
> There was nothing to be done about this one-sidedness of Freud's. Perhaps some inner experience of his own might have opened his eyes; but then his intellect would have reduced such an experience to "mere sexuality" or "psychosexuality." He remained the victim of one aspect he could recognize, and for that reason I see him as a tragic figure; for he was a great man, and what is more, a man in the grip of his daimon.
>
> (1965: 152–153)

One's virtue is one's own Self. When one's image as reflection is used as an antidote to feelings of fragmentation and shame, the person who is looking may be quite unaware of the sustaining power his own image holds for him. The child must free himself from his mother's reflections of her own image of her son, and in turn recognize the object (or really subject) of his dependency – a task at which Freud fails. He remained in mother's omnipotence which was later disguised through the paternal superego and identification with cultural moral values. The man of genius repeats the narcissistic inflation of the infant. When Jung re-visioned Freud's resolution of the Oedipus Complex, he walked right in on Freud's deepest shame, and the area most blindly defended by his power and authority – as well as Liriope and Jocasta.

Chapter 5

Siegfried to Salome: Jung's heroic journey

Leading up to and in the aftermath of his split with Freud, Jung nearly went mad. He lost a mentor and a reliable father figure – confirmation of his phallic being. A man who strove for a life of individuation and wholeness realized that he did not have a myth of his own. He lost one of his closest friendships. He rejected and was rejected by what he knew to be the foundation of his professional life. His whole being had become fragile, he lost his footings, and was dropping into an experience of non-being that verged upon annihilation. Cut off from all the activity that the outside world brought, he was driven to investigate the things within himself. He plunged into the depths of his soul in search of the ancient roots of man's being in the Incest Phantasy, the symbols of libido at the core of the Oedipus Complex. For a long time nothing helped him, but in the end, Jung says, "all my work, all my creative activity, has come from those initial fantasies and dreams."

Throughout the entire text of *Symbols* (1955), Jung stares into the eyes of the succubus, trapped in the distortions brought about by repression. All roads in Jung's unconscious lead to the seductive world of incest – with no way out. Trees, fish, serpents and snake eyes, great dragons, all the goddesses in the Greek pantheon or simply the Great Whore of Babylon – all images are interpreted in light of the Terrible Mother's most flagrant seductive charms from which Jung cannot pull himself away.

Through his confrontation, Jung came to believe that a man must bring himself to recognize and come to terms with a hidden, terrifying feminine part within. It is through forging this relationship that one obtains transcendence and the chance of greater consciousness. His lack of vision, however, lies in the fact that Jung romanticizes his confrontation with insanity. Even though he felt menaced by a psychosis that threatened his very existence, Jung's inner journey, like most other renowned heroes, reads like a mythological version of a descent into the underworld. He says:

> I was sitting at my desk once more, thinking over my fears. Then I let myself drop. Suddenly it was as though the ground literally gave way beneath my feet, and I plunged down into dark depths. I could not fend off a feeling of panic . . . I even made several attempts to get to the very bottom. The first time I reached, as it were, a depth of about a thousand feet; the next time I found

> myself at the edge of a cosmic abyss. It was like a voyage to the moon or a descent into empty space…
>
> (1965: 179–181)

Rivers of blood, deep caverns and dark water depict a world of the Terrible Mother, and the ground giving way beneath one's feet is the quintessential image of plunging into shame (Ayers, 2003: 82).

Here is the succubus as regressively charged inner image of the incestuous mother from whom the heroic in man must free himself. The task in this hostile but seductive maternal atmosphere is to survive the overwhelming power of his unconscious, libidinal fantasies: "I had to take the chance, had to try to gain *power over them*; for I realized that if I did not do so, I ran the risk of their gaining *power over me*" (italics mine) (Jung, 1965: 178). This one sentence epitomizes Jung's approach to the mother, what made him blind to his shame, and the resulting dualism and determinations of femininity that are most problematic with his theories. Jung's need to establish power over results in his pursuit of conquest; this leads to the creation of a barrier between himself and conscious knowledge of the absent, terrible mother of his infancy. Moreover, the psychic energy of the self cannot manifest when a man seeks to experience his feelings while maintaining control.

The psychological birth of Jung: the Siegfried complex

Jung's great triumphal struggle for male individuation is played out against the backdrop of the re-engulfing, seductive mother. Jung's journey takes him to the maternal realm of the dead, a place "where young men die." The unconscious itself is the living representative of the Great Mother, and the hero's reason for descent, primary source of deeds, and greatest danger is always some form of the Terrible Mother:

> I am with an unknown, brown-skinned man, a savage, in a lonely, rocky mountain landscape. It was before dawn; the eastern sky was already bright, and the stars fading. Then I heard Siegfried's horn sounding over the mountains and I knew that we had to kill him. We are armed with rifles and lay in wait for him on a narrow path over the rocks.
>
> Then Siegfried appeared high up on the crest of the mountain, in the first ray of the rising sun. On a chariot made of the bones of the dead he drove at furious speed down the precipitous slope. When he turned a corner, we shot at him, and he plunged down, struck dead.
>
> Filled with disgust and remorse for having destroyed something so great and beautiful, I turned to flee, impelled by the fear that the murder might be discovered. But a tremendous downfall of rain began, and I knew that it would wipe out all traces of the dead. I had escaped the danger of discovery; life could go on, but an unbearable feeling of guilt remained.
>
> (Jung, 1965: 180)

I would like to change the word guilt to shame, for the words in which the dream is told, as well as its images, are more related to his struggle with shame – it was simply not a word in Jung's vocabulary (i.e. shame is not a word in the *General Index* to his 20-volume *Collected Works*). Nevertheless, the presence of this affect is supported by the central fear of the self being revealed, that the murder "might be discovered" – rather than Jung feeling badly about having committed the crime which would point to guilt. Jung, or his shamed self, lays in hiding to murder Siegfried, the German tribal hero who comes proudly blowing his horn. So the hero, slayer of dragons and rescuer of the fallen Valkyrie Brunhilde, has to die at the hand of Jung's shamed self, an unbearable feeling that surfaces upon Siegfried's death and remains despite the rain "wiping out all traces" to escape "the danger of discovery." The rain cannot erase Jung's feelings of disgrace. The fact that Siegfried is assassinated is also true to the story: he was murdered by a perfidious traitor from among his closest associates.

In Jung's dream, the hero is shamed by not being felled in a fair fight. His is not a noble death but a treacherous one. This murder fills Jung with feelings of shame, revealed in the words "disgust" and "remorse." These feelings compel a fight or flight survival anxiety; Jung turns to flee in the face of the destruction of the hero, but instead rain "wipes out" any traces of the act. The shame that has surfaced is repressed, and its denial and petrifaction is also indicated in his feeling that "life can go on" only if the danger of discovery is erased.

At the outset of his confrontation, Jung articulated the meaning of Siegfried to be what the romantically nationalistic Germans wanted: to heroically impose their will. He realized that the attitude embodied by Siegfried no longer suited him. He deposed his superior function. He could no longer follow in Freud's footsteps, and this is why Siegfried was shot: "This identity and heroic idealism had to be abandoned, for there are higher things than the ego's will, and to these one must bow" (1965: 181). The heroic image that displays all of the essential elements that make a man a man no longer suits Jung. He professes to put an abrupt end to his proud egoism; a savage, primitive shadow self leads the charge, and Siegfried, shot, "plunges down, struck dead."

The heroic self, however, lives on in Jung's determination to have power over the content of his dreams and visions, indicating that perhaps his interpretation of Siegfried is only partially true. In his June 1925 seminar, Jung is commenting on the nature of the "killing of the hero dream." He begins by noting that "dissolving an image means that you become that image" (1989: 88). The libido invested in the image moves into the unconscious, and one is forced into the hero role by it. He goes on to say that when a power motive is behind a fantasy, one can be aware of a fantasy system, and yet have its activity persist in the unconscious. When power is the motivating factor, "the killing of the hero … means that one is made into a hero and something hero-like must happen" (p. 89). In other words, murdering Siegfried means that Jung becomes Siegfried – and in repressing his shame he does indeed.

Sabina Spielrein

It is not possible to move on in Jung's story without giving further amplification to the meaning of Siegfried, so central is this image to Jung's work prior to his split with Freud and the mythic system he shared with Sabina Spielrein, a woman who fit into Jung's personal quest like a hand in glove. In fact, she was the occasion for his descent into incestuous sexual fantasy. In his book entitled *A Most Dangerous Method*, John Kerr (1993) details the documentary record of Spielrein's intimate relationship to Jung (and Freud as well, which will not be emphasized in this summary). His research reveals several amazing facts: Spielrein had been closest to Jung during his personal transformation that first made Jung a Freudian; she was at the center of the developing relationship between Freud and Jung; and last but not least, she stirred up a hornet's nest by revealing Jung's secret, polygamous self that didn't think like Freud. Her revelations, however, only fueled an inevitable eruption between Freud and Jung.

So why does our first glimpse of her importance come six decades later with the publication of the Freud–Jung correspondence in 1974? The letters implicate Jung and Spielrein in a potentially disastrous scandal, barely covered up between Freud and Jung, an affair which could have had fatal consequences for the science of psychoanalysis – and the very thing Freud was avoiding in 1896 when he switched his focus from reality to fantasy. Rather than being caught up in his vision of Jung as the son and heir of psychoanalysis, mirror to his narcissistic object, Freud should have been scrutinizing Jung's emotional stability. "In retrospect, it becomes clear why it was not accidental that her name has not come up before now . . .;" her story is an exemplar of the "insidious silence that gradually overtook psychoanalysis at this time" (Kerr, 1993: 13).

No one would have wished Spielrein more silent than Jung, a woman with whom he succumbed to enacting his incestuous desires, and with whom he had come to feel weak and exposed; he had indeed attempted to "erase the danger of discovery." For example, Jung's new interpretive scheme in Part II of *Symbols* entitled "Sacrifice" had originated in reaction to his personal involvement with Spielrein (Kerr, 1993). And despite the fact that Spielrein was the first to go into print with data supporting Jung's phylogenetic contention, he neglected to reference the fact that there was another theory of the unconscious that paralleled his own. Spielrein's considerable contributions, like her earlier protests as a patient and a lover, were ignored and then deliberately erased. And in order to make his own misconduct non-existent, Jung projects the succubus onto her. However, the demon kicked out the front door always finds its way in through a back window; Jung, caught up in a intense conflict within his own being, claimed innocence of any wrong doing, only to find himself later, in his descent, struggling with the magnified echoes of his own protests. Jung concealed the true nature of his relationship with Spielrein, which means that his enactments in relation to her exemplify the relationship between power and the projection of shame through the image of the succubus – the focus of the following explication of Jung's relationship with her.

Jung first met Spielrein when she was a hysterical patient at the Burgholzli Psychiatric Clinic in Switzerland, at that time the foremost psychiatric teaching hospital in the world. Spielrein's wealthy parents had brought their daughter all the way from Russia for a cure, and Jung was the physician put in charge of the case. She eventually became his first psychoanalytic test case when Jung began seeing her on an outpatient basis. To make the long story of her two-year cure very short, Spielrein's burgeoning self-confidence and recovery from psychotic hysteria was leading her in the direction of becoming a psychoanalyst. This was paralleled by the appearance of Siegfried in her dreams. In Spielrein's own words:

> it was Wagner who planted the demon in my soul with such terrifying clarity. I shall omit the metaphors, since you might laugh at the extravagance of my emotion. The whole world became a melody for me: the earth sang, the trees sang, and every twig on every tree.
>
> (Carotenuto, 1983: 107)

Spielrein wanted to have the love-child Siegfried with Jung. The appeal of Wagner's Siegfried seemed to lie in the fact that although Siegfried is a sun hero in a cosmological struggle, he is also an innocent orphan who needs the self-sacrificial protection of a woman who he, in turn, rescues and loves.

> Thus Siegfried came into being; he was supposed to become the greatest genius, because Dr. Jung's image as a descendant of the gods floated before me, and from childhood on I had had a premonition that I was not destined for a mundane life. I felt flooded with energy, all nature spoke directly to me.
>
> (Carotenuto, 1983: 108)

Spielrein felt strongly that a great destiny awaited her. Another important dimension of Spielrein's Siegfried complex was a psychic intuition and the production of prophetic dreams. In addition to foreseeing the future, Spielrein felt she could see the hidden complexes of people, most especially Jung. She could see into his secrets, a place where shame hides. For example, among her prophetic dreams was one that revealed Jung's secret wish to have the son Siegfried. Spielrein believed in it – and Jung believed in it. Her imagined magical omnipotence with symbiotic overtones is revealed in the idea that she was "able to read Dr. Jung's thoughts both when he was nearby and *a distance*, and he could do the same with me." Jung interpreted the similarity of their work as a manifestation of telepathy, and thought that they had "swallowed part of each other's souls." Yet this "secret penetration of thought" was not for the public.

Spielrein plays right into Jung's incestuous, heroic fantasies. For Jung, Siegfried became the Oedipal drama of incestuous attachment as well as the mother-imago of his birth:

> If only I knew
> What my mother was like!
> But that will my thought never tell me!
> Her eyes' tender light
> Surely did shine
> Like the soft eyes of the doe.
> (Wagner quoted in Jung, 1955: 363)

This maternal longing is reflected in how he responds when she first tells Jung about Siegfried in early 1907:

> When I confessed to Dr. Jung for the first time, he treated me with tenderest friendship, like a father, if you will. He admitted to me that from time to time he, too, had to consider such matters in connection with me (i.e. his affinity with me and the possible consequences), that such wishes are not alien to him, but the world happens to be arranged in such a way, etc., etc. This talk calmed me completely, since my ambitia was not wounded and the thought of his great love made me want to keep him perfectly "pure."
>
> (Carotenuto, 1983: 108)

Jung ends up writing a letter to Freud in July of 1907 admitting his illegitimate wish for a male child "that had better not see the light of day:"

> A hysterical patient told me that a verse from a poem by Lermontov was continually going around in her head. The poem is about a prisoner whose sole companion is a bird in a cage. The prisoner is animated only by one wish: sometime in his life, as his noblest deed, to give some creature its freedom. He opens the cage and lets his beloved bird fly out. What is the patient's greatest wish? "Once in my life I would like to help someone to perfect freedom through psychoanalytic treatment." In her dream she is condensed with me. She admits that actually her great wish is to have a child by me who would fulfill all her unfulfillable wishes. For that purpose I would naturally have to let "the bird out" first. (In Swiss German we say: "Has your birdie whistled?")
>
> (Freud, 1974: 72–73)

> A pretty little chain, isn't it? Do you know Kaulback's pornographic picture: "Who Buys Love-gods?" (Winged phalli looking like cocks, getting up to all sorts of monkey-tricks with the girls.)
>
> (p. 150)

The Siegfried fantasy was a shared incestuous fantasy of brother-sister/ mother-son; interpretations, fantasy and lived experience all merge together. "Siegfried stood simultaneously for the son she would give Jung and for Jung himself, with Spielrein in the role of the protective, self-sacrificing mother. By the same token … Jung was fathering himself through her" (Kerr, 1993: 227).

Jung obviously did not come to terms with the need to sacrifice his ideals and conscious attitude or will. There was no surrender in his heroic quest and acceptance of "incomplete masculinity." Jung plainly conceals the truth of the meaning of Siegfried in a 1925 seminar when he is talking about his dream:

> Siegfried was not an especially sympathetic figure to me, and I don't know why my unconscious got engrossed in him. Wagner's Siegfried, especially, is exaggeratedly extraverted and at times actually ridiculous. I never liked him. Nevertheless my dream showed him to be my hero. I could not understand the strong emotion I had with the dream. I can tell it here appropriately because it connects with the theme we have been discussing with respect to art, that is, with the change in values.
>
> (1989: 56)

Hidden in Siegfreid is the instinctual incestuous desire of a hidden part of himself – his infantile desire for the forbidden mother through the birth of a child. This primitive content lies behind Jung's abandonment of his role as Spielrein's analyst. Jung was a hopeless romantic, but now the romanticized hero merges with a romanticized succubus and the child killer. Seduced by the idea of Spielrein's love for him and fulfilling his wish for a male genius child, Jung begins sexualizing his relationship with Spielrein.

In the late Spring of 1908, he could no longer resist what he perceived to be her seductive temptations, a positive transference turning into uncontrollable infatuation. Spielrein records the moment in her diary:

> I told him [Jung] how my exams had gone, but was deeply depressed that he displayed no pleasure at hearing I was capable of doing good work after all and was now an official candidate for the medical degree. I was ashamed of having believed in any prophecies and told myself: not only does he not love me, I am not even a good acquaintance, whose welfare matters to him. He wanted to show me we were complete strangers to each other, and it is humiliating if I now go to see him. But I decided to go the following Friday, but to act completely professional. The devil whispered other things to me, but I no longer believed them … Now he arrives, beaming with pleasure, and tells me with strong emotion … about the great insight he has just received (i.e. about polygamy); he no longer wants to suppress his feeling for me, he admitted that I was his first, dearest friend, etc., etc. (his wife of course excepted), and that he wanted to tell me everything about himself. So once more this most curious coincidence that the devil so unexpectedly turned out to be right.
>
> (Carotenuto, 1983: 107)

After seeing her at a boating party, Jung writes to her:

> I must tell you briefly what a lovely impression I received of you today. Your image has changed completely, and I want to tell you how very, very happy it makes me to be able to hope that there are people who are like me, people in whom living and thinking are one; You can't believe how much it means to me to hope I can love someone whom I do not have to condemn, and who does not condemn herself either, to suffocate in the banality of habit.
>
> (Carotenuto, 1983: 239)

The projective, infantile nature of Jung's love is obvious. Jung and Spielrein were merged and he felt no shame. There is no hero who has to die, no hiding or hoping the ground beneath your feet opens and swallows you up. He wants to live with her in a heavenly, magical paradise beyond reality. He wants to reveal everything about himself and never feel powerless. He wants to bring this inner world into reality in the outer world. On August 12, 1908 he writes: "I happen to be terribly suspicious, and always think other people are trying to exploit and tyrannize me ..." The world is not perfect infantile bliss, and Jung was entangling himself in a complex web as he began to act shamelessly. He had become an official representative of psychoanalysis with his installment as the editor-in-chief of the new *Jahrbuch* and could not afford a public spectacle. Nevertheless, he compromised too much of what others were fighting for when he attempted to introduce Spielrein into his household.

Then Jung began to have second thoughts, which led to the withdrawal of his affections. In December 1908 Jung writes to Spielrein:

> My dear, I regret so much; I regret my weaknesses and curse the fate that is threatening me ... My mind is torn to its very depths ... Will you forgive me for being as I am? For offending you by being like this, and forgetting my duties as a doctor towards you? ... Give me back now something of the love and patience and unselfishness which I was able to give you at the time of your illness. Now I am ill.
>
> (Carotenuto, 1983: 240)

Spielrein writes back: "You are trying to suppress all the stronger feelings you have towards me. As a result you are surviving on mere diplomacy and lies" (p. 240).

Spielrein turned to Freud in search of help. She sent a single long letter to Freud in late June of 1909 incoherently detailing her relationship to Jung. Spielrein was part of Jung's clandestine world so that she ended up revealing his "secret career as a sorcerer's apprentice" (Kerr, 1993: 222). Meanwhile, Jung is afraid that Spielrein is spreading scandalous rumors about him.

When Jung gets caught, he projects his shame onto Spielrein. In his description of her to Freud where he attempts to maintain his secret, she has gone from *femme inspiratrice* to succubus. The following is Jung's first (1909) explanation to Freud:

> The last and worst straw is that a complex is playing Old Harry with me: a woman patient, whom years ago I pulled out of a sticky neurosis with unstinting devotion, has violated my confidence and my friendship in a most mortifying way imaginable. She has kicked up a scandal solely because I denied myself the pleasure of giving her a child. I have always acted the gentleman towards her, but before the bar of my rather too sensitive conscience I nevertheless don't feel clean, and that is what hurts the most because my intentions were always honourable. But you know how it is – the devil can use even the best of things for the fabrication of filth. Meanwhile I have learnt an unspeakable amount of marital wisdom, for until now I had totally inadequate idea of my polygamous components despite all self-analysis. Now I know where and how the devil can be laid by the heels.
>
> (Freud, 1974: 207)

And further on he writes:

> At the moment I don't know what to say. Spielrein is the person I wrote to you about.... She was, so to speak, my test case, for which reason I remembered her with special gratitude and affection. Since I knew from experience that she would immediately relapse if I withdrew my support, I prolonged the relationship over the years and in the end found myself morally obliged, as it were, to devote a large measure of friendship to her, until I saw that an unintended wheel had started turning, whereupon I broke with her. She was, of course, *systematically planning my seduction*, which I considered inopportune. Now she is seeking *revenge* ... Now of course the whole bag of tricks lies quite clearly before my "eyes" [italics mine].
>
> (pp. 228–229)

Jung had indeed lost pride, and is weakened by this loss of honor. But his eyes are blindly projecting his shame to maintain an intact ego and the power to mask his weakness and fragility.

Spielrein meets Jung face to face to proclaim that she had not started the scandalous rumors, and demands a settlement: he would write to Freud and admit that he was largely to blame for the "high flying hopes of his former patient" and apologize for his cowardly behavior. Jung was exposed in a most uncomfortable situation and forced to explain more. Incited by her confrontation, Jung admits that he seduced Spielrein, and that he had attempted to hide his shame behind her. Jung writes another letter to Freud on June 21, 1909 admitting his cowardliness:

> Caught in my delusion that I was the victim of the sexual wiles of my patient, I wrote to her mother [Frau Spielrein had asked Jung for an explanation] that I was not the gratifier of her daughter's sexual desires but merely her doctor, and that she should free me from her. In view of the fact that the patient had

> shortly before been my friend and enjoyed my full confidence, my action was a piece of knavery which I very reluctantly confess to you as my father.
>
> (Freud, 1974: 235)

Freud acts in unison by moving to protect the future of psychoanalysis and keep his "crown prince" clean and unblemished. He acts to protect psychoanalysis from a downfall: "if I am Moses, then you are Joshua and will take possession of the promised land of psychiatry, which I shall only be able to glimpse from afar" (McGuire quoted in Carotenuto, 1983: 241). He advises Jung not to become too contrite, and understands the trouble as a hazard of the countertransference. He concurs with Jung's assessment of feminine seduction and forgives all. In other words, the complicity between Freud and Jung is accomplished through the projection of their shame onto the succubus. Freud absolves Jung of any wrongdoing. It was not that Jung was powerless, but that he had succumbed to Spielrein's seductive charm. In a letter to Jung, Freud writes: "The way these women manage to charm us with every conceivable psychic perfection until they have attained their purpose is one of nature's greatest spectacles" (1974: 231); and he adds a quote from Mephisto to support his statement: "And another thing: 'In league with the Devil and yet you fear fire?' "

Discussion of the matter ended in a letter from Freud to Jung in 1909. "Don't fault yourself for drawing me into it; it was not your doing but hers. And the matter has ended in a manner satisfactory to all ..." (1974: 238). Spielrein felt otherwise:

> To suffer this disdain at the hands of a person whom one loved more than anything in the world for four, five years, to whom one gave the most beautiful part of one's soul, to whom one sacrificed one's maidenly pride, allowing oneself to be kissed, etc., for the first and perhaps the last time in my life, because when he began my treatment I was nothing but a naïve child ... Miserable good for nothing, let Siegfried die...
>
> (Carotenuto, 1983: 93)

And for Jung, it spelled the beginning of the end of his relationship to Freud. Kerr writes:

> But beyond both his loss and whatever self-recriminations may have haunted him, the most important aspect of the Spielrein affair was the change it occasioned in his relationship with Freud. For Jung had been quite earnest in trying to broaden both his theoretical outlook and the professional audience to which he was addressing himself. Even now, he was making plans to attend the Sixth International Congress ... His personal resentment – "neurotic ingratitude" – toward Freud had been no less real. To be sure, Freud had stood by him in the crisis and that counted for a great deal. Yet gratitude was a mantel that a man like Jung could only chafe under, and Freud's various

> remarks of the last few months could not have gone down easily ... their personal relationship, so crucial to Jung's early enthusiasm, was decisively altered.
>
> (1993: 230)

The "mantel" that Jung could only "chafe under" is his rivalry and plain competitiveness with Freud. Jung, a particularly shame-sensitive person, has shown himself in a cowardly light and is completely humiliated. In his 1925 seminar, Jung tells the killing of Siegfried dream a little differently, and in a way that ties the hero to Jung's cowardice with Spielrein and collusion with Freud:

> Presently, around a bend in the trail he came upon us, and we fired full into his breast. Then I was filled with horror and disgust at myself for the cowardice of what we had done. The little man with me went forward, and I knew he was going to drive the knife into Siegfried's heart, but that was just a little too much for me, and I turned and fled. I had the idea of getting away as fast as I could to a place where "they" could not find me. I had the choice of going down into the valley or further up the mountains by a faint trail. I chose the latter, and as I ran there broke upon me a perfect deluge of rain.
>
> (1989: 56–57)

In admitting his shame to his "father," he was momentarily unmasked and stripped of the grandiosity that hid an empty self. He was able to see that he "imputed all the wishes and hopes entirely to (his) patient without seeing the same thing in himself." Nevertheless, through Jung and Freud's complicity to dismiss Spielrein, Jung had escaped the danger of exposure by going up the mountain and being cleansed by the "perfect deluge of rain" – but shame always catches up. Ironically, Spielrein – who in her agony over Jung's disdain towards her prayed "to let Siegfried die" – got her wish.

In their collusion to preserve their personal aims, both Jung and Freud look with blind eyes. This means that their loss and shame will be pushed into the unconscious. Acting in their own interests, they dismiss the damage done to a then 21-year-old (but considerably mature) woman who not too long before was a patient diagnosed with psychotic hysteria. They misjudge her true worth, don't see the value of her brilliant theory on repression, and justify their dismissal of her by casting her again in the role of patient – as though the presence of an illness precludes an individual from having a voice or vision. When driven by the ego pursuits of prestige and power, a man can't help but rise in defense of himself. Both Freud and Jung were compelled to win the great race to systematize psychoanalytic theory, and both ended up acting spinelessly. Jung writes to Freud:

> I'll gladly take Spielrein's new paper [*Destruction as a Cause of Coming Into Being*] for the first number of Jahrbuch 1912. It demands a great deal of

> revision, but then the little girl has always been very demanding with me. However, she's worth it. I am glad you don't think badly of her.
>
> (Carotenuto, 1983: 77)

And on April 1, 1912, Jung begins with a quote from Horace:

> I was working on Spielrein's paper just before my departure. One must say: "*desinat in piscem mulier formose superne*" (What at the top is a lovely woman ends below in a fish; Horace). After a very promising start the continuation and end trail off dismally. Particularly the "Life and Death in Mythology" chapter needed extensive cutting as it contained gross errors and, worse still, faulty, one-sided interpretations. She has read too little and has fallen flat in this paper because it is not thorough enough. One must say by way of excuse that she has brought her problem to bear on an aspect of mythology that bristles with riddles. Besides that her paper is heavily overweighted with her own complexes. My criticism should be administered to the little authoress in *refracta dosi* only, please, if at all. I shall be writing to her myself before long.
>
> (Freud, 1974: 77–78)

The woman with whom he felt no shame, the woman who loved him and whom he loved in return, the woman with whom he wanted to give birth to the love child Siegfried, is now diminished and finally dismissed as a demanding little girl. Their contempt is made all the more outrageous when one considers the significant impact that her work had on both Freud and Jung's. *Destruction as a Cause of Coming Into Being* is the unspoken other half of Jung's thinking in Part II of *Symbols*, and Spielrein inspired Freud's landmark insights on transference and countertransference, as well as his concept of the death instinct (Kerr, 1993).

Despite their depreciation of her, however, through the "transference cure" of her psychosis with Jung and her friendship with Freud, Spielrein was able to give voice to her true self. Spielrein seemed to conceive of her own contributions, and was anything but a woman out for revenge. She remained deprived until 1974 of the one thing she wanted – recognition – despite demonstrating great psychic strength in its pursuit. Foremost amongst her admirable handling of the whole disastrous affair is her commitment to stay true to her resolve to separate from Jung in a loving way – in a way true to the story of Siegfried. She tries not to take sides in Freud and Jung's split, despite Freud's insistence for her to choose sides; in a letter to Spielrein he states: "My personal relationship with your Germanic hero has definitely been shattered" (a word reminiscent of "torn" or "smashed to pieces"), and "of course I want you to succeed in casting aside as so much trash your infantile dreams of the Germanic champion and hero" (Freud quoted in Carotenuto, 1983: 122). She takes care that Jung is not seen as a rogue by Freud, whom she eventually consults to resolve her feelings for the man who "smashed her whole life." Even after Freud and Jung's complicity disintegrated into hatred for each other, she continued for the next decade to seek their mutual recognition: in a letter to Freud she writes, "in spite of all his wavering I like Jung and would like to lead him back into our fold. You, Professor, and he have not the faintest idea that you belong together far more than anyone might suspect" (quoted in Carotenuto, p. 112). At the very least, Freud and Jung belonged together in their shame, and Spielrein, among anyone else, would be the one to suspect. The cover of John Kerr's book, *A Most Dangerous Method*, depicts the three faces of Jung, Spielrein, and Freud, in that order. Jung and Freud's face meets the onlooker directly and fills the entire frame, while Spielrein's image is distinguished by its placement between Freud and Jung's and depicts her small and at a distance, sitting and reading, head down as though in shame. If the idea that the medium contains the message is true, then the photos convey the idea that she carries their shame.

Jung's descent was as much precipitated by his loss of Spielrein as it was about his loss of Freud – two objects of dependence Jung had to omnipotently destroy. This is the double meaning of the murder of Siegfried. It is hard to fathom how Jung wrote *Memories, Dreams and Reflections* so many years later without so much as mentioning Spielrein's name.

Salome and Jung's anima

The dream of killing Siegfried has now given way to an area of Jung's unconscious where the figures of Elijah, Salome and a serpent meet him. Before him lays a passage into the depths of ubiquitous, dark maternal images that again give him the feeling of being "in the land of the dead." In this other world,

> near the steep slope of a rock I caught sight of two figures, an old man with a white beard and a beautiful young girl. I summoned up my courage and approached them as though they were real people ... The old man explained that he was Elijah, and that gave me a shock. But the girl staggered me even more, for she called herself Salome! She is blind ... They had a black serpent living with them which displayed an unmistakable fondness for me.
>
> (1965: 181)

The disparity between the wise old man and the beautiful young woman stands out immediately, but Elijah assures Jung that he and Salome "belonged together for all eternity ..." The paired image of the old man with the young girl could certainly reflect Jung's relationship to Spielrein – he her wise 30-year-old doctor and she his 19-year-old psychotic, infantile patient. In a letter explaining his cowardly behavior to Spielrein's mother, Jung writes:

> You do understand of course, that a man and a girl cannot possibly continue indefinitely to have friendly dealings with each other without the likelihood that something more may enter the relationship.
>
> (Carotenuto,1983: 94)

Jung took the figures to be images that amplified the nature of some unconscious process.

> Salome is an anima figure, blind because, though connecting the conscious and the unconscious, she does not see the operation of the unconscious. Elijah is the personification of the cognitional element, Salome the erotic. Elijah is the figure of the old prophet filled with wisdom. One could speak of these two figures as personifications of Logos and Eros very specifically shaped.
>
> (1989: 89)

Jung, unlike Elijah, is truly a male of the dominance mentality who must maintain a separate subjectivity premised on the denial of his association with the feminine. He chose to stick "close to Elijah because he seemed to be the most reasonable . . . and to have a clear intelligence . . . Elijah and I had a long conversation, which, however, I did not understand" (p. 181). Perhaps Jung could not understand because he could not fathom Elijah's choice of Salome as a companion, of whom Jung was distinctly suspicious. Jung is dissociated from some painful affective state symbolized by Salome. If one considers the following comment, it is no wonder Jung splits her off, for nothing feels heroic when one is engulfed in blood:

> When Elijah told me he was always with Salome, I thought it was almost blasphemous for him to say this. I had the feeling of diving into an atmosphere that was cruel and full of blood. This atmosphere was around Salome, and to hear Elijah declare that he was always in that company shocked me profoundly.
>
> (p. 93)

If one examines Jung's imagery of Salome as the point of contact, however, connections between Salome and Lilith surface. The bloody atmosphere is identical with Lilith's lair, which is said to be "drenched in blood." Lilith does indeed seem to belong with Elijah for all eternity, for she is coupled with him in several Hebrew legends. For the most part, Lilith's encounters with Elijah depict her in her guise as blood-sucking child killer. These stories depict Elijah as another male hero: a female demon is vanquished by a lone prophet, then rendered harmless and driven away. The woman is delivered up, defenseless, to the demon without a fight. There are certain Kabbalistic traditions that have Elijah seduced by Lilith, and this prevents his entrance into heaven. One such meeting is described in an anti-Gnostic text from 375 to 377 A.D.:

> There came, so people say, a female demon, who stopped him and said to him: "Whither do you go? For I have children by you and you cannot ascend (to heaven) and abandon your children." And he replied: "How can you have children by me, have I not lived in the way of holiness?" She said: "Yes, in

> sleep, in your dreams, you were often emptied by the outflow from your body. Then I received your sperm and bore you children."
>
> (quoted by Hurwitz, 1999: 104)

Most interesting of all the associations to Elijah is the fact that John the Baptist is identified in the Gospel of Luke as Elijah come down to earth in fulfillment of the prophecy made in the very last verse of the Old Testament (Mal. 4:5):

> Behold, I will send you Elijah the prophet before the great and terrible day the Lord comes. And he will turn the hearts of fathers to their children and the hearts of children to their fathers, lest I come and smite the land with a curse.

That Elijah and Salome appear together for all eternity points to the relationship between the succubus and man, Salome and John the Baptist, Lilith and Elijah.

One of the main theses of this book is that masculine shame is dissociated through the male's identification with the warrior hero, and the primitive content projected makes a succubus of the maternal feminine. This phenomenon has been occurring for at least seven thousand years. So if the hero with whom Jung is "secretly identified" is murdered, and Jung is then, according to his autobiography, no longer identified with Siegfried and the heroic ideal, where is Jung's shame?

The "talented psychopath"

Jung's rejection of Salome is a case of the hero split off from his maternal feminine side. Yet he is led to an important discovery from her appearance – the feminine soul image in the male psyche, his own inner femininity:

> I was greatly intrigued that a woman should interfere with me from within. My conclusion was that she must be the "soul" in the primitive sense, and I began to speculate on the reasons why the name "anima" was given to the soul . . . At first it was the negative aspect of the anima that most impressed me.
>
> (Jung, 1965: 186)

His first writings on the anima and the feminine inevitably mirror Jung's primitive disturbance. There is precious little of Jung's appreciative attitude towards the anima overall in his telling of his confrontation with the unconscious.

The anima is formed not only by the male's personal experiences with the maternal feminine, but with the archetypal ones as well, genuine experiences beyond the male projection upon a woman. This archetypal figure gets unconsciously projected onto certain feminine figures (when projections become operative), who in turn hold a correspondingly strong fascination for a man. "The projection-making factor is the anima, or rather the unconscious as represented by the anima" (Jung, 1970: 13). And Jung is the one who warned that if one is not conscious of his internal contradictions, he will project them outward, hence inflicting them upon himself in the form of fate (and "the instrument of fate is always woman, who knows and reveals [a man's] secret thoughts" (Jung, 1955: 361). In normal development, the man's feminine side is largely repressed, and this contributes to the constellation of the anima which, when projected, makes contact with a woman possible. The anima is also a factor of the utmost importance in the feeling life of a man where she "intensifies, exaggerates, falsifies, and mythologizes all emotional relations with his work and with other people of both sexes." For Jung, the anima matches two different kinds of libido: one infantile, incestuous and backward looking, the other adolescent, procreative and forward looking. This theoretical version of Freud's libido theory was one he could accept.

According to Jung, mother and anima form a reciprocal dynamic: experiences of mother form a core component of the anima, while "the numinous qualities which make the mother image so dangerously powerful derive from the collective archetype of the anima, which is incarnated in every male child" (Jung, 1951: 13). Patriarchal masculine development of consciousness conditions the constellation of the anima figure and its differentiation from the mother archetype. Because of the difference in anatomical sex, a son's mother complex never appears in pure form. In every masculine mother complex, right alongside the archetype of the mother, a significant role is played by the image of a man's sexual counterpart, the anima. The anima is a preexisting psychic image of woman, which means that a male's perception of mother will always be obscured by the anima archetype. This emotional obscuring is behind a man's statements about the mother, in the "sense of showing 'animosity'" (Jung, 1955: 345–346). Anima experience overlays a man's real experience of mother, which is then split off under the spell of ego repression for established men. This is where the patriarchally driven images of woman have particular relevance, which results in the anima's appearance as a power figure from the very beginning.

To his credit, Jung intellectually understood that he experienced his own femininity through his projection upon women. This insight, however, doesn't change the fact that most of what he has to say about the anima is the result of projection which he consequently takes to be real. While Jung could objectively see that the woman a man deals with most of the time is a projection of his own anima, he remains blind to the shame he unconsciously projects in order to maintain his position of power.

Spielrein was just one of many women held hostage to Jung's anima projections, but her voice was the one that Jung's inner anima figure adopts. The fact that the voice is Spielrein's underscores her connection with Salome and amplifies the meaning of Jung's visions. As a scientifically trained doctor, Jung wondered about the processes he was undergoing, and whether they could still be called science – or were they art? Was psychoanalysis a science, in which case rival hypotheses were essential to a meaningful examination of the data? Or was it an art, in which case the original artist had the right to enforce his own view as to how his creation is to be completed. At this point, a female voice intruded itself and said "it is art." Jung recognized the voice as belonging to one of his "patients," "a talented psychopath who had a strong transference to me ... she had become a living figure within my mind" (1965: 185).

Jung's act of matricide

Jung took the position that if he viewed his fantasies as art (associated with femininity), they would carry no more conviction than visual perceptions of the surface. Moral obligation and integrity would be lost. "The anima might then have easily seduced me into believing that I was a misunderstood artist, and that my so-called artistic nature gave me the right to neglect reality" (1965: 186). This seduction will result in his diminishment. Jung imagines that if he allows himself to be influenced by her thoughts, she will undermine his authority and power. He proves his own theory on the anima's projective functions with the thought "If I had followed her voice, she would in all probability have said to me one day, 'Do you imagine the nonsense you're engaged in is really art? Not a bit.'" Thus, he concludes, "the insinuations of the anima, the mouthpiece of the unconscious, can utterly destroy a man. In the final analysis the decisive factor is always consciousness, and (one must) take up a position toward them" (1965: 187).

In his confrontation, one of the ways Jung attempts to gain control over his dreams and visions was to make his images scientifically comprehensible and relevant. This meant drawing concrete conclusions from his insights, thus trespassing on the line between reality and psychosis – just the place where the succubus resides. Jung was driven to defend his conscious, ego, patriarchal male power, and wrote to his anima every evening so that her negativity could not get into his fantasies and "twist them into intrigues:"

> What I did then to get at this inferior, unconscious side of me was to make at night an exact reversal of the mental machinery I had used in the day. That is to say, I turned all libido within in order to observe the dreams that were going on.
>
> (1965: 186)

Jung determined that the only way to "strip the power" from unconscious contents was to bring them into relationship to consciousness. One gets the feeling that Jung's determination not to be blindsided by the anima's deep cunning, and his need to maintain power over her, became its own kind of enslavement.

In *Memories*, Jung fails to mention that the argument contains important personal referents to himself and his "psychopathic patient" during a time when analysis and fantasy, incest and myth, had started to merge into each other. First and foremost, "art" (and poetry) was a metaphor which had special meaning known only to Jung and Spielrein; from their writings, we know only that they came very close to "poetry," Spielrein's word for "what happens when a couple, both enamored of mysticism, move backward from it to a sexual realization – and keep psychoanalyzing" (Kerr, 1993: 227). Spielrein also defines the terms in her inner dialogues:

> The dissolution of a complex through empathic sharing (with attendant sexual attraction) is but one of the avenues open to the instinct for transformation. Other are "art" and "science," both ways of objectifying complexes; art in particular allows complexes "to express themselves to the utmost."
>
> (p. 197)

It is no wonder, then, that Spielrein's voice becomes the voice of Jung's anima.

Jung's mother

Jung's suspiciousness of Salome in relation to his own authority feelings compelled him to hold her with such disregard. His mistrust of maternal feminine containment stems from his early attachment issues with his mother, who figured large in Jung's early life with her depression and dissociative tendencies. Jung (1965) describes his mother as a "kindly fat old woman" who had two distinct personalities: he found the second to be far more compelling. He shares several ways he experienced her dissociation.

> She held all the conventional opinions a person was obliged to have, but then her unconscious personality would suddenly put in an appearance. That personality was unexpectedly powerful; a somber imposing figure possessed of unassailable authority – and no bones about it. I was sure she consisted of two personalities, one innocuous and human, the other uncanny. This other emerged only now and then, but each time it was unexpected and frightening. She would then speak as if talking to herself, but what she said was aimed at me and usually struck to the core of my being, so that I was stunned into silence.
>
> (p. 48)

> All sorts of things were happening at night, things incomprehensible and alarming. My parents were sleeping apart. I slept in my father's room. From my door to my mother's room came frightening influences. At night Mother's room was strange and mysterious.
>
> (p. 18)

> There was an enormous difference between my mother's two personalities. That is why as a child I often had anxiety dreams about her. By day she was a loving mother, but at night she seemed uncanny. Then she was like one of those seers who at the same time is a strange animal, like a priestess in a bear's cave. Archaic and ruthless; ruthless as truth and nature. At such moments, she was the embodiment of what I have called the "natural mind."
>
> (p. 50)

The natural mind was one that "is the sort of mind which springs from natural sources, and not from opinions taken from books; it wells up from the earth like a natural spring, and brings with it the peculiar wisdom of nature" (Jung, 1965: 50). From what Jung relates of his maternal memories of personality number two, it is easy to understand his literary analog for the anima, She Who Must Be Obeyed (the main character in H. Rider Haggard's *She*) and an image for his shame (Ayers, 2003: 158–160).

Part of mother's "welling up" appeared to include confiding her troubles to her son. Jung would take her seriously and overreact to her concerns, so he decided to divide everything his mother said by two. "My confidence in her was strictly limited." His world came to be full of "vague and incomprehensible perils." "Therefore, I always wanted to know at the start to what and to whom I was entrusting myself" (1965: 30).

Jung's mother was hospitalized for a severe depression when he was just three years old. It was thought that her depression stemmed from difficulties in the marriage, and she went away for several months. During this time Jung was unable to identify with his mother's soothing and containing function, evidenced by his development of severe eczema. He describes his experience of his mother's absence: "I was deeply troubled by my mother's being away. From then on I always felt mistrustful when the word 'love' was spoken. The feeling I associated with 'woman' was for a long time that of innate unreliability" (Jung, 1965: 8). The sudden appearance of his sister nine years later left him with the same sense of distrust.

Jung shares the first dream he remembers from when he was three or four, his "first great secret" that he thought critically important in his development (1965: 27). Feldman argues, however, that because the dream is highly complex and structured, Jung probably had this dream in the Oedipal stage at the age of five or six (Feldman, 1992: 265). He is in a meadow and discovers a stone hole in the ground which he descends into an ornate, underground chamber. He discovers

> a magnificent throne, a real king's throne in a fairy tale. Something was standing on it which I thought at first was a tree trunk twelve to fifteen feet high and about one and a half to two feet thick. It was a huge thing, reaching almost to the ceiling. But it was of a curious composition: it was made of skin and naked flesh, and on top there was something like a rounded head with no face and no hair. On the very top of the head was a single eye, gazing motionlessly upward.
>
> It was fairly light in the room, although there were no windows and no apparent source of light. Above the head, however, was an aura of brightness. The thing did not move, yet I have the feeling that it might at any moment drawl off the throne like a worm and creep toward me. I was paralyzed with terror. At that moment I heard from outside and above me my mother's voice. She called out "Yes, just look at him. That is the man-eater."
>
> (pp. 11–12)

Jung identifies the enthroned glowing phallus with the eye on top as a subterranean God "not to be named." He says of it "that is the handicap I started off with" (Jung, 1965: 8). Jung amplified the dream later as a descent into the earth, the realm of the dark mother, and an initiation into its secrets – the place described in Part II of *Symbols* entitled "The Sacrifice" and the place he got lost – and the same place he tried to find himself when he took the matter up again in his descent into the unconscious.

So what is a disembodied penis with the single eye on top doing deep in the bowels of the mother's realm? Perhaps the eye on top connects the maternal dimension of the succubus to the chthonic phallus, the negative and destructive elements as opposed to its solar ones. This image could connect the phallus to matriarchal times, a time when the man's powerful male member belonged to the mother. According to Melanie Klein, the mother's body holds all that is desirable, including the father's penis. Lacan, in his essay on psychoses, put it this way: "As to the child, there's not a shadow of doubt – whether male or female, it locates the phallus very early on and, we're told, generously grants it to the mother" (Lacan/Griggs, 1993: 319). The mother proves to be a powerful castrator, just as she is in Freud's theory of the Oedipus Complex, combining Oedipal and infantile, narcissistic shame. His fear of potential castration by the father's penis inside the mother could have made it difficult for him to relate in a productive way to his own childhood sexuality, and this may provide an explanation for his early renunciation of Freud's theory of childhood sexuality (Feldman, 1992: 266). Jung's encounter with the penis as Medusa is similar to Freud's Medusa and castration anxieties, the *vagina dentata*, in the form of his mother's voice saying "that is the maneater." Of father, Jung could only say, " 'father, on the other hand, meant reliability and – powerlessness."

Jung was aware of suffering shame and a strong sense of inferiority all the while growing up. By Jung's own account, he suffered difficulties in the interpersonal realm. One reason was that his mother had a bad habit of calling out to him on the street, humiliating him while he was feeling the dignity of his purpose and public appearance. She would yell belittling things after him, like "have you washed your hands?"

> And so on. It struck me as definitely unfair that the inferiority feelings which accompanies my self-importance should thus be exposed to the world when I had taken every care, out of *amour-propre* and vanity, to present as irreproachable an appearance as possible … I felt important and dignified … The picture changed radically, however, as soon as I came in sight of the house I was visiting. Then a sense of the grandeur and power of those people overcame me. I was afraid of them, and in my smallness wished I might sink fathoms deep into the ground … I felt as timid and craven as a stray dog. It was ever so much worse if mother had prepared me properly beforehand.
>
> (Jung, 1965: 26)

Jung's absolute shame is the smallness which made him wish he would sink "fathoms deep into the ground." He felt it in all areas of his early life, and he refers to it frequently in his autobiography.

> But my fear of failure and my sense of smallness in face of the vast world around me created in me not only a dislike but a kind of silent despair which completely ruined school for me.
>
> (p. 29)

> The neurosis became another of my secrets, but it was a shameful secret. A defeat.
>
> (p. 32)

> I had a certain physical timidity which I was not able to overcome until much later on. This timidity was in turn linked with a distrust of the world and its potentialities.
>
> (p. 29)

> When my mother once said to me, "You have always been a good boy," I simply could not grasp it. I a good boy? This was quite new to me. I often thought of myself as a corrupt and inferior person.
>
> (p. 41)

And last, Jung once had an image of God befouling a cathedral by dropping a feces on the roof that he resisted thinking for days. This image became one of his closest held secrets: "at last I had something tangible that was part of the great secret ... My entire youth can be understood in terms of this secret. It induced in me an almost unbearable loneliness" (p. 41).

To cope with his deep shame, Jung utilized autistic and encapsulating defenses which point to very early wounding. Behind Jung's focus on the inner, archetypal realm and the world of nature is his attempts to get the soothing, holding and containment that mother could not give him due to her severe depression. He could cling to his isolated, sensory world of nature and the awesome power of the archetypes for security in the face of psychotic anxieties. Mythology provides a marvelous place for dissociation, but this contact could not humanly soothe, nourish and provide the real tenderness he needed.

A threat to the hero is the risk of giving into his secret thoughts and wishes, to give into his instinctual, feminine nature and seek solace with the mother. Jung's shame, therefore, is repressed through lots of hiding places, and in his autobiography he makes consistent references to secrets. Jung states that he did not discuss his early childhood material with anyone until he was 65 years old (except with Spielrein, but then he couldn't mention her). He reserved these memories to contain his developing self, and felt they provided him with a "secret truth."

The restoration of Salome's vision

The serpent

In Jung's second vision of Elijah, Salome and the serpent, the figure of Elijah drops out of view, and the serpent and Salome, who played small roles in the first vision, move into the foreground. Jung is now leaving ascent and the mountain ranges of Elijah to descend into Salome's alluring world, the "Eros" side. This is much different from Elijah's world of intelligence and knowledge, or the "Logos" side (which became Jung's conversations with Philemon, now available to the public with the recent publication of *The Red Book*). Jung is entering the place of his fears and "suspicions" in his pursuit to penetrate the incest barrier, conceived of as an obstruction to self knowledge, and to make contact with the deepest libidinal well springs of his mind.

Jung says that the unconscious hero takes shape once again, this time in the huge black snake. With the punctuation of the snake the vision becomes more primal, and culminates with the snake playing a major part in the "primal scene of Western religion" – the crucifixion of Christ (Miles, 2001). Mythology is full of the relationship between the hero and the snake, and Jung recites them endlessly in *Symbols*. For example, a northern myth says the hero has snake eyes. Many other myths depict him being worshipped in the form of a snake, and others say he transforms into a serpent after death. "The hero who sets himself the task of renewing the world and conquering death personifies the world-creating power which, brooding on itself in introversion, coiled round its own egg like a snake, threatens life with its poisonous bite, so that the living may die and be born again from the darkness" (1956: 543). The hero is himself the snake, the sacrificer and the sacrificed. The presence of the snake, then, points to the idea that this vision is going to be another hero story (Jung, 1989: 89). The serpent also points to the serpent force that will enable Jung to expand his consciousness into other worlds.

The snake symbolizes the dead, buried, chthonic hero; but since the hero, once deceased, is back in the mother, the snake also stands for the Mother of Death in conjunction with the hero, the entwining animal connected to her earth aspect. The serpent also relates to the seductive function of the anima, another negative aspect of the Great Mother in the male psyche, although related to the Oedipal period. The *Zohar* cites the serpent as a symbol of the sinful, destructive Lilith, Queen of the Succubi: "The female of Samael (the devil) is called Serpent, Woman of Harlotry …" And it is this dark feminine element that leads psychological movement astray into the shadows, into the dead and wrong places, into concretization – and for Jung, into a love affair with Spielrein. Lilith made his thoughts real, made them come into being, and put him on a false track. After all, it was Lilith in her form as serpent who tempted Eve to eat an apple from the Tree of Knowledge.

Just before emerging from his confrontation with the unconscious, Jung felt compelled to write an overblown, petrified tract which he entitled *Seven Sermons to the Dead.* Sermon VI provides a vivid description of Lilith as serpent anima, and most certainly amplifies the meaning of the serpent in Jung's visions:

> The daimon of sexuality approacheth our soul as a serpent. It is half human and appeareth as thought-desire.
>
> The daemon of spirituality descendeth into our soul as the white bird. It is half human and appeareth as desire-thought.
>
> The serpent is an earthly soul, half daemonic, a spirit, and akin to the spirits of the dead. Thus too, like these, she swarmeth around in the things of earth, making us either to fear them or pricking us with intemperate desires. The serpent hath a nature like unto woman. She seeketh ever the company of the dead who are held by the spell of the earth, they who found not the way beyond that leadeth to singleness. The serpent is a whore. She wantoneth with the devil and the evil spirits; a mischievous tyrant and tormentor, ever seducing to evilest company. The white bird is a half-celestial soul of man. He bideth with the Mother, from time to time descending. The bird hath a nature like unto man, and is effective thought. He is chaste and solitary, a messenger of the Mother. He flieth high above earth. He commandeth singleness. He bringeth knowledge from the distant ones who went before and are perfected. He beareth our word above to the Mother. She intercedeth, she warneth, but against the gods she hath no power. She is a vessel for the sun. The serpent goeth below and with her cunning she lameth the phallic daemon, or else goadeth him on. She yieldeth up to the crafty thoughts of the earthly one, those thoughts which creep through every hole and cleave to all things with desirousness. The serpent, doubtless, willeth it not, yet she must be of use to us. She fleeth our grasp, thus showing us the way, which with our human wits we could not find.
>
> With disdainful glance the dead spake: Cease this talk of dos and daemons and souls. At bottom this hath long been known to us.
>
> (1965: 388–389)

Descent

Jung's second vision begins with a deep conflict over descending. He wants to go up towards the sun again, the male principle striving upwards by nature, instead of down into the cruel, dark, bloody, feminine place below. From the outset Jung is identified with the sun hero, the subject of his long excursus in *Symbols*. His conflict is imaged as "two dark principles" that take the form of serpents in battle.

> There was a mountain ridge, a knife edge, on one side a sunny desert country, on the other side darkness. I saw a white snake on the light side and a dark snake on the dark side. They met in battle on the narrow ridge. A dreadful conflict ensued. Finally the head of the black snake turned white, and it retired, defeated. I felt, "Now we can go on."
>
> (1989: 95–96)

Dualities are opposing each other in the light/dark atmosphere. Yet the brutal conflict is between "two dark principles." This may point to the maternal and the anima, terrible and seductive, dual aspects of the succubus archetype. The *Zohar* usually calls Lilith "the black one, the false one ..." The head of the serpent turning white could be linked to shame and defeat, as when one "turns white as a ghost" and "loses face" with the petrifaction of shame. Jung's vision depicts the black serpent undergoing the whitening of his head, and this instigates the light symbolism, the victorious white serpent that gradually develops and intensifies as the vision evolves into the sacrificial transformation of the sun hero and the restoration of Salome's vision.

The above and the below

Once the serpent battle is over Jung goes through a process of alternating size perceptions until it slowly dawns on him that he is in a crater "at the bottom of the world." The *krater* (mixing vessel) is a feminine vessel of spiritual transformation "that had no place in Freud's patriarchal world" (Jung, 1965: 200). In the *krater*, the feminine plays a role equal to that of the masculine. Elijah and Salome are there together, and Elijah climbs up onto a Druidic altar, foreshadowing a sacrifice. Upon his realization as to where he is, Jung announces the basic premise of the teachings on equivalence, a Hermetic axiom common throughout the whole of antiquity, "Why, it is just the same, above or below." This means that to ascend or descend makes no difference. The interface between the opposites is the place of psychic transformation. Heaven and hell, the higher and the lower, are unified when the masculine and the feminine are equal. Spielrein had this to say about the above and below:

> The extension into the dark sea corresponds to the forging ahead into the dark problem. The merging of air and water, the mixing of above and below may symbolize that, in the Mothers (as Mephistopheles pictures it), all times and all places are fused. There are no boundaries between above and below. For this reason, Mephistopheles can say to the departing Faust, "Plunge then. – I could even say soar."
>
> (1994: 155–186)

According to the *Gospel of Thomas*, Jesus speaks directly to the concept of the above and below in a passage which amplifies the content in Jung's vision:

> When you make the two one, and when you make the inside like the outside, and the outside like the inside, and the above like the below, and when you make the male and the female one and the same, so that the male be not male nor the female female; and when you fashion eyes in place of an eye, and a hand in place of a hand, and a foot in place of a foot, and a likeness in place of a likeness, then will you enter [the Kingdom].

For Jung it was not much different: to ascend to the sun hero is to descend into the dark (castrating) mother. This descent is a necessary prelude to the death of his ego and an ascent into higher consciousness, and yet can only be accomplished when the gaze is confident of an indissoluble bond with the regenerating Mother of the Mysteries.

Salome

> Then a most disgreeable thing happened. Salome became very interested in me, and she assumed that I could cure her blindness. She began to worship me. I said, "Why do you worship me?" She replied, "You are Christ." In spite of my objections she maintained this. I said, "This is madness," and became filled with skeptical resistance. Then I saw the snake approach me. She came close and began to encircle me and press me in her coils. The coils reached up to my heart. I realized as I struggled, that I had assumed the attitude of the Crucifixion. In the agony and the struggle, I sweated so profusely that the water flowed down on all sides of me. Then Salome rose, and she could see. While the snake was pressing me, I felt that my face had taken on the face of an animal of prey, a lion or a tiger.
>
> (1965: p. 96)

From beginning to end, the possibility of the resolution of Jung's shame and fears of an equal female completing him lies in the imagery of ancient mystery rites of Mithraic and Christian origin. Salome focuses her seductive intentions on Jung in order to regain her vision, and this contact sparks an initiation/deification mystery. Jung sees her only as the "side of the inferior function which is surrounded by an aura of evil" whose attentions can precipitate madness (the psychotic core of absolute shame). And yet it was Jung himself who maintained that revelation comes through the inferior function: it takes hold of us where we are most vulnerable and insecure. Jung fears that his identification with the figure of Christ, fashioned through the serpent's seduction and penetration of his heart, will make him insane. This feeling is really coming from his loss of ego and his power over stance, the self-justification of cosmic heroism.

The serpent's deification performance is reminiscent of Salome's dance for her stepfather, King Herod, and the only mythological association Jung addresses. Here is Salome and John the Baptist's story:

> [Herod had had John] chained up in prison because of Herodias, his brother Philip's wife [and his own niece], whom he had married. For John had told Herod, "It is against the law for you to have your brother's wife." As for Herodias, she was furious with [John] and wanted to kill him, but she was not able to do so because Herod was in awe of John, knowing him to be a good and upright man, and he gave him his protection. When he heard him speak, he was greatly troubled, yet he liked listening to him.

> Herodias got her chance on Herod's birthday, when he had a banquet for the nobles of his court, for his army officers, and for the leading figures in Galilee. When the daughter of the same Herodias came in and danced, she delighted Herod and his guests; so the king said to the girl, "Ask me anything you like and I will give it to you." And he swore an oath to her: "I will give you anything you ask, even half my kingdom." She went out and said to her mother, "What shall I ask for?" And she replied, "The head of John the Baptist." The girl at once rushed back to the king and made her request: "I want you to give me John the Baptist's head, immediately, on a platter." The king was deeply distressed, but, thinking of the oath he had sworn and in front of his guests, he was reluctant to go back on his word to her. Next thing, the king sent one of the bodyguards with the orders to bring John's head. The man went off and beheaded John in the prison; then he brought the head on a platter and gave it to the girl, and the girl gave it to her mother. When John's disciples heard about this, they came and took his body and laid it in a tomb.
>
> (Mark 6:17–29)

Had Jung cared to probe any deeper into Salome's significance, he might have discovered her roots in the myths of the succubi, most especially Lilith, the meaning of the serpent in connection to her, and their striking similarity to Mithraic imagery. In *Symbols*, Jung does make a cursory connection between the entwining serpent Lilith and Mithras (and his only mention of Lilith in his *Collected Works*):

> The tree entwined by the snake may therefore be taken as the symbol of the mother who is protected against incest by fear. This symbol is frequently found on Mithraic monuments. The rock with a snake coiled round it has a similar meaning, for Mithras (and also Men) was born from a rock. The threatening of the new-born infants by snakes (Mithras, Apollo, Heracles) is explained by the legend of Lilith and the Lamia. Python, the dragon of Leto, and Poine, who devastated the land of Crotopos . . .
>
> (1955: 260)

As her serpent aspect encoils, it becomes the dance, the "art" which Jung needs to integrate. She is the instrument of a sacred act that creates an attitude of sacrifice, images as Christ's crucifixion. Salome's worship is less the expression of an erotic situation, as it was with the Baptist, than a ritual act of the greatest numinous significance. The following is a passage Jung quotes from Holderlin in *Symbols*, words which amplify the meaning of his vision.

> . . . shamefully
> A mighty force wrenches the heart from us,
> For the heavenly each demand sacrifice.
>
> (p. 414)

Christ and sacrifice

When dealing with the image of Christ, we are dealing with a Mediterranean culture in which the supremacy of the male had been established for millennia. It is intriguing that Salome, the succubus figure responsible for the murder of the man who revealed the identity of Christ to the world, appears in Jung's vision as the instrument of his realization that he is Christ. Something has been turned around. It is as though the serpent, the succubus aspect of Salome, has transformed the meaning of John the Baptist's beheading and her actions in the bible. By his own hand at having to grant Salome's wish, Herod develops a conscience and later cannot sentence Jesus to death; instead, he sends him on to Pontius Pilate. Through his sacrifice, Jesus becomes the human form of the Christ principle, the unity of the above and below, the victim expressing compassionate love for the perpetrator to facilitate an integration of shame and the development of conscience.

The link between Jung's Christ transformation and the restoration of Salome's vision brings an often overlooked detail in the story of John the Baptist's beheading clearly into view. Salome is herself a victim of child abuse at the hands of her mother, Herodias. Burning with the sting of shame over John's finger pointing at her incestuous marriage to Herod, it is she who seizes the moment with her own wish, and instructs her daughter to request the head of John the Baptist. Salome accedes to her mother's evil request blindly and without question. The restoration of Salome's vision, in this respect, means no longer being blind to the victimizing, succubus mother.

The meaning of sacrifice was in contention between Spielrein and Jung, and this remained true to the end of their (at least external) relationship. For Jung, sacrifice was an act of moral repression, a "phylogenetically acquired moral imperative, a symbolic archway through which one can gain access to the 'total energy of countless generations'" (Kerr, 1993: 334). This makes sense, and appears to be rooted in his polygamous nature (which, in fact, was enacted throughout his life). In *Destruction as a Cause of Coming Into Being*, Spielrein argued that all sexual attraction involved destruction. The feeling of dread, ultimately a fear of dissolution and death, was surely not an obstacle for love; it was merely the price demanded by the destructive component of the libido. Self-destruction is replaced by sacrificial destruction. "Death in the service of sexual instinct, which includes a destructive component, is a salutary blessing since it leads to a coming into being" (1994: 183). New creation somehow requires in turn the death of the creator, and surrender to destruction leads to transformation. Spielrein had clarified the essential interconnection between death and rebirth – "transformation" in her language, and its relation to incestuous sexuality. The symmetry of Christ and Salome reflects the same symmetry between Jung and Spielrein's ideas on the nature of sacrifice.

> In short, while Jung was describing an inner confrontation with a maternal image felt to be "destructive," Spielrein was explicitly arguing for "destruction"

> as a necessary part of love. The two texts, his and hers, adjoin each other like severed halves of a forgotten conversation.
>
> (Kerr, 1993: 3)

More particularly for a man, sacrifice is the necessary prerequisite for a restoration of vision of the maternal feminine and the completion of the hero's journey (more on this in Chapter 8). In order to include his love for Spielrein and the meaning of her ideas – hence, in order to become whole – Jung needed to look deep into his heart and face the shame which had been projected onto her. Spielrein, the woman who dared Jung to be Siegfried, was right: transformation, in her system, was accomplished through the surrender of the hero.

Herein lays the meaning of sacrifice and submission, to give into the annihilation of oneself and become nothing. "No creature," writes Ananda Coomaraswamy, "can attain a higher grade of nature without ceasing to exist" (1973: 92), and ceasing to exist is the very essence of a plunge into absolute feminine shame (Ayers, 2003). Even God, with his own descent and incarnation into man, had to become nothing:

> Christ Jesus,
> who, being in the form of God
> did not count equality with God
> a thing to be clung to,
> but emptied himself,
> taking the form of a slave,
> being born as men are born
> And being in every way like a man
> he humbled himself further and was obedient unto death,
> even death on a cross.
>
> (Phil. 2:5–8)

The image depicts Jung needing to place his own destruction into creation's service, imaged as "coming into being" through the realization that he "is Christ," and healing Salome's blindness through a unification of Mithras and Salome's succubus nature – restoring sight was just one of the many miracles Jesus could perform. Restoration of vision is also a secret of the matriarchal mysteries, the secret of the immortality of the divine luminous son of the Great Mother who is resurrected physically in death. In early Christian art Christ is not nailed to the cross, but is shown standing before the cross with open arms, just as Jung imagines himself coming to stand as the serpent penetrates his heart. The body posture speaks of its reconciliation with death. By becoming the victim, through sacrifice, man resolves his shame and wins through to the all-transfiguring vision of human death becoming a whole and eternal self. The fountainhead of all the pairs of opposites, the unification of male and female, Mary and Jesus, mother and son, creates the bringing and receiving of redemption.

Baptism

The experience of "sweating so profusely that the water flows on all sides" is a return to the image in the murder of Siegfried dream, the "deluge of rain that wiped out all traces of the dead" – and the death of the hero. Jung must give up his warrior stance, expose what was wiped out without a trace, and allow Salome, his projection of shame onto Spielrein, into his own shamed and cowardly heart. Jung's transformation into Christ is in the image of water that "flows on all sides;" this implies baptism, an initiatory immersion into water that serves as a symbol for repentance and the forgiveness of sins, a ritual cleansing of shame before reform. Baptism is also the way Christ is revealed: "my purpose in coming to baptize with water was that he might be revealed to Israel" (John 1:31).

> Then cometh Jesus from Galilee to Jordan unto John, to be baptized of him. But John forbad him, saying I have need to be baptized of thee, and comest thou to me? And Jesus answering said unto him, Suffer it to be so now: for thus it becometh us to fulfill all righteousness. Then he suffered him. And Jesus, when he was baptized, went up straightway out of the water: and, lo, the heavens were opened unto him, and he saw the Spirit of God descending like a dove, and lighting upon him: And lo a voice from heaven, saying, This is my beloved Son, in whom I am well pleased.
>
> (Matthew 3:13–17)

Baptism creates Jesus' as well as our own recognition of Christ. The story of Jesus' baptism is told at the beginning of every gospel in the New Testament, underscoring baptism as the quintessential manifestation of the Christ.

Christ and Mithras

According to Jung, the animal face that he felt his own transformed into is the famous *Deus Leontocephalus* of the Mithraic mysteries. This lion-headed god encoiled by the snake is also called *Aion,* or the eternal being achieved through a reconciliation of opposites. In his own analysis of the image, Jung (1989) amplifies its meaning through the Mithraic amphora: a lion is on one side and the snake is on the other; both are trying to get at the fire. The lion, he says, is the young, hot, dry July sun and the culmination of summer. The serpent is humidity, darkness, the earth and winter. Again, the opposites of the world are attempting to come together, this time through the flame, a mediating, reconciling symbol, the "eternal fire" of Christ and the Holy Spirit. He says of this symbol:

> It is of course a man's symbol, a symbol of the womb – the creative womb of the man out of which rises the fire. When the pairs of opposites come together,

> something divine happens, and then it is immortality, the eternal, creative time. Wherever there is generation there is time, therefore Chronos is God of Time, Fire, and Light.
>
> (1989: 99)

Jung sounds the leitmotif of the male initiation mystery of the hero's survival of the awesome miracle of a second birth after traversing the threshold of self annihilation. This threshold is the emptiness that is "a great feminine secret." It is something absolutely alien to man; the chasm, the unplumbed depth, the yin" (1954: 98). The hero goes inward and descends, dying to time in the world womb to be born again. The purpose of such a journey, specific to my focus on shame, is to separate the male from the mother in both her earth and sexual dimensions; the passage requires a confrontation with shame and the development of humility on both Oedipal and infantile levels.

Jung's vision depicts the transformation of his depths into light. To realize that he too is Christ is to come forth separated from the mother as a child of God who recognizes his need for woman to incarnate his only Son. Realizing a vision of Christ is the consummation of Dante's Canto 32, 85–88:

> look now upon the face that is most like
> The face of Christ, for only through its brightness
> Can you prepare your vision to see Him.

A confrontation with shame is a necessity if one is to fully separate from the mother in both her earth and sexual aspects, meaning the sacrifice of the whole man and a transformation of his sources for power:

> Truly I tell you,
> No one can see the Kingdom of God
> Without being born anew.
>
> (John 3:1–3)

Another avenue for amplification of the lion is also possible. The lion of Mithras is one of Lilith's cult animals, and, also like Mithras, she has the face of a lion (and has been depicted with the body of a snake and the head of a beautiful woman) (Hurwitz, 1999: 43). Lamashtu, the historically older root of Lilith, is described in the Labartû text:

> Her abode is on the mountains, or in the reedbeds. Dreadful is her appearance. Her head and her face are those of a fearsome lion, white as clay is her countenance ... she roars like a lion ... A whore is she.
>
> (quoted in Hurwitz, 1999: 36)

Another passage links Lilith to the lion and the entwining serpent:

> Dreadful is she, headstrong is she, she is a goddess, terrible is she. She is like a leopard, the daughter of Anu. Her feet are those of (the bird) Zu, her hands are dirty, her face is that of a powerful lion … she slides in like a snake.
>
> (quoted in Hurwitz, 1999: 43)

Jung goes on in his 1925 seminar to explain the connections between Mithras and Christ. Mithras is the brother of Christ, so they have a lot in common. To the early Christians, Christ was identified with the sun, and Christmas meant the resurrection of the sun. The name Mithras is related to Modern Persian *mihr*, meaning "love" and "sun." The self-sacrificial hero Mithras is a god of enormous power who, like the sun, has a shining countenance. As the god of light, he guards against evil. The Persian sun god Mithras is even equipped with an immense number of eyes for just such a purpose.

Both Mithras and Christ sacrifice their animal nature, their instinctual side. Both are gods of life and death. Mithras is represented on monuments as carrying the bull, meaning the animal side of himself that he has to sacrifice. The bull sacrifice is a divine sacrifice. But the animal is, as it were, only a part of the hero; he sacrifices his animal attribute, his instinctuality. It is both voluntary and involuntary. By sacrificing the valued objects of desire and possession, the instinctive desire, or libido, is given up in order that it may be regained in a new form. His inner participation in the sacrificial act is perfectly expressed in the anguished and ecstatic countenance of the bull-slaying Mithras. He slays it willingly and unwillingly at once, hence the rather pathetic expression on certain monuments, not unlike the somewhat mawkish face of Christ in Guido Reni's *Crucifixion* (Jung, 1925).

Christ carries the symbol of the cross, and is then hung on it. His entire being is the sacrifice. This act of supreme courage and renunciation is a crushing defeat for not only man's animal nature and ego, but for his entire life. It is completely involuntary. Yet such a deed alone seems equal to the task of expiating Adam's, hence all of mankind's, sin of unbridled instinctuality. Christ is the "Lamb of God," but unlike the lambs sacrificed in the Jerusalem temple for certain kinds of sin, Jesus is a man, meaning that the sacrifice is of his manhood; "the place where opposites cross is a place of crucifixion for the male" (Thompson, 1981: 114). Jesus the human being is treated more like an animal, unlike the bull that substitutes for Mithras. Towards the end of "The Sacrifice" in *Symbols*, Jung began to reverse his identification with Mithras and attempts to educate us on the sublimation of the libido:

> The comparison of Mithraic and Christian sacrifice plainly shows wherein lies the superiority of the Christian symbol; it is the frank admission that not only are the lower wishes to be sacrificed, but the whole personality. The Christian symbol demands complete devotion; it compels a veritable self-sacrifice to a higher purpose…
>
> (1955: 478)

Mithraic symbolism depicts a sacrifice that suggests that when instinct is killed, one will become conscious. When Mithras conquers his animal nature, he arrogates to himself the strength of the sun and becomes its lord (Jung, 1989). Being both animal and man, he paradoxically represents instinct as well as the prohibition of instincts. Man becomes the sun through conquering his animal instinctuality.

The death of Christ signifies a different meaning of sacrifice. Man is cleansed of his shame, his original sin, making sacrifice the very reverse of regression. Sacrifice produces a successful canalization of the libido into a symbolic equivalent of the mother – hence, a spiritualization of her. The hero's journey undertaken to separate from the mother must include not just the sacrifice of Mithras, which only leads to the sun, the masculine, but the sacrifice of Christ, a descent into darkness and nothingness – the absence – of maternal femininity; this leads to light-giving empowerment of shame and the development of conscience.

Jung's ascent

Jung says that Salome is the erotic element, blind because she does not see the meaning of things. In the second vision, this problem would appear to be corrected: Salome's vision is restored, which means that now she does see the meaning of things – after all, what good is a blind anima? Common blindness passes from the ordinary into the spiritual domain as the meaning of Salome, previously a projective version of an internal object, is now internalized. The anima is restored as a bridge to the soul, serving as unifier for the above and below. The secret alchemy between Mithras and Salome achieves a synthesis of the Christ numinosum at the heart of nature and psyche. With Salome's vision restored, or the transformation of the seductive component of the succubus, Salome as anima assumes her rightful place in the operations of the unconscious. The principles of transformation contained in the image of Christ are identifiable with the maternal feminine because her body is the source of incarnation, birth, and rebirth.

> Whenever we encounter the symbols of rebirth we have to do with the matriarchal transformation mystery, and this is true even when its symbolism or interpretation bears a patriarchal disguise.
>
> (Neumann/Mannheim, 1974: 60)

It seems that his entrance into the bloody lair of Lilith helped Jung to begin to integrate Salome – a necessary prerequisite to any possibility of emerging from his descent. The mysterious menstrual blood of Lilith becomes the blood of the mysteries of Christ. The restoration of Salome's vision is a process of coming face to face with the goddess, an idea paralleled in Apuleius' *The Golden Ass*, where Lucius is undergoing an initiation (turning into an ass) into the mysteries of Isis.

> Thou shalt understand that I approached neere unto Hell, even to the gates of Proserpina, and after that, I was ravished throughout all the Element, I

> returned to my proper place: About midnight I saw the Sun shine, I saw likewise the gods celestiall and gods infernall, [above and below] before whom I presented my selfe, and worshipped them face to face....
>
> (Apuleius/Adlington, 1639: 277)

In his confrontation with the unconscious, Jung has two visions that he states he spent 20 years trying to realize. After great losses, he is striving to reconcile himself to the world and the world to himself; in this struggle Jung tastes death. The internalization of his human vulnerability deep in the core of his instincts, his human helplessness before an uncontrollable impulse that nearly destroyed psychoanalysis and contributed significantly to his loss of the paternal Freud plunges Jung into the depths of his mother complex – the mother of his infancy and the Oedipal mother – hence, into the dual aspects of the succubus, the child killer and the seductive demon lover.

Jung believed that a man – specifically the heroic ego in man – must make two sacrifices before the transformation of individuation can occur. The first is in the area of childish longing for the past; most especially, longing for the mother and the comfort and security she represents. The second entails an adult pride in one's accomplishments. The metabolization of the seductive aspects of the succubus and his shame is ritually acknowledged through a vision of sacrifice and sublimation, depicting a process of freeing the anima from the mother archetype: withdrawal of projections, hence the restoration of vision, and a transformation of shame into a realization of his humanity in the Christ principle. This separation is reflected in Jung's admission of his love for her in a revealing and honest confessional letter written to Spielrein on September 1, 1919 – simultaneous to his realizations on the meaning of mandalas.

> The love of S. for J. made the latter aware of something he had previously only vaguely suspected, that is, of a power in the unconscious that shapes one's destiny, a power which later led him to things of the greatest importance. The relationship had to be "sublimated" because otherwise it would have led him to delusion and madness (the concretization of the unconscious). Occasionally one must be unworthy, simply in order to be able to continue living.
>
> (Carotenuto, 1983: 190)

Jung was never man enough to openly admit what Spielrein meant to him personally or professionally. He did not name her in *Memories*, at least not beyond her being called the "talented psychopath" that became the voice of his anima. Yet to be sure, Jung is no longer heroically unrepentant. Jung restored his personal connection to the qualities of being that he associated with the feminine and which we as a culture have so badly neglected. A more stable psyche is achieved by illumination from the higher feminine, expressed in Jung's concept of the anima, a cornerstone of analytical psychology. Some time in the later days of his life, Jung sculpted a last testament to Spielrein. At Bollingen, the simple stone house where Jung spent his time rock carving, is a sculpture on the subject of the anima. The first panel depicts a bear bending down with its nose nudging a ball. The inscription reads "Russia gets the ball rolling" (Kerr, 1993: 507).

Mandalas

Near the end of his life, Jung describes his emergence from his confrontation with the unconscious as being marked by two events. One was that he "broke with the woman who was determined to convince me that my fantasies had artistic value; the second was that I began to understand mandala drawings" (1965: 195). His love for Spielrein had been sublimated into mandalas and given expression through a form of art – the very idea he sought to conquer and have power over. Jung was very willing to take the time for such foolish things as the study of fairytales, the creation of mandalas, and collecting colored stones in order to animate his unconscious. Art, which has no earthly purpose and is left out of the world of science, provides Jung with his most precious commodity, a sense of true freedom for "recreation," to create from the "streams of lava" that came from the depths of his insides for the remainder of his life. For Jung, however, "reality meant scientific comprehension" from which he "had to draw concrete conclusions." His revelations became what we know as Analytical Psychology, a system that contains the imagination Jung rescued from the trash heap of Western science, the intermediate realm where the unintelligible is rendered into the sensible, the "stuff of psychosis" that is also "the matrix of a mythopoeic imagination that has vanished from our rational age" (p. 188). What Jung does not mention is that the mythopoeic is the language of the matriarchal age. Robert Graves contends that originally the poet gave myth its connection to religious impulse, and its poetic language is bound up with ceremonies in honor of the Great Mother, the Muse-poet who dies for the Goddess, some of them dating back to the Old Stone Age (this language, he states, remains the language of true poetry). This language is essentially an "invocation of the goddess, the Muse, the Mother of all living things, the ancient power of fright and lust – the female spider or queen bee whose embrace is death" (1966: 24). This has been kept secret because in late Minoan times, when invaders from Central Asia began to substitute patrilinear for matrilinear institutions, Greek myths were remodeled or falsified to justify the social changes.

Similarly, and even more important to point out about mandalas, is their little known connection to the round, circular womb of the Paleolithic Great Mother, and so, by extension, container for life and the mother of his infancy. The circle mandala as a psychic integrator arose with the spread of mother goddess figurines. With the increased division of labor that came with agricultural advances – hence the increased psychic demand for a more complex organizing image for the maintenance of cohesion as well as social and self differentiation – the mandala became more complex. It then became a masculine symbol of the hieratically organized city-state yet retained its essential nature as an image of the Great Mother within the celestial order, the "generative and nourishing, 'female' powers of the tilled earth" (Campbell, 1969: 146). The emergence of the mandala, in other words, points to the idea that civilization was conceived of as a sociological imitation of the celestial order; in its center is an artifact of matriarchal culture. In Campbell's words:

> We have, therefore, to recognize what now appears to be the demonstrated and documented fact that all of the high civilizations of the world are, finally, but so many variants and developments of a single marvelous monad of mythological inspiration – and that, where as the history and prehistory of the human race covers some one million seven hundred and fifty thousand years, this monad was constellated and brought into a living form in the mud flats and among the reeds of Mesopotamia hardly more than five thousand years ago.
> (p. 154)

Jung painted his first mandala in 1916 after writing Seven Sermons to the Dead. But it was not until 1918–19, when Jung woke every morning as commandant in a British prisoner of war camp and drew a mandala, that he really began to understand the nature of these images.

> I sketched every morning in a notebook a small circular drawing, a mandala, which seemed to correspond to my inner situation at the time. With the help of these drawings I could observe my psychic transformations from day to day ... Only gradually did I discover what the mandala really is: "Formation, Transformation, Eternal Mind's eternal recreation" (Faust, II). And that is the self, the wholeness of the personality, which if all goes well is harmonious, but which cannot tolerate self-deceptions. My mandalas were cryptograms ... in which I saw the self – that is, my whole being – actively at work ... in time I acquired through them a living conception of the self. The self, I thought, was like the monad which I am, and which is my world. The mandala represents this monad, and corresponds to the microcosmic nature of the psyche.
> (Jung, 1965: 195)

Jung's discovery of the mandala provides a key to understanding his entire system of analytical psychology.

> I had to abandon the idea of the superordinate position of the ego ... I had to let myself be carried along by the current, without a notion of where it would lead me. When I began drawing mandalas, however, I saw that everything, all the paths I had been following, all the steps I had taken, were leading back to a single point – namely, to the mid-point. It became increasingly plain to me that the mandala is the centre. It is the exponent of all paths. It is the path to the centre, to individuation ... I began to understand that the goal of psychic development is the self. There is no linear evolution; there is only a circumambulation of the self ... This insight gave me stability, and gradually my

> inner peace returned. I knew that in finding the mandala as an expression of the self I had attained what for me was the ultimate.
>
> (pp. 195–196)

Jung sublimates Spielrein, or Salome, or the anima, or the succubus into art. The original tension between Jung's ego and the unconscious is annulled and replaced by a creative act of spirit. Yet Jung attempts to transcend the incest barrier without looking at its roots in the earliest stages of development and the infant's real, personal experience of a life and blood mother. For Jung mother is still an archetype, this time at the center of a mandala. This theme belongs to a much earlier phase of development – an area in which Jung (and Freud) failed to produce any theory. The problem is that Jung stays purely transpersonal, no doubt a result of his creative predisposition with its natural preponderance of the archetypal and an autistic, dissociative tendency to detach from the ordinary human environment. It is probably for this reason that Winnicott, the man who opened our eyes to mothers and babies, pointed to Jung's blindness in this area. He diagnosed childhood schizophrenia and concluded after reviewing Jung's autobiography that "at the end of a long life Jung reached the centre of his self, which turned out to be a blind alley" (1964: 483).

The absence of the pre-oedipal mother may account for Jung's strange split around art and science, claiming as he emerges with his realization to "be carried along by the current of mandalas," while having to maintain power over his anima:

> now the prisoner, or the well-protected dweller in the mandala, does not seem to be a god … but rather an apparently most important part of the human personality. One might also say that man himself, or at least his innermost soul, was the prisoner of the protected inhabitant of the mandala … It is evident that in the modern mandala, man – the complete man – has replaced the deity … A mandala is an involuntary confession of a particular mental condition. There is no deity in the mandala, and there is also no submission or reconciliation to a deity. The place of the deity seems to be taken by the wholeness of man.
>
> (Jung, 1953: 171)

Man has taken over the role of deity, the soul of an individual, and the soul is a part of a "complete" human personality with its goal of psychic development being a whole self. Jung had attained his "ultimate," a condition in which there is "no submission or reconciliation to a deity." He conquers the mother of infancy and roots of the mandala in the Great Mother, the "generative and nourishing, 'female' powers of the tilled earth" (Campbell, 1969: 146). Developmentally and psychologically, the real flesh and blood mother is our first object of love and therefore our first object in search for wholeness – how can wholeness be achieved without her? Joseph Campbell had this to say of such attitudes: "One cannot but think of the words of Paracelsus: 'I under God in his office, God under me in mine'" (1969: 156). Jung claims totality in the self, and such arrogance implies a shame beyond the power of his explanation – the same reason he could never visit Rome.

As to whether Jung ever addressed his earliest attachment issues we cannot conclusively know from his writings. Jung knew that the resolution to the Oedipus Complex entailed a return to the mother. Yet he seems to remain stuck in his main fascination with the anima as an image for the Oedipal mother alone. He succeeds in a successful canalization of his omnipotence at the level of Salome, yet the mother figure of infancy and the hetaira anima figure, two inseparable sides of the same problem for Jung, remained split.

Jung and the maternal feminine

This psychic split is an inevitable outcome of his polygamous relationships, which are in turn reflective of his early experience of a nurse who took care of him during his mother's hospitalization. No one can dismiss Toni Wolf as a mere *femme fatale*, the woman with whom Jung lived more or less openly as his mistress for nearly 30 years. She was called the "anima type," a woman well suited to carry Jung's projections and one over whom he has power (at least according to Jung, and she was a former patient). She is credited with keeping him grounded during his confrontation with the unconscious. She played a pivotal role in Jung's conversations with his anima which led to his profound insights on the anima archetype. Yet together they concretized the anima into a man–mistress relationship which prevented Jung from dealing with the elemental aspects of the succubus – the Terrible Mother with the Evil Eyes whom heroes can't hope to conquer. Where Jung lived openly with Toni as his mistress his knowledge of maternal elements was blocked. This prevented Jung from receiving wisdom from the maternal feminine – exactly what is missing in his theories.

Had Jung truly integrated the maternal feminine, his system of individuation imaged in mandalas would have shifted from a patriphallic to a matriphallic consciousness – he would have realized the Great Mother in the heart of the mandala – yet this did not occur. Self alone became the deity at the center of the mandala, and "a god" replaced the goddess. His focus, of course, was the need for a sacrifice in order to cut the hero away from the power of the unconscious and give him his individual autonomy. Jung's form of sacrifice is somehow assured of conquering, while a sacrifice of his whole self, where he is "Christ," would have required complete submission, completely beyond his ego command and control. The Great Mother is preponderant over the anima; for Jung, detachment of the anima from the Terrible Mother remains incomplete.

It is for this reason that Jung by no means escapes the power of the cultural attitudes towards the feminine, and remains at the very least theoretically bound to masculine dominance structures. Jung's model, depicting as it does the masculine entering culture by splitting off from the mother, creates for the masculinist ego an inherently negative relation to the mother. The connection he makes is one that repudiates the mother so that the hero can enter culture, similar to Freud's identification with paternal authority to enter fully into the world of power and intellect. Yet Jung's thinking is in some ways even more repressive to women than Freud's condemnation. Jung's concept of the feminine had the result of limiting women, although he seemed to think that he was trying to get it a better place in patriarchal thinking. According to El Saffar,

> despite the great following that Jung has enjoyed among women for his sympathy with and interest in those aspects of the psyche traditionally linked to the "feminine," his gender ideology is in fact more conservative, for being archetypally based, than Freud's. The notion that "femininity" is an adaptation to a cultural requirement that women become reproductive objects locked out of the institutions and power structures of society is more openly acknowledged by Freud, who sees femininity as acquired, than by Jung, who tends to regard the psychological structures that lead to femininity in women as innate.
>
> (1994: 47)

Jung's inability to fully metabolize his shame (at least until he could realize the meaning of his visions) naturally leads to his dualistic world view that distinguishes between inner and outer, the rational and the irrational, the anima and the animus, man and woman, autonomy and dependency. Dualism is a form of thinking that eliminates the possibility of recognition, and its persistence alerts us to the unchanging image of the mother of infancy in the deepest strata of Jung's psyche. Behind Jung's dualistic thinking was a nearly explosive temper (evidence of unresolved Oedipal material) and a fear and hatred of women that leads to a desperate attempt to restrict and silence them:

> No matter how friendly and obliging a woman's Eros might be, no logic on earth can shake her if she is ridden by the animus. Often the man has the feeling – and he is not altogether wrong – that only seduction or a beating or rape would have the necessary power of persuasion [shame is the deepest affect behind violence to women] ... No man can converse with an animus for five minutes without becoming the victim of his own anima. Any who still had enough sense of human to listen objectively to the ensuing dialogue would be staggered by the vast number of commonplaces, misapplied truisms, clichés from newspapers and novels, shopsoiled platitudes of every description interspersed with vulgar abuse and brain-splitting lack of logic.
>
> (Jung, 1951: 15)

It is clear that Jung remained plagued by a deep feeling that a woman could destroy him. In the same way that Oedipus tries to get a glimpse of his own origins without confronting the brutal maternal forces of nature, Jung enters onto a path of self-knowledge that has a huge blind spot: his autistic attachment and difficulties with premature separation, object loss and abandonment.

Toni Wolf dies very late in his life (in 1953), and Jung continued on. But with the shock of Emma Jung's death on November 27, 1955, Jung realizes that a "great illumination" took him by surprise two days before she died. The content of the revelation is unknown; Jung only says of it

> I can only think that the illumination came from my wife, who was then mostly in a coma, and that the tremendous lighting up and release of the insight worked back upon her and was one reason that she could die such a painless and regal death.
>
> (Jung quoted in Wehr/Weeks, 1987: 424)

Yet perhaps it is behind his later comments on the hetaira. In a letter of June 18, 1958, simultaneous to the beginning of his work on *Memories, Dreams and Reflections*, Jung writes:

> It is unfortunately true that when you are wife and mother you can hardly be the hetaira too, just as it is the secret suffering of the *hetaira* that she is not a mother. There are women who are not meant to bear physical children, but they are those that give rebirth to a man in a spiritual sense, which is a highly important function.
>
> (1975: 455)

In a field near his beloved Bollingen tower, in the same garden where his tribute to Spielrein is located, sits a phallic milestone engraved with an inscription in Greek: "To the most beautiful Attis." Attis is the son lover of the "regal" Queen Cybele, the mother of the god who personifies the longing for the mother of early infancy alive in every psyche. Attis holds the impulse to sacrifice but lives on through being the ideal child of the mother. Eventually driven insane by his mother's mad love for him he castrated himself, symbolic of a man's resistance to incest in protection of the mother. Jung connects Attis' auto-castration with subservience to the Great Mother; "This is the dream of the mother in matriarchal times, when there was as yet no father to stand by the side of the son" (1955: 259). Indeed, Attis' castration symbolizes a very different expression of male sexuality for Jung, the kind that is naturally included as a part of marriage.

Psychic development moves to a higher level: from the darkness of blind instinct to a feminine anima that brings illumination – although for a full resurrection of the maternal feminine, Jung would have had to let the anima, which for Jung remained dominated by a preponderance of the maternal, be the one to take the lead.

Notwithstanding all his faults, Jung ultimately sought truth above all else, and felt that a man must bring himself to recognize and accept a hidden and terrifying feminine part of himself. Jung believed that the repression of the feminine is bad for the whole human race, and that if it is not restored to its archetypal place in Western religion the results would be catastrophic. This conviction is surely reflected in the restoration of Salome's vision. His whole work was a self-unfolding of his individuation process, and he stayed devoted to the inner forces guiding his existence – two of which manifested in his visions. Jung quotes the words of St. Paul, "I live; yet not I, but Christ, liveth in me."

In Jung's concept of the anima, the feminine remained other and became a place where Jung was able to differentiate himself. This higher union of opposites transcends opposition, in turn facilitating a transformation of power over into creative empowerment. He was buried with a tombstone inscribed with a saying from the great resurrection chapter of the First Epistle to the Corinthians (I Cor. 15:47):

> The first man is of the earth and is earthly,
> the second man is of heaven and is heavenly.

Lilith has presence in "the first man" of the earth. Lilith is the female of Adam, the first man, or Adamah, the Hebrew feminine word for earth or soil.

Chapter 6

The blinded eternal feminine

Freud and Jung agreed on the importance of the Oedipal in male development and the necessity of separating from the mother. In many ways, these concerns formed the centerpiece for both of their theories, and became the measure of effective individuation. It is in this way that they engendered a heroic ego that forces the unconscious to flow into an Oedipal model, the identification of masculinity with a culturally created patriarchal ideal. They rightly theorized that infantilism needs to be relinquished in order for life to go on, otherwise libido stays fixed in an incestuous bond with mother and individual freedom is lost. Yet they believed that the first act of liberation from the mother must be matricide so that the ego can fully develop – an act on which patriarchal culture, with its basic structure of the slain mother, was founded. "Patriarchal development of consciousness [of which the ego is the center] has an indisputable inner need to 'murder the mother,'" that is, "as far as possible to negate, exclude, devalue, and repress the 'maternal-feminine' world which represents the unconscious" (Neumann Mannheim, 1974: 58–59).

In the patriarchal world of Freud and Jung, the great triumphal struggle for male individuation is played out against the backdrop of the re-engulfing, symbiotic mother. In order to maintain separate subjectivity, the hampering, forbidding, and punishing mother, she who clings to the growing child who is trying to push away, or the desired but forbidden mother whose presence is a lure to dangerous desire (castration complex) becomes the mother of focus, and maternal goodness is denied. Heroic honor is considered a masculine virtue because it is split from the devouring mother.

It is at this point that Freud and Jung part ways. Freud remained the Father of Psychoanalysis, and theorized the same theme in all stories, so much so that the Oedipal lost its full meaning. Moreover, his theory determined the meaning of the story of Oedipus, rather than the other way around. The Oedipal ideal entails proving oneself a man, a universal theory of development centered on a projected masculine image which has its roots in shame. Jung, who formed his own school of thought he named Analytical Psychology, theorized that a man must be willing to temporarily forsake his ego strength for the higher aim of a unity with the feminine; this alone makes the hero a hero, that is, a higher, ideal representative of mankind. Yet despite his inclusion of the feminine, he somehow manages to remove the mother of infancy. This theoretical environment of repressed maternal complexes was fertile ground for the succubus to emerge, that container for masculine shame repressed through unseeing eyes. In Freud and Jung's pursuit of power, each became guilty of attempting to bring phenomena under their control – and so personally succumbed to the succubus.

Basically what their split comes down to is this: Freud's secret over his incestuous affair was affecting his theory, and Jung could not reveal the personal sources (Sabina Spielrein) of his own theoretical turnaround in the writing of *Symbols*. Each had a secret seduction that profoundly affected his theoretical thinking. Both must have feared being overcome by shame and ridicule – at least somewhere in their being. What was hidden was not for the eyes of the public in order to maintain the medical standing of psychoanalysis and the reputations of its founders, yet it is also true that shame motivates the wish for concealment and both were fighting to protect themselves. Freud knew Jung's secret, and Jung resented it; he probably took solace in what he knew Freud was hiding. Freud may or may not have known what Jung knew. Even more important is that their secrets were tied to the loss of their powerless fathers and deep self-reproach that went all the way back to incestuous death wishes and symbiotic attachment to the pre-oedipal mother. Given the power of such regressive forces as the source of their shame, the two men could not remain friends, could not share in their humanness, because they were not really free to say what was real (a sure sign of a lack of separation from the mother). And in their power split the same basic dualities of a superior-inferior paradigm – the same that exists between men and women – come into play. Ultimately human qualities and humane behavior disappear, and their vexed relationship ended without another word into the silence of shame.

Freud's repression represents the masculine need to kill off femininity due to fears of Medusa and castration anxiety, when the real problem was his struggle against the adoring mother and symbiosis – the psychic place where he loved himself in her loving. Jung took the process of individuation for a man one step further and rightly interpreted the danger as a falling into the terrible mother complex instead of facing arduous tasks, but he prescribed the work and trials of the hero pursuing death defying feats as the antidote. One of man's arduous tasks is to take power over woman, a desperate attempt on Jung's part to claim love and recognition from the danger of his mother's "personality number two." He nevertheless remained plagued by a deep feeling that a woman could destroy him. Jung's myopic focus on mythic symbolism was probably so attractive because it was the perfect realm for dissociation and heroic identification.

Freud and Jung, petrified by shame, remained embedded in the impasse between each other and what became their different schools of thought – the backlash for their primordial act of matricide. Their shame could not be revealed to others and has become the pernicious silence which splits the body of depth psychology five generations later. Due to this repression, the subterranean streams of the succubus archetype feed the wellsprings of the study of the unconscious, atrophying movements within the field and driving the constriction of interpretive ranges and integration of Freudian and Jungian thought.

Nevertheless, together and apart, Freud and Jung transformed modern man's conception of life. Freud made important contributions to the understanding of infantile sexuality and narcissism, and had a life preoccupation with the hero-motif in the core Oedipus Complex; Jung made important contributions to our understanding of the hero in relation to masculine development and his considerations of femininity through his construct of the anima. Freud got the basics of instinctual, bodily development in relation to self and ego development; Jung got psychology's archetypal dimensions and emphasizes the self as soul. While raw sexuality was the issue for Freud, the numinosity of sexuality was it for Jung. Freud's approach was linear, rational and masculine, Jung's was circular, symbolic, and feminine. Freud started with the theory of early sexual trauma, and then abandoned it on empirical grounds (Freud's place of repression); Jung made a parallel case for going beyond the theory of fixation in early fantasies, and moved to transform the sexual into the spiritual (Jung's place of repression) (Kerr, 1993). The value of their work endures. If we can recognize both sides through an examination of the relationship between the two, we may discover the seeds of a new language to talk about the dangerous realities confronting us today – but that subject will be taken up in my Epilogue.

Matricide, however, does not constitute the life of humanity – male or female. It does not teach humankind how to create and sustain a self and a life. Due to their theorizing the universal experience of dependence and its psychic meaning is contraindicated, forcing neediness into a place of shame and weakness. From infancy on, patriarchal culture teaches a boy to forget the mother of his beginnings. He is taught to shut out information and intuition so that he can operate within the consensual domain of our inherited masculine world. The expectation to enter a macho world of power so far removed from the maternal feminine complicates the already traumatic experience of disruption that attends the passing of the symbiotic stage. Shame solidifies in the emotional disconnection required.

Psychoanalysis has had a tremendous effect on how we think about gender and sexuality. In their matricidal theorizing, Freud and Jung engendered an ego that channels unconscious energies into a paradigm, and thereby facilitated the creation of a succubus world that warns against the upsurge of mother's subjectivity because it will destroy the male. Disavowal of dependence comes to be deeply repressed in masculine psychic life with a number of tragic results, a topic to be taken up in the following analysis of current masculine gender ideas.

The social construction of the patriarchal hero

We can only understand masculine shame if we understand the gender roles, socially constructed distinctions based on sex, into which a male is socialized. The male socialization process is founded upon the concept of separation from the mother. Masculine development is all about the denial of the mother, an expectation that derails the development of a masculine self in a number of significant ways. Boys are expected to mature out of "infantile" dependence and their maternal needs very early (which will be discussed in the next chapter in more detail), before most boys are emotionally ready. Boys are taught that staying close to their mothers is something shameful, and so they are shamed into withdrawing from her more than necessarily wanting to. At the heart of society's male gender ideas, from the very beginning, is the male need to achieve "masculine autonomy." Maternal loss dissociates a boy from his inner space; upon the loss of his connection to his insides a boy turns to conquer outer space, and this forces the tiny child to become a man long before his time. Boys have to be more independent sooner or their peers will call them sissies and ridicule them. As Tolstoy observed, by the time he is five a boy can be taking on the whole existential burden of the human condition.

The heroic in man

The devaluation of his need for the mother becomes the male's way of maintaining machoism, the touchstone of masculinity. The main message of masculine development is that there can be no weakness, and so the boy must focus intensively on power in one form or another. In his desperation to become fully autonomous and independent, he seeks to reinforce his sense of masculinity, and society offers any number of means to accomplish this. No matter what form this achievement takes, the basic principle at work is the expansion of the ego as the individual wields the kind of power which will inevitably go to his head.

The heroic in man is intent on achievements, glory, and domination, dissociating his real feelings by identifying with symbols of power and control (i.e. nation, money, leader, doctor, lawyer, Olympic Gold Medalist). Sports are a huge fraternity that teaches physical prowess, aggression, and the need to win and dominate at any cost (especially the contact team sports). Sports have achieved mythic proportion in our culture, forms of ritualized warfare Spartan style. Hung on the walls of many a men's locker room is the saying, "Winning isn't everything, it's the only thing."

In the corporate world power takes form in the pursuit of money, and forms of financial and political winning. Today, lots of money equals a large penis – and nothing to be ashamed of. To be poor, of course, means "to be without a penis." This idea is creating a shameless corporate culture of mega profits at any price, real or false, where men choose power over the other, domination, risk and extravagance. This form of phallic omnipotence is shown in the sheer magnitude of the greed, deception, deceit and lying that was inherent in most of Wall Street's "accounting irregularities" and fiscal sleight of hand. The self-destructive priority given to winning is exemplified by the men of Enron Energy Corporation's upper management who called themselves the "Masters of the Universe" and filed the largest bankruptcy in the history of the U.S. They considered money the measure of a person's very being. Their slogan was "you can break the rules, you can cheat, you can lie, but as long as you make money, it is all right" (Henning, 2006: 130). An employee's ability to adhere to this principle separated the men from the boys. Human greed replaces human vulnerability to make mistakes when materialism and the accumulation of wealth for the attainment of power take the lead.

The idea of manhood lies in the will to dominate others. Patriarchal culture has forged powerful beliefs in physical force and the elite entitlement of men. Enduring pain is also a very big aspect of masculinity, but it is a particular kind of pain. It is an omnipotent pain, a conquering through the identification with the aggressor who caused the pain. A military slogan is "pain is weakness leaving the body," and only real men are good at soldiering. In an article entitled "Why Men Love War," William Broyles (1984) writes: "war is, for men, at some terrible level, the closest thing to what childbirth is for women: the initiation into the power of life and death."

Manhood is a relentless repudiation of the feminine. One of the most important things about being a man is not being a woman. Being masculine means devaluing the feminine, a powerful male imperative to be unlike females and repudiate anything that smacks of maternal caretaking, a hardening process of repression that creates a succubus culture, and turns masculinity into a brittle achievement. Feminine types of needs will raise doubt as to whether or not one is a real man. Men are chided not to be women, not to be "sissies" or "pussies." Being a sexually adequate male means not being loving.

The hero and shame

Above all, however, the highest expectation of masculinity and the development of power are to destroy any vulnerability to shame. What this means, unfortunately, is that humiliation is used by both mothers and fathers to turn boys into men, to toughen them up and make them more masculine. This idea is all too current and appears daily in the paper. A *Washington Post* article entitled *The Undercover Lawman Who Went Hog Wild* tells the story of Zemen, an undercover cop who became a member of the notorious Mongol biker gang. Zemen quotes the Mongols as having little concern over being portrayed as violent and mean; he says, "they said 'just don't make us look like wimps' " (2002: c9).

The idea that masculinity and power has to be devoid of shame is also epitomized in the work of a man who was nicknamed the "Tyrant's Lobbyist" (Bernstein, 2005). Edward von Kloberg III was one of Washington's political image-making machines; he raked in millions of dollars sanitizing the reputations of some of the twentieth century's barbarians of unimaginable cruelty, including Saddam Hussein, Mobutu Sese Seko of Zaire and Samuel Doe of Liberia – a few of the endless legion of mass murderers and human rights violators no one else would touch. Von Kloberg embraced the slogan "shame is for sissies" and thoroughly lacked a conscience, expressed in his complete lack of ethical or moral concerns in regards to his work. His actions epitomize how rational self interests can only blind one to the reality of those forms of violence that have been most horrendously destructive to human life around the world. It is no surprise, then, that "the Baron" scripted his operatic end, a dramatic descent into death from the top of Castel Sant'Angelo in Rome.

A grim consequence of the masculine repression to shame is violence, another way of maintaining manhood (Gilligan, 1992). "Violence is primarily men's work; it is carried out more frequently against man." It is also a means for denying love and renouncing the feminine. Men are driven to batter and abuse their women, the masculine way of showing off death-defying superiority. The culture of contact sports like football and macho masculinity is a breeding ground for rape. Warshaw (1994) states that "there is a masculine peer group dynamic, which affirms that the domination and control of women is a mark of manhood and the entitlement of men. This dynamic creates the rape culture" (p. 16).

Absolute shame results in violence when its presence causes an absence of feelings of love or conscience – absent in oneself and towards the other. According to Benjamin (1988), domination is the by-product of the self's denial of its dependent relationship to the Other: "If I completely control the Other, than the Other ceases to exist" (p. 53). Ultimately, killing is the one act that will prevent the other forever from either telling or receiving shameful secrets. In fact, the greater the feeling of the sting of shame, the greater the attempts to destroy it, meaning the more aggression and killing is necessary. The Columbine boys, the students who shot teachers and classmates in Columbine, Colorado, were loners, taunted and ridiculed by their fellow students. They simply snapped under the strain. One investigator was quoted as saying "these boys were crying with bullets" (Henning, 2006: 65).

The degree of shame that a man needs to be experiencing in order to victimize another is so overwhelmingly intense and painful that it threatens his self-coherence. This shame-driven experience is quite separate from the precipitator which can be imperceptible to the observer; in fact, the feeling is most often described as coming from "a look in the eye." It also occurs most commonly where the male feels threatened with losing.

Behind the mask of cool self assurance that many men clamp onto their faces – with a desperation born of the certain knowledge that they would lose face if they ever let it slip – is a person who feels vulnerable to the disintegration of his identity, his selfhood, personhood, rationality, and sanity. Maintaining an intact ego is even of far greater concern than the death of the body; a man can willingly sacrifice his body if he perceives it as the only way to avoid shame. But shame is an inescapable fact of our humanity; for Darwin, it is the affect that distinguishes humans from other animals. A man is not invulnerable to shame no matter how much blood is spilled trying to demonstrate it.

The weakening of the hero

Dependency is the best word to describe the basic survival mechanism of the human organism – and so the repression of fundamental dependency needs leads to disastrous consequences. Masculine gender ideas leave a man wounded in the deepest reaches of his psyche. He is dissociated from a feeling self, separated from maternal feminine qualities and life-giving energies. Men are oppressed by their own expectation to conquer everything from their baser animal and emotional natures to the world at large. Under all the narcissism, however, men are at war with themselves with nothing to win. In his book *The Hazards of Being Male*, Herb Goldberg writes:

> Oppressed by the cultural pressures that have denied him his feelings, by the mythology of the woman and the distorted and self-destructive way he sees and relates to her, by the urgency for him to "act like a man," which blocks his ability to respond to his inner promptings both emotionally and physiologically and by a generalized self-hate that causes him to feel comfortable only when he is functioning well in harness [remember Freud's Pegasus in Harness], not when he lives for joy and personal growth.
>
> (1976: 4)

In actuality, behind all the mastery is a constant attempt to recapture or conquer the mother in the outer world. "False self" acts substitute for creativity because they make a male feel acutely awake and alive, an illusion of holding onto the mother that provides something vital to his self. Compulsive greed and power lust are simply manifestations of a false manhood. Narcissism provides the defense for infantile energies and emotions grounded in the unconscious tie to the maternal object. It is the presence of this attachment, in fact, that makes the eradication of shame unattainable, and results in the phenomena that men, long at the pinnacle of power in our cultural hierarchy, can become infantilized by small imputations of their inadequacies. In Dinnerstein's words, "If he lets her, she can shatter his adult sense of power and control; she can bring out the soft, wild, naked baby in him" (1977: 66–67). The consequences for the repression of shame are grim: a man becomes a prime candidate for possession by the succubus, the repository for his shame.

When a boy avoids separation, he fails to recognize his dependency which warps into a hidden shame that follows the laws of magical rather than rational thinking. He comes to use blinding and diabolizing as prevention from seeing what he has learned are bad things about himself. When a man suffers a sense of personal insignificance, of being helpless and of no real value as a person, of being mocked or treated with scorn and contempt, an urgent and desperate need to reinforce a sense of manhood and personal worth is created. He is quick to seek revenge for any humiliation. He may be compelled to punish those who look at him the wrong way, meaning in a way that makes him feel small and powerless. For men, the power of shame is inversely proportional to the magnitude of the precipitating cause: the more insignificant the precipitator, the more shameful it becomes to even acknowledge that one feels so ashamed. In fact, it is precisely for this reason that whatever leaves a man feeling so ashamed, he will be more ashamed of being ashamed and project his feelings of being so slight, trivial and unimportant – and the infantilized part of the male self can distort anything way out of proportion. As Gilligan puts it, "the most dangerous men on earth are those who are afraid that they are wimps: wars have been started for less" (1992: 66). Further on he writes

> truly, the more tiny and trivial the cause, the more powerful, deadly, and violent the result. The Great Chain of Being may go from atoms to God, from the smallest to the greatest, but the Great Chain of Non-Being goes in exactly the opposite direction.
>
> (p. 136)

Shame and the eyes

Shame dwells in the eyes. On both a collective, archetypal level and an individual, developmental one, shame manifests itself most through the eye. It is mediated and conveyed by vision, and cannot arise without this perceptual element. When a man feels shamed by another person, when he is taunted and ridiculed, feels small, weak, inferior, inadequate, rejected, and insulted – or any other number of near synonyms for shame – an aggressive impulse to put out the other's eyes in one form or another is created. Shame motivates an individual to conceal or hide himself from public view to save the self from further insult. His shame cannot be revealed to others, and so he thinks that if he rids the world of eyes, he eliminates shame. Erikson describes this idea very well:

> one is completely exposed and conscious of being looked at ... One is visible and not ready to be visible ... He who is ashamed would like to force the world not to look at him, not to notice his exposure. He would like to destroy the eyes of the world.
>
> (1950/1985: 252–253)

The bible is full of images of eyes being cut out in response to words or actions that expose someone to disrespect, insolence, haughtiness, boasting, or anything else that may constitute a shaming experience. For example, what did the angels do to the men of Sodom who tried to rape (and thus dishonour) them? "They smote the men that were at the door of the house with blindness" (Genesis 19:11). The penalty for mocking, despising and scorning (three synonyms for shaming) is to have one's eyes picked out and eaten: "the eye that mocketh his father, and despiseth to obey his mother, the ravens of the valley shall pick it out, and the young eagles shall eat it" (Proverbs 30:17). The mortified Oedipus tore his own eyes out. Shame is the motive that leads Delilah to have Samson blinded. "Behold, thou has mocked me. I see you have made a fool of me" (Judges 16:10, 13–15).

Blinding is in effect a masculine response for feeling shame. A few years ago, a Columbia graduate student was victimized over an 18-hour period of time. The ex-gang member raped and sodomized her over and over again. Most poignant in this crime is that he slit her face and eye lids in "unspeakable ways" and then poured bleach in her eyes in an attempt to blind her. This blinding is a grotesque denial of shame: a real gang man can take pride in not being demeaned by what is most clinging in human nature.

The synthesized experiences of mother–infant attachment and eye contact form a structure anchored deep down in the male psyche (Ayers, 2003: 34–60). So what happens when the boy is expected to separate through a complete disidentification with mother, and the bond to her through eye contact is the core of his developing, relational self? A boy must cut himself off at his roots, alienating himself in an obliterating emptiness that ultimately lacks subjective existence. What happens when the cultural and psychological action for male separation from the mother is matricide, a repression of the mother unconsciously motivated by the sting of shame which is evoked as the male sees his "felt" dependency? One must close one's eyes and go blind, or gouge out the eyes of the mother. This gouging can consist of anything from destroying, to killing, to exterminating, to butchery, to dismissing – all forms in one way or another for demonizing mothers' eyes through the projection of shame.

The patriarchal thinking of Freud and Jung intensifies feelings of shame and denies dependencies which reverberate powerfully and painfully in the male psyche all of his life. Does Freud and Jung's theorizing speak to the fact that the mother's contribution goes unrecognized simply because it is so immense and deep, and this makes a needy boy feel very small? And isn't small the quintessential synonym for masculine shame, the feeling a man wants to remain blind to, and destroy the eyes of the world? The patriarchally driven notion of matricide creates a mother blinded by male projections of shame. This, in turn, reverberates back onto the male, who in destroying maternal feminine vision is made blind himself.

The blinding of the maternal feminine

The painting by Paul Cezanne (see cover) named *The Eternal Feminine* depicts a psychological phenomenon of central importance to humankind: the shocking spectacle of a desirous woman in the parturient (squatting birth) position with eyes gouged out. Her eye sockets echo Aeschylus' vision of the feminine in the words of Orestes:

> Ah, Lord Apollo, how they grow and multiply,
> Repulsive for the blood drops of their dripping eyes.
> (Aeschylus, 1969: 161)

Made visible through art and depicted in human form is the intrinsically formless archetypal structure of male and female shame. A naked, blinded female who depicts the masculine nature of shame, squats before men who don't seem to know she exists, an image for the nature of female shame (Ayers, 2003). Men standing around the woman stare blindly at her unseen and unseeing face and bare body.

They display a seeming indifference to her plight as they offer bread and wine or paint her. In the painting, the elemental linking capacity between subject and object, male and female, is reduced and debased while perpetrator and bystander collude in the obfuscation of this woman. An interesting detail about this unusual painting is that it has embarrassed scholars because it suggests aspects of Cezanne's personality that many commentators in the past would rather "repress." The bald figure along the bottom center foreground edge is thought to be Cezanne himself, positioned to convey what he is showing the spectator, as if to say that this image comes from the back of his head, in other words, what he cannot see. Indeed, in his depiction of all the men around her with closed or even missing mouths, vacant eyes, and no ears, Cezanne seems to be saying that all of mankind has dulled their most vital senses to the Eternal Feminine. His depiction echoes the words of Psalm 115:5–7:

> They have mouths, but cannot speak,
> Eyes but cannot see;
> They have ears, but cannot hear
> They can make no sound in their throats.

The Eternal Feminine's exposed genitals convey the idea of shame. In contemporary English, the use of the word "privates" to refer to the genitals conveys the idea that nudity is a source of shame and should remain concealed. Adam and Eve's discovery that they are naked is the genesis of shame in the Story of Creation, the Western world's depiction of the beginning of human history. This idea has its roots in the etymology of our language. The words shame and genitals are inextricable in most languages (Gilligan, 1992). In Greek, for example, *pudenda* means both shame and genitals: the French word for shame, *pudeur*, and the English word for genitals, *pudenda*, both derive from the Greek. In German, one expression for the genitals is *schamteile*, "part of shame." In early translations of the bible, according to the Oxford English Dictionary, the word shame was used to refer interchangeably to the genitals.

Exposure of certain body parts makes one vulnerable to shame. Full nakedness in the face of gawking men, therefore, exposes the feminine to the maximum amount of shame possible.

A dark shadow line creeping up the woman's belly looks like a serpent emerging from her vagina, hinting at Freud's Medusa and fears of castration. The serpent, black with a white head, is like the black serpent undergoing the whitening of his head as he is victorious over another black serpent in the opening scene of Jung's second vision. The serpent line extends down the woman's right leg, connecting the serpent to the Pope's miter, the top of which mimics the lines of the opening of the lady's legs. It is as if Cezanne is saying that *The Eternal Feminine*'s vagina is the place from whence the Pope derives his power. Her vagina, the birthplace for all human beings, with the emerging serpent is echoed still in the meeting of the Pope's staff with the serpent line on the left leg, also a symbol of the Vicar of Rome's power.

That the Pope's power is actually linked to the Eternal Feminine is an idea that is alive and well today. While lying in his hospital bed recovering from five gunshot wounds – the bullets all narrowly missed vital organs – Pope John Paul II ordered that all of the documentation associated with the Lady of Fatima's predictions be brought to him. (The Lady of Fatima is the presentation of the Virgin Mary the 13th day of May through October, 1917 before three children in Fatima, Portugal. The Virgin revealed three prophecies; her revelations have been recognized by the Catholic Church as a true miracle.) The Pope realized that the assassination attempt on his life was part of the Lady's third and last prediction, and stated that she "guided the bullets through my body." For the rest of his life the Pope worked to restore "dignity to the feminine." In his Apostolic Letter *Mulieris Dignitatem* he wrote "I am seeking the eternal feminine..."

The serpent seeping from *The Eternal Feminine*'s vagina captures the idea of a man's dread of being called a pussy, a slang term for the female genitals and a word that means being a non-man in every possible way. For men, the specter of being feminine is based on the perception that femininity emerges when the annihilation of masculinity occurs. Intact genitals symbolize honor and pride, and raped or castrating serpent genitals symbolize shame and confer disgrace (Gilligan, 1992: 144). It is for these reasons that castration (or emasculation) and rape are two of the most powerful ways of inflicting ultimate shame and humiliation upon another person – the same way Medusa came to be demonized.

The victim

The painting of *The Eternal Feminine* reveals, at an archetypal level, a victim at the heart of absolute masculine shame. Accomplished looking men from all walks of life, led by the ultimate man of God, strain to gaze blindly at a woman who has been violently blinded: the purpose of transferring shame onto the victim is achieved. The maternal feminine becomes victim in the masculine attempt to replace shame with heroic pride.

This cultural and psychological expectation creates a remarkable and profoundly tragic distortion: it is shameful to suffer violence, yet it is a source of pride and honor to be the one who dispenses violence to others. There is good in harming others. Domination is superior to submission, and becomes the means through which violence becomes a noble crime that co-opts the higher self and its conscience. Shame and dependency is hidden in the bond between those who inflict it and those who endure it. It is an ideology that has taken such a profound toll on human life. The tragic fatality of power is that it "leads to a fundamental distortion of reality of man's relationship to nature – and so can undermine his own well being" (Becker, 1975: 99).

Exterminating his helplessness through the victim remains a magnetizing fact of masculine shame, even if momentarily obscured by the individual's fraudulent superiority maintained by brute acts of power: not even killing someone or having all the money in the universe can eradicate shame.

The hero and the mother

The real task of the male hero is to separate from the mother and the powers of neediness and dependency that she represents. Mother's provision and protection make the losses due to the call for matricide unimaginable. Boys lose a special kind of nurturing and loving interaction when qualities connected to the good mother are cast off. Her mirroring capacities, emotional attunement, sharing states of mind and reverie, empathy, and imaginative perceiving of the child's needs and feelings are lost. "For all of society's mandates to boys to act like invulnerable superheroes, among all the subtle messages given to boys to downplay their sadness and pain, premature separation is the deepest hurt of all" (Pollack, 1998: 26).

For two decades, William Pollack (1998) researched why boys are sad, lonely and confused despite appearances, what he calls "this generation's silent crisis." Contrary to cultural determinations, one of his groundbreaking discoveries is that boys benefit tremendously from the love of their mothers, especially the kind of non-shaming mothering that can bring out the best in them (1998: 81). Pollack recognizes the connection between maternal separation and shame:

> the trauma of separation is one of the earliest and most acute developmental experiences boys endure. An experience which plays a large role in the hardening process through which society shames boys into suppressing their empathic and vulnerable sides.
>
> (p. 27)

Because of patriarchal expectations, masculine separation from the mother is a relational rupture, a devastating disruption in a boy's emotional life, a "trauma [that] profoundly affects the psychology of most boys – and of most men – forever" (p. 27). The truth is that by empowering the mother you empower the son.

> Far from making boys weaker, the love of a mother can and does actually make boys stronger, emotionally and psychologically. Far from making boys dependent, the base of safety a loving mother can create – a connection that her son can rely on all his life – provides a boy with the courage to explore the outside world.
>
> (p. 81)

Pollack's research shows that it is in fact the absence of a close relationship with a loving mother that hinders a boy's autonomy, undermines his self-confidence and independence, and his ability to form loving attachments with others in his adult life. When mother is internally absent, a male can only engage in heroic acts to regain and possess her in the outside world. With her inclusion, castration becomes a metaphor for the destruction that comes from being separated from mother as a source of goodness, a holding container that provides the means for mutual recognition, internal space, reverie, creativity, the symbolic function and transcendence. This mother is the real hero described in the following passage from *Gates of Fire*:

> There is a clue here. The seat of this highest valor, I suspect, lies in that which is female. The words themselves for courage, *andreia* and *aphorbia*, are female, whereas *phobos* and *tromos*, terror, are masculine. Perhaps the god we seek is not a god at all, but a goddess.
>
> (Pressfield, 1998: 233)

The bottom line is that the kind of separation from the mother theorized by Freud and Jung is not really even possible. Scientific research supports what is imaged at creation's core: nature depicts the male element going on a death-defying quest for ultimate dissolution in the Great Mother, just as a sperm flagellates its tail to cross the vast fallopian distance for a life-giving dissolution into the female's egg. In other words, wishing to remain connected to the maternal realm is actually normal.

In the next section, I will be attempting to elucidate the male infant's relationship to the mother in conjunction with masculine shame. At this early stage of psychic development lives the child-killing aspect of the succubus and the infantile shame behind Freud's castration fears and Jung's identification with the hero. This aspect of the mother is engaged when the boy has to renounce his identificatory maternal love; in this repudiation of the maternal feminine the original source of goodness is lost through its placement outside of his self.

I will argue that male separation from the mother requires not an annihilating act of matricide, but the restoration of the element of recognition, a movement which includes male shame and transforms its projection and distortions into sight. In this shift the focus moves from the independence and autonomy of Freud and Jung, to an intersubjective relatedness with others. The transition from power driven by the fear of castration, to phallic empowerment driven by the male self, lies in building a foundation that includes the mother who gives shape and form to all of life.

When Nietzsche said "supposing truth is a woman, what then?" he may have intuited the mother from whom males cannot really separate, the woman whose loss hurls one into a narcissistic wound that derives from the loss of fusion and omnipotence. It is only by coming face to face with psychotic shame at the earliest layers of being that a man can transform the narcissism contained in images such as King Oedipus or Siegfried into a realization of masculinity that restores sight to both the masculine and the feminine. This balance constitutes the mature resolution of the Oedipus Complex.

Part III

From the succubus as child-killing mother to the restoration of the eternal feminine

Who dares misery love,
And hug the form of death.
Dance in destruction's dance
To him the Mother comes.
(Vivekananda)

Thus conscience does make cowards of us all,
And thus the native hue of resolution
Is sicklied o'er with the pale cast of thought,
And enterprises of great pitch and moment
With this regard their currents turn awry
And lose the name of action. Soft you now!
The fair Ophelia! Nymph, in thy orisons
Be all my sins remember'd.
(*Hamlet*, Act III, scene 1)

I look into frost's face, alone:
It's going nowhere,
Which is where I come from.
Miraculous! The breathing plain all ironed,
Without a crease.
The sun screws up its eyes in laundered destitution,
Finds calm and consolation...
Innocent as bread, snow crunches in one's eyes.
(Osip Mandelstam)

By the little that can satisfy the needs of the human spirit we can measure the extent of its loss.

(Hegel, *Phenomenology*)

Chapter 7

The succubus of early infancy

We are leaving the Oedipal world of Lilith, the beguiling seductress with the evil eyes, and entering an earlier phase of development, the world of infancy where the succubus manifests in an evil form of the Terrible Mother. In this dark aspect of her maternal being, Lilith's widely spread archetypal motif centers on an infant stealing and killing female demon, symbolic of the destructive component of the archetypal feminine in her earth aspect. As the devouring mother she is called "the strangler" who attempts to harm pregnant women, and drinks the blood and sucks the marrow from the bones of infants. In one of her earliest Babylonian forms, she has the ability to take out her eyes so that she can remain on watch and keep a lookout while she sleeps (Hurwitz, 1999: 43).

Sequences typical of hero myths are recapitulated in her stories, yet astonishingly Jewish texts depict Lilith being vanquished by the Great Father and hero Elijah through a simple act of recognition:

> Once, as the prophet Elijah was walking along, he met Lilith and her host. He said to her: O evil Lilith, whither do you go with your unclean host? And she replied: My Lord Elijah, I am about to go to the woman who has born a child to bring her the sleep of death, to take the child born to her away from her, to drink its blood, to suck the marrow from its bones and to leave its flesh over (alternative version: to gobble up its flesh). Elijah answered and said: I place you under the great ban, so that you may be turned into a speechless stone through the will of God. And Lilith said: My Lord, for God's sake, lift this spell so that I may fly away. I swear in the name of God that I will avoid the paths that lead to a woman with a newborn child. Whenever I see or hear my name, I will disappear at once. I will tell you my (secret) names. Whenever you pronounce these, neither I nor my host will have the power to enter the house of a woman in childbirth and torment her. I swear to you to reveal my names so that you may write them down and hang them in the room in which a newborn child lies ... Whosoever knows these names, and writes them down, ensures that I will flee from the newborn child. Therefore, hang this amulet up in the room of a woman in childbirth.
>
> (quoted in Hurwitz, 1999: 130)

Lilith tells Elijah her secret names. In Babylonian invocation texts one is Abizio and another is Ailo. To Lilith's earnest entreaty, Elijah responds:

> I conjure you and your host in the name of YHWH, the God of Israel, Abraham, Isaac and Jacob, in the name of the divine Shekhinah ["supreme woman in whose secret all that is female in the earthly world is founded"], in the name of the ten Seraphim, Ophanim and the divine beasts, may their names be praised, that you and your host do no harm to this woman . . . Sanai. Sansanvai, Semangloph. Adam and Eve. Out with Lilith.
>
> (p. 131)

Lilith and Elijah are negotiating a resolution as to how best to deal with evil. Applying the will of God with the great ban in an attempt to simply conquer will create the very thing that Elijah wants to avoid, and what makes Lilith revengeful and evil. All she wants to do, just as she did with Adam, is to be separate and fly far away. A child's life will be protected and the mother will be kept alive only so long as Lilith's hidden names are pronounced or written. In other words, life, humanity and empowerment against evil are conditional upon Lilith being revealed, recognized and given existence as real. In Lilith's own words, "do not curse me, for I have twelve names. Whosoever writes them down has no fear" (Hurwitz, 1999: 137).

By divulging her secret names, Lilith becomes harmless and so departs. When Lilith is recognized, she is no longer hidden as a vengeful, reactionary figure; instead, her beneficence is revealed. Elijah will be able to ensure protection for both mother and child against the evil acts which originate from Lilith's dismissal through her recognition. This is the guiding idea in the following analysis of mother–infant attachment and the psychic processes that lead to masculine shame, its projection, and the necessary role of recognition in the male's journey from dependence to independence. In the next chapter, the evil that results from an absence of the development of recognition will be explored.

Recognition

Recognition is so organic to the human experience of feeling in existence that its ubiquitous presence goes unseen. It is naturally present from the moment of birth, for the first object of desire is to be recognized by the mother, a fact which becomes all too clear when one bears witness to the first moment of eye-to-eye contact between a mother and her baby at birth (see Ayers, 2003: 37). Recognition confirms our very humanity, ourselves to ourselves. It is of pivotal importance throughout all events and phases of maturation and development. Benjamin uses the idea of sunlight as a metaphor for recognition, the essential element in photosynthesis that provides the necessary energy for the plant's constant transformation of substance. She offers a long list of "near-synonyms" for the word recognition: affirm, reverie, validate, acknowledge, know, accept, understand, empathize, take in, tolerate, appreciate, see, identify with, find familiar, belong, love (1988: 15). Not one of these words completely captures the word's depth of meaning.

Essentially, recognition brings to life that which is real. It makes one feel authentic and true, and facilitates the acceptance of responsibility, self-mastery and ownership in a real way. Recognition is necessary to agency, coherence, affectivity and continuity of being, all important variants that contribute to a core sense of self and sense of being with another. Contained in the principle of recognition is the development of a whole and integrated self.

Mother–infant attachment and recognition

Mother is the infant's symbiotic world of absolute dependence (Winnicott, 1971: 84); dependencies are central to infancy and to coming into being as a person, so much so that separateness during this early period threatens the infant's survival. The infant is totally dependent but does not differentiate himself cognitively from his environment; he is merged and continuous with his caring habitat. Narcissism during this time is the baby loving himself in his mother's love. Recognition at this level of development becomes mother's ministrations, responses and mindfulness of her baby, her "knowing her baby's" needs – when he wants to sleep, eat, have a diaper change, needs a bath, or wants to play alone or together. Recognition is present in everything that an ordinary mother does naturally just by being herself. As provider, caregiver, nurse, nourisher, container, significant other, and mirror, mother is the infant's first object of attachment. His initial exposure to the world of humanity consists in what the mother does with her face, eyes, voice, body and hands. The baby is attaching to the touch and warmth of mother's skin, the sight of her face, the smell of her body, the taste of her breast and milk. Infant researcher Daniel Stern (1985) makes the point that the infant develops very early a core sense of self and core sense of other during the period of time. Winnicott, Mahler and other theorists have posited a prolonged period of a lack of differentiation. With this concept of a distinct self and other, a subject and an object, recognizing and being with an other is an active act of integration rather than passive failures of differentiation. Combining these two points of view results in a "self/other" or of a "we self."

No matter what words are used, however, the infant is clearly embedded in a social matrix. This mutual recognition is a vital factor in the dialogue between child and mother, there from the beginning in the simultaneity of mother–infant interaction, two subjects in synchronous union and mutual exchange that say "I recognize you as my baby who recognizes me … I recognize that you are real" (Benjamin, 1988: 15).

Vision is vital in setting up a relationship of recognition between self and other, baby and mother, the fundamental elements in the creation of a world. Attachment behavior is the effort to retain one's connection to mother, especially through the maintenance of physical closeness. It is through smiling, eye-to-eye contact, and playful face-to-face interaction that attachment between mother and infant proceeds. The literature on infant research is full of the language of recognition. It details the elements of psychic life that demand a living, responsive other, a progression that has been best studied through vision in the earliest days of life. The direct study of development and attachment observes the infant as a remarkably interactive partner, born with an innate curiosity and responsiveness to elements that are incipiently social, including sight, sound, face and voice.

The baby is a self who requires others' selves. Eye contact has survival value for the infant, being critical to the development of good, harmonious maternal feelings that bring mindfulness of her baby's independent existence. From the moment of birth, the sight of an infant's searching eyes will magnetically attract mother's gaze. When her baby looks deeply into her eyes, the mother experiences the very certain reality that her infant is really looking at her, and even more, into her eyes. With the feeling that her baby can see her, a new level of dramatic connection can be experienced, and she seems to spend much more time with her baby. The need to feel that her baby knows and prefers her to all others facilitates her abilities to meet all the necessities of her child. The relationship she is forming to her baby sustains her from moment to moment through the gratification she feels when the baby responds to her. The mother who feels recognized in turn by her child is not simply projecting her own feelings into the child. She is also "linking the newborn's past, the inside of her, with his future, the outside of her, as a separate person" (Benjamin, 1988: 13).

The visual motor system comes immediately into operation, and infants are born with innate preferences for certain visual features that add up to a human face (Stern, 1977). An infant reacts differently to human and non-human objects, indicating that they have "inborn pre-coordinates" for these two types of interactions (Lichtenburg, 1991). The infant has an inbuilt bias to respond to features that have human significance, and mother's is the first face to be recognized. When presented with mother, the neonate will "open his mouth, circle and purse his lips, and sustain this for several seconds. This is often accompanied by tongue thrusts as well as body quivers and small thrusts of the head forwards ... These responses, especially when accompanied by the widening of the eyes, are as compelling as the social smile at six weeks" (Bennett, 1971: 87). This well known "smile of recognition" is in all likelihood self affirming as well as world affirming. The infant's responsiveness to his environment is considerably heightened and his communicative capacities expand (Stern, 1985: 92–93).

By two months, both mother and infant have the same visual facility over the same behavior. This gives each equal measure of control over perceptual input. In other words, through eye contact each is alive in the presence of an equal other. The infant's world is now one of mutual gazing, an important milestone in the journey towards recognition. Eye contact is the cradle of human perception. According to Robson (1967), if the bond through eye contact is not established, or if it is characterized by disruption or distress, the infant's ability to form human relationships will be damaged. He quotes Ahrens who says: "the absolute stimulus which must stand at the root of social behavior is the eye part (of the observer's face)" (pp. 17–18). Robson goes on to quote Schaffer and Emerson, who have observed with increasing frequency during the first year of life that situations in which "visually maintained contact" is interrupted are the most provocative of separation protest (p. 18). A mother who cannot provide her baby with significant amounts of eye contact is not providing him with a good attachment, and vice versa: for example, if the infant demonstrates gaze aversion, a failure to achieve the optimal level of social stimulation is indicated.

Already at three to four months, the infant has the capacity to interact in sophisticated facial play which appears to be motivated by social interests. Stern (1977) points out that the baby's social world is limited to a face-to-face one, and "as a way of interacting with others and reading their behavior, it will last all his life" (p. 47). The baby can initiate play and periods of eye-to-eye contact that become conversational games. Also, by controlling his own gaze direction, he self-regulates the level and amount of social stimulation to define his self. Infants can avert their gaze, shut their eyes, stare unseeing, and become glassy eyed. Through the decisive use of his gaze behavior, he is able to reject, distance, defend and separate from mother (Stern, 1977, 1985). Through gaze control, the infant basically regulates the mother in order to maintain his own internal physiological states, particularly arousal and affect, and it is for this reason that it is considered to be an early ego mechanism to accomplish coping and defensive strategies in an interpersonal situation. The infant can reduce his state of arousal by turning away from a stimulus that is too intense, complicated or conflicting. He can close his eyes to escape a boring stimulus and open them to seek a more exciting one. The infant's gaze initiations and terminations which accomplish this regulation appear to be a functional adaptation of an intrinsic biological process of gaze alteration.

Face and eyes are of primary importance in mother–infant attachment and the development of recognition. Eyes are organs of perception and the anatomical base for recognition; the need for recognition is the instinctual aim that drives the infant's searching for eye contact with mother. Moreover, the infants' innate perceptual systems are pre-designed to perform cross-modal transfers of information that allow them to recognize a correspondence across the senses (Stern, 1985: 49). This means that data received through vision, for example, transfers innately to tactile or auditory modes; or information gathered through touch transfers to a visual perception of shape. Infants are also pre-designed to forge certain global integrations, the most important of these for my purposes being the integration of self and other (p. 52). Memory itself is an act of recognition, and the infant has an extraordinary capacity for registering perceptual and affective events in memory. There is what is called a "recognition memory," a synthesizing element that melds mother's milk, face and voice, all the elements of a nourished self, which seems to operate across the birth gap (p. 92).

In these basic elements of the early experience of eye contact, we can see a link to Freud's concept of the body ego, the idea in his structural view of the mind that a part of the ego is unconscious, and that the body is a place from which both external and internal perceptions arise that facilitate the formation of ego. The body is metaphorically a mental container. The current focus on mother–infant interaction can be seen as working back from speech to the body (Benjamin, 1988: 26). Affect is expressed through an infant's entire body; for example, newborns are described as expressing anger by moving face, arms, and whole body in concern when he experiences a lack of air from nasal occlusion at the breast (Stern, 1985: 66). This global subjective world of emerging organization is and remains the fundamental domain of human subjectivity, from which perceived forms and identifiable acts will come. It is also a mythopoeic place of coming into being, the source for Jung's "streams of lava," the "ultimate reservoir that can be dipped into for all creative experience" (p. 67). Past this point everything is culturally invented.

It is through maternal eye contact that the infant becomes aware of his own eyes, and begins to develop an eye ego with its potential for the interiorization of mother's reflections. It is also eventually through vision that image comes into being, and the first image that an infant forms is that of the body of his mother. From her body and the identification with his own reflection the infant gains an image of his own body as both self and other, and will eventually identify his body with the ego and his maleness. This is the beginning of ego development, the centerpoint of consciousness that is capable of communicating with a subject. The stronger the ego develops, the better able he will be to give his own personal meanings creative form.

Being seen, or the need to make one's existence as a human being real through reflection, is an instinctually based, key and universal human concern (Ayers, 2003: 34–49). It is in part through seeing and being seen that the matching can occur between our own self-concept and the concept that others have of us. Eyes and faces are amongst the most important objects that can be seen and are indispensable for relations of any kind. A supportive social environment facilitates pleasure in one's own assertions. Feelings, intentions, and the actions of the self become meaningful when seen through the eyes of others.

The infant is paradoxically both independent and dependent. The nascent self holds the independently existing inherited potentials and maturational processes which depend upon a good maternal environment for their evolution (Winnicott, 1971). At the same time, the infant is absolutely dependent and unable to know about dependence: environmental provision is taken for granted. In this state, "the environment is holding the individual, and at the same time the individual knows no environment and is at one with it (Winnicott, 1992: 283). Mother gives the gift of life through the sharing of her body, her womb and breasts, and her mind. Winnicott once said (during a discussion at a Scientific Meeting of the British Psycho-Analytical Society, *circa* 1940)

> "There is no such thing as an infant," meaning of course, that whenever one finds an infant one finds maternal care, and without maternal care there would be no infant.
>
> (Winnicott, 1960)

From her own subjectivity she knows with a certainty that her baby is a unique individual, and that he depends upon her for an emotional reflection and affirmation of himself as a nascent person. Her child is both inside and outside, other and together. He is utterly unfamiliar, new and unknown and yet totally a part of herself at the same time. She says, in essence, "I recognize that you are real." It is under these paradoxical conditions that the mother's face serves as mirror, and her reflections give back to the infant his own self. In Winnicott's words:

> What does the baby see when he or she looks at the mother's face? I am suggesting that, ordinarily, what the baby sees is himself or herself. In other words, mother is looking at the baby and what she looks like is related to what she sees there.
>
> (1971: 112)

The good enough mother looks at, admires, and reflects her infant in her mind as shown in her eyes, and this in turn facilitates the creation of the infant's mind to constellate a sense of self. The infant looks into mother's face and gets back evidence that he is recognized as a being. Seeing oneself reflected in another's eyes is to know one's self and to exist. Here is the nucleus of human identity.

The primary mirror for the emerging self of the infant is the mother. In the state of narcissistic bliss and omnipotence before the child has consciousness of his distinctness from mother, the child craves recognition. The baby, who has a unique personality from the start, is an active participant with mother, driven by his need for a contingent response that fosters a sense of mastery and agency. When we recognize ourselves in the other our sense of effective agency is enhanced; the responsive world makes one feel effective. As Stern (1985) says, recognition is both self affirming as well as world affirming.

Through mother's reflection and responsiveness the infant is able to come to know his own emotions. The synchrony of mother–infant eye contact builds the infrastructure for the deepest levels of empathic contact with another (Stern, 1977). At this point the child seeks to be the sole object of mother's desire. Unlike Freud and Jung's separate ego of the habituated world, the "I" of the child at this stage is desire for the mother; he consumes her through her breast and eye contact, absorbing her love, attention and admiration. It is from this desire that the self begins to emerge.

Masculine emotional shaping and the shame-based hardening process

Infant research on early mother–infant facial interactions, shown above as playing a significant role in interpersonal communication, illustrate plainly how the process of masculine genderizing (what Pollack (1998) calls "straightjacketing") begins from the start. At birth, male infants are naturally more emotionally expressive – boys startle, cry, fuss and are more excitable than girls. In their studies, Professors Haviland and Malatesta (1981) found that in order to defuse what is perceived as emotional intensity – rather than eagerness or something more positive, as off-balance or unwell instead of enthusiastic – mothers unwittingly mimic and overly enforce smiling. In other words, mothers teach their sons to smile whether they like it or not. Hoping they'll just "snap out of it," mothers will ignore their son's sad faces. They hope to avoid pushing them towards more distressful emotions. It is in this way that a mother can convey the subliminal message that it is dangerous or shameful to express spontaneous and vulnerable feelings. Emotional messages are led by the face, and what this facial interplay says is negative feelings are not important in the mother–son relationship. Without realizing it, a mother can narrow her son's emotional expressiveness, and suppresses his tender, related side.

Haviland and Malatesta (1981) also studied how mothers respond to their babies' expressions of "special interest" or surprise. Here they found that mothers more accurately reflected their son's feelings by mimicking their facial expressions. She provided no additional stimulus other than raising her eyebrows when he did, or acting startled along with him, and kept the interaction emotionally neutral. Without intending to, and thinking that she is going "to great lengths to ensure that their sons remain contented," a mother pushes her son towards premature disconnection from the wide range of inner experience and teaches him that some emotions are unnecessary or inappropriate. With girls, on the other hand, mothers did not mimic their daughter's emotional expressions, but rather stimulated, broadened and deepened their expressive range. What Pollack has found, however, is that boys are no different from girls in their emotional needs. He states that what "'real' boys actually need from infancy forwards – and what mothers in their hearts are longing to offer – is complete and unconditional empathy and understanding for a full range of feelings" (1998: 42).

In addition to having to suppress their vulnerable sides, research also demonstrates that boys are pressured to express the one strong feeling allowed them – anger, and the reason shame hides behind violence. Even in the earliest days of life, vulnerability has become shameful. When coupled with the demands of separation, boys turn most to anger in order to mute and rein in the full range of emotional responsiveness they might otherwise exhibit. This shame-hardening process will continue throughout childhood and into adulthood. It comes not from a boy's desire to be courageous or coldhearted, but from a deep wish to protect himself from losing face, from being disgraced. Once they've been shamed enough for failing to be masculine, the psychic wounds scar over. The petrifaction of shame sets in, and will create a barrier to the development of recognition, a necessary ingredient for the development of an autonomous self.

Looked at scientifically, mothers appear to be uncaring or neglectful; yet they are simply fulfilling patriarchal cultural expectations, their actions created from the same kind of emotional shaping they are forcing their sons to undergo. They are concerned that if they let boys express too much pain or vulnerability they will be "less than a fully functional male" (Pollack, 1998: 41). Society expects mothers to push their sons away so that they can survive in a culture that will shame them for showing the very feelings they are longing to teach boys to express.

Recognition of the mother

Historically there has been a lack of understanding of the necessity for recognition. From a depth perspective, early infancy is mother and narcissism, "twin streams calling us back to infantile bliss." As Benjamin (1988) puts it, implicit in the Oedipal model is "oneness = mother = narcissism" (p. 148). Narcissism at this stage is an emotional cathexis highly charged by its embeddedness in total dependence and fusion with the mother. The child is completely unaware of relying upon her for everything.

We now have a much greater depth of knowledge about the original psychic situation. The repressed mother of psychoanalysis's beginnings has been remembered by Klein, Winnicott, Mahler, Fordham, Bowlby, Stern and others who have given us psychologically sensitive and rich accounts of the mother–infant relationship, as well as its unique and singular role in development. Expanding the clinical scope has made us much more cognizant of the pre-oedipal stages of development and the object relations issues of mother–infant attachment and early trauma, principals of containment and mirroring (Winnicott), attacks on linking and early separation psychoses (Bion), and the internal differentiation of self and object. Infant research on human psycho-social growth makes these concepts scientifically trackable: we can isolate and investigate each side of the mother–infant relationship – the infant's experience of his mother, and the mother's experience of her child.

These many contributions have transformed the way we see early life. By working backwards through direct observation of the baby and his mother, behaviors are subject to close examination at the time of their occurrence. As Eigen (1984) puts it, "There is a sense in which we can say that we have entered the Age of the Baby and that sectors of humanity are now as intent on decoding babyhood as they are the origins of the universe" (p. 93). The focus on infancy has prompted a shift from the intrapsychic and subjective to the subjective in conjunction with the intersubjective. Symbiosis and the infant being born into an undifferentiated unity has become self and other, independence and dependence simultaneously, a distinction which according to Stern (1985) and Winnicott (1971) exists in some respects from the beginning. Given these revelations, the issue of separation becomes not how an infant separates out of symbiotic oneness (the one-sided act of matricide), but how he can actively engage and make himself known to another subject in the relationship. An exclusive focus on physiological regulation has become an understanding of the infant's mutual exchange of social behavior. Classic psychoanlaysis' asocial, unresponsive infant has become the social infant seeking engagement with others. This shift has transformed Freud and Jung's dismissal of the mother into a focus on her as the organizing principle of experience that rivals the Oedipus Complex. And with the inclusion of this emphasis on the pre-oedipal mother and intersubjective theory on the early growth of self in relation to other, the goal of the transition from dependence on the mother to independence from her in order to become a man changes from pure autonomy and the definition of self in terms of a movement away from dependency, to differentiating self in the world and external reality so that the individual and environment become interdependent (a psychological shift on which our human survival now seems to depend, but more on that in my Epilogue). Adaptation, in fact, is relative to dependence.

Separation between mother and infant

In the course of normal development, narcissism gives way to object relations. As the child differentiates between himself and his mother, he suffers the loss of narcissistic bliss rooted in omnipotent gratification. The self's wish to preserve a narcissistic identity clashes with the self's need for recognition and the creation of an inner self with symbolic functions. As the drive for separation and the demands of the environment penetrate the world of fusion and omnipotence, of dual unity and magical, autistic thinking, the child is torn in two: one part seeks autonomy and freedom, the other clings to paradise, merger and infantile bliss. As the mother responds and descends to the infant's level, she provides him with a differentiated kind of human reflection. He is learning object relations as well as self-regulation and attunement. Stern explains:

> The issue at stake is momentous. The infant requires the integrative experience to successfully restructure the world – that what he does changes the other. Since these acts are also charged with emotion, with pleasure or pain, acting on the world also means being able to change one's own feelings "in the desired direction."
>
> (1977: 116)

When mother gives her child a positive, nurturing introduction to existence, things go well. Nurturance includes soothing, reassuring, and facilitating the development of confidence, as well as his enthusiasm and joy in life. Under these circumstances the child builds up a good mother representation. The developing self of the child comes to attach to his particular mother with all the intensity and absoluteness of primary love and infantile dependence; the mother is no longer interchangeable with any provider. Winnicott (1965: 29–36) suggests that a good relationship between an infant and his mother allows him to develop a separate sense of self – a self whose existence does not depend on the presence of another – at the same time as he develops a sense of basic relatedness. The infant begins to disidentify himself from the original unity with mother through the frustrations he inevitably suffers and through the aggression called forth by those frustrations. The infant, who starts out in a symbiotic condition of absolute dependence, gradually begins to perceive the mother as separate – as "not-me." The son begins to become subject, the mother becomes object, and then the baby splits into good and bad objects.

In the stage of adaptation Winnicott called "relative dependence," at about the age of six months, the child is beginning to realize that his mother's mind is necessary. The infant oscillates between perceptions of his mother as separate and as not separate. The self originates in the mother and separation from her is the beginning of differences and perceptions of limitation. The child's first crisis is his perception of mother as a separate being. The infant achieves a differentiation of self only insofar as its expectations of primary love are frustrated. The infant will inevitably undergo tension, discomfort, and pain as the reality principle begins to penetrate emotional and cognitive levels. The child comes to recognize that mother has different interests and activities. He uses his developing physical and mental capacities to adapt to her interests and her modes of behavior in attempts to retain his connection to her. Changes are gradual in the infant's cycle of fusion, separation, and re-fusion through which he progressively differentiates himself.

In the normal course of things, if separation is done in conjunction with the infant's inner experience of continuity in the midst of changing instances and events, an experience of self is formed. As absolute dependence decreases, the child gains increasing awareness around his actions and can connect them to personal impulse. Gradually thereafter, the child no longer experiences the environment as totally acting upon it. Not only is he influenced by the social, political, economic and biological world, but the child influences his world in turn. The development of this factor is critical in Freud and Jung's masculine model of development.

Eventually the child is able to populate the world with samples of his own inner life. His object relationships, as well as the nature of his self, develop through his awareness of mother's separateness: this development points to the fact that there is a part of the individual that wants to see the mother separately, as an independent subject. This creates an anxiety that spurs the development of ego capacities as well as the creation of ego boundaries. For this part of the child, total merging and dependence are not desirable. The phase where the child is struggling to maintain his connection to mother and at the same time struggling to get some distance from her is an extremely difficult one. While the child has gained a certain sense of himself as a separate and permanent being, he does not yet have an emotional certainty of the mother's permanence, nor the emotional certainty of being an individuated whole self, or what Mahler called "libidinal object constancy." While he has attained perceptual and cognitive recognition of separateness and object permanence, he does not yet have an emotional certainty of being an individuated whole self.

At about the age of nine months, the child begins to sense that he has an interior subjective life of his own and that others do too. In the same way that vision sets up a relationship of recognition between self and other, it facilitates a separation between the two. Eye-to-eye contact is strikingly like the interaction between mother and infant carried out with locomotor behaviors during the 12- to 18-month period of separation (Stern, 1985). Early eye contact can mimic the child walking away from and returning to mother's side. The child continues to need mother's emotional support while learning to walk: "The child walks alone with his eyes fixed on his mother's face, not on the difficulties in his way ... In the very same moment that he is emphasizing his need for her, he is proving that he can do without her" (Mahler, 1975: 41).

With the locomotor shift and the child's awareness that he can be physically autonomous, he also becomes aware that the contents of his own mind can be shared with another. It is not a time, as previously thought, that the child exerts all his efforts to separating, individuating, and getting free from mother. Separation is indeed occurring, but this period of time is equally devoted to creating an intersubjective union with mother, of forming new ways of being with another which continues throughout the life span. From this point on, all future developments of self-knowledge depend equally on the mediation of the other. The paradox of recognition is the need for acknowledgment that turns us back to dependence on the other: this is the natural, organic course of human development. Basically one is faced with dependency on others outside of one's control. The success of transition depends on the stability of one's self image and identifications, and the level of distinction between object and self.

The nature of a boy's self and object relationships change with a growing recognition of the mother's separateness and a lessening of dependence on her. As development occurs over the passing months and years, the child turns to substitutes – transitional objects that facilitate his movement away from the relationship with his mother, and that also enable him to continue in that relationship at the level of fantasy and emotion. He is moving in two developmental directions at the same time. The child learns to use objects around him in the culture to preserve his secure tie to the maternal figure, while he struggles to achieve a measure of his own power and control.

The development of recognition is often accompanied by feelings of rejection which mark the psychic loss of mother's security and protection. Shame is not only an affect in evidence as early as the first six months of life (Ayers, 2003), but the core of the pain in the separation which results from a loss of symbiosis and the demands to be autonomous. Shame is primarily object relational, ultimately about the self and other, and so it becomes intensified at the point of differentiation due to the felt dependence on the other. Sartre put it this way: "shame is the feeling of an original fall, not because of the fact that I may have committed this or that particular fault but simply that I have 'fallen' into the world in the midst of things and that I need the mediation of the Other in order to be what I am" (Sartre, 1956: 288). From an intersubjective perspective, the issue involved in a boy's separation from the mother is not only how he can free himself, but also how he can engage her in seeing him which necessitates that he in turn look at her. It is in this way that the need to face shame becomes an inescapable necessity for recognition.

The shift from object relations to object usage

A necessary adaptation in the movement from dependence to independence from an intersubjective perspective is from object relating, a subjective phenomena, to object usage, a more sophisticated capacity in which the object is realized as being a completely separate part of external reality (Winnicott, 1971: 88). Male separation from the female mother of a different gender is fraught with difficulties that are only compounded by the need to transition from object relations to object usage.

As separation proceeds, the fact that recognition is made up of essentially two parts comes into play; feeling recognized by the other who is recognized as separate and distinct. A necessary part of the process of separation, therefore, is the perception that the mother exists as a person in her own right. Here is encountered the not-me part of the mother, an independent other who responds autonomously and in her different ways. The infantile ego grows with the capacity for a different kind of object love as long as the child recognizes mother as a separate person with separate interests (a prototype for attachment to later, separate objects).

In order to truly receive recognition and feel seen by the other, a boy must recognize the other as a separate human being; in other words, a boy must see his mother as real and external to himself. These two elements are essential; they make for all the difference between object relations, which turns the other into a bundle of projections, and object usage, which allows for the destruction of the other, hence the other's separate, autonomous existence. The child needs to discover that the real mother is not simply an object for his omnipotent demands; she is another subject whose independent center must be outside his self if she is to be rendered capable of granting the recognition he himself needs from her to become a self. It is in the face of this need for intersubjectivity as separation proceeds, the fact that two subjects require a separate existence, that recognition becomes so crucial as to allow for the assertion and agency of each self. Indeed, as the child increasingly establishes his own independent center of existence, mother's recognition will be increasingly meaningful only to the extent that it reflects his developing awareness of her own equal separateness.

Differentiation of self and other has all to do with those elements of psychic life that demand a living, responsive other, and is, therefore, difficult to sustain. If one destroys the other, then there is no one to recognize oneself. A condition of our own independent existence is recognizing the other. Heidegger argued the point this way: the relationship between existence and world is not that of contained and container, but the world as it is "cast forth" in the very process of existing itself. In other words, to exist means to cast forth a world, and we are utterly incapable of bringing forth a world alone. There is no such thing as self sufficiency. It is only through the other, through the mother, that one is able to be himself and cast forth a world. Yet the self requires the opportunity to act and have an effect on the other to affirm his own existence. In order to exist for oneself, one has to exist for another. It would seem there is no way out of this dependency. Social stimulation, warmth and affective interchange are indispensable to human survival and growth and humans' natural state of being. One cannot know without a world, and seeing the world means recognition of the mother.

Object relations, the psychic place where the object remains a bundle of projections, is very different from object usage, in which the externalization of the other is achieved. This occurs, according to Winnicott (1971), only as the subject destroys the object. He explains: from "'subject relates to object' comes 'subject destroys object' (as it becomes external)" (p. 90); destruction must be followed by "object survives destruction by the subject," by which he means that the other does not retaliate. Projection mechanisms enable the subject to take initial cognizance of the object. This is not the same as claiming that the object exists for the subject because of the operation of the subject's projection mechanisms. Such activity is particularly active around the male separating from mother through repudiation, the core of "liberation through matricide."

Separation and omnipotence

Complicating development is the fact that separation from the mother brings with it a catastrophic anxiety that she will not return. Mahler observed that the decline of symbiosis, or the increasing awareness of separation on the part of the infant, will be experienced as a loss of self. Merging, however, also brings the threat of a loss of self. Hence, there is no way out of this annihilating experience with a still fragile continuity of self.

The most difficult aspect of the transition to object usage is that the subject must place the object outside his omnipotent area of control. This means that in order to become an independently existing subject, the other must come to exist as an independent subject as well. For this to occur, the boy must accept dependence as a state of being. This demand comes at a time when mother and child are in an all-powerful symbiotic system, and the child must realize his smallness. Another important factor in relinquishing omnipotence is that otherness and omnipotence are always mutually constituting, meaning that awareness of omnipotence occurs only when the self recognizes a possible threat that can only be felt when one is a subject. In other words, the boy only feels threatened when he realizes his dependence.

Recognition and the other

The only way through the transition to object usage is to recognize the subjectivity of the other so that the subject can use the object that has survived. This means the loss of omnipotence and recognition of dependence (and this point is just where shame is catalyzed); the inseparable dualism of subjectivity is that the subjectivity of otherness is essential for the manifestation of the subjectivity of self. Opposites are to some extent unavoidable because of an inherent psychic tendency to split. The critical issue at hand, however, is to maintain tension in order to overcome splitting. The result of this simultaneous equality and division is the setting of boundaries, the exertion of control, and the struggle for power. Separation and connection must remain in balance, transforming complementarities into tolerable paradox (a lack of balance and merger with omnipotence results in antimonies that compel evil choices, but more on that in the next chapter). True independence means sustaining the essential tension of these contradictory impulses; that is, both asserting the self and recognizing the other. When there is difference there is otherness.

Through recognition of the other the object finds externality, which means that "projective mechanisms assist in the act of noticing what is there, but they are not the reason why the object is there" (Winnicott, 1971: 90). Benjamin (1988) articulates Winnicott's line of thinking this way: if the child misses the encounter with mother's independent subjectivity (she has gone away), he also misses the opportunity to work through pain that has the potential of becoming an emotional reality (I am sad, I am abandoned, I have destroyed her) which facilitates a differentiation from external reality (she has returned, she loves me, she knows my grief, she has survived my destruction of her). Winnicott concludes that "the destruction of the object becomes the backcloth for love of a real object; that is, an object outside the area of the subject's omnipotent control ... In this way a world of shared reality is created which the subject can use and which can feed back other-than-me substance into the subject" (p. 94).

A subject-to-subject relationship must be formed for object usage to occur. This means a struggle for recognition that includes the male and female elements, both son and mother existing at the same time. The real backdrop of male individuation is that his acts will have to be meaningful to his mother, not that he will repudiate her. Her subjectivities, the organizing principle of psychological life that has traditionally been most rigorously censored, create his sense of a felt existence. He must be able to find himself, as though looking in a mirror, in his mother, and yet – and this point is unique to male issues of separation – she is the opposite of him.

Matricide and the absence of recognition

Object relations theory has shown that healthy maturational development depends upon an ever growing awareness of others (mother being the first), outside the area of one's own subjective phenomena (omnipotence). The conflicts between separation and merger, to be an autonomous, separate person and at the same time retain one's connection to significant others – two of life's most powerful needs – not only dominate the life of the infant, but extend far beyond infancy and childhood. This process of individuation reverberates throughout the course of life and is always active. According to Mahler, the achievement of a separate identity as a separate being lies at the very core of the self. The paradox is that in order for this to be accomplished, the mother must give the child persistent, uninterrupted feelings of continuity.

When male consciousness identifies with power, it is split off from the emotional life of feeling and intuition. Ego development and linear thinking become overemphasized. A boy acculturated into patriarchal thinking does not separate from the mother to form two subjects; he repudiates her and all her feminine attributes, which are redefined as a threat to his autonomy. The need for her continued repression manifests in the diabolization of her eyes and blindness in masculine shame to maintain the original illusion of omnipotence that denies dependence on external sources of gratification. The male is to come into being in a narcissistic structure, a state of inflation full of entitlement derived from a complete identification with the omnipotent mirroring mother who gazes upon him endlessly.

The dissociation of shame, therefore, inevitably leads to narcissism. The individual gratifies his fantasies of completeness and omnipotence through fantasies of admiration that the mother shined on the infant during the earliest days of life. Blinding mothers' eyes creates deep narcissistic vulnerability, a condition of low self-esteem, self-doubt, and fragility of self-cohesion that twists as development proceeds into the will to dominate, to conquer the other as a means of relating.

The fantasy of omnipotence is the result of early splitting which is replicated at many levels of cultural and social experience where it takes the form of power, a monument to the ego which has been built on a foundation of maternal resources.

When matricide is an expectation, omnipotence becomes a central problem of the self. His sense of omnipotence is maintained by projecting any unpleasurable stimuli or perception, whatever its origin, beyond the boundary of his symbiotic unity with mother. This feature of omnipotence is the lack of reality sense and perception of the mother as a godlike creature, the miraculous source of all of life. In the face of the helplessness resulting from the real loss of mother's protection, separation becomes an attempt to recapture omnipotence which leads right back to fusion with the mother who then requires more repression. The child stays petrified, making the two subjectivities necessary for the generation of mutual recognition impossible. When the development of masculine traits is emphasized, omnipotence becomes the only way out.

The attainment of object usage is complicated for the male trying to establish his self as an independent entity with his mother of a different gender. The inability to move from object relations to object usage lies in the defensive use of discharging shame into an object. This driven activity is masculine mastery that demands a feminine object to take up the feelings of shame. Mother is used as a container for his discharges of the evacuated shame. This urgently driven relation to the object lacks recognition and so allows neither separation nor boundaries, hence the creation of authorship or ownership, the qualities of a genuine subjectivity that allows space for another. The maternal feminine remains an object without subjectivity – a mass of projections and what make men blind in Cezanne's *The Eternal Feminine*.

The feminine need for recognition is distorted into her emasculating, infantilizing desire to possess power and control. The absent, unattainable mother, against whom frustrated aggressive fantasies are directed; the hampering, forbidding, punishing mother; the mother who would hold to herself the growing child trying to push away; and finally the desired but forbidden mother whose presence is a lure to dangerous desire: these are the elements which overtake the images of mother in her repression. Here lays the destructive power of the succubus archetype today.

The male self transfers his infantile omnipotence to the sphere of sexual feelings during the Oedipal. This reconstitutes the Oedipal situation in a manner that prevents the paternal figure from impeding the omnipotent merger with mother. Exclusive identification with the father accomplished at the expense of repudiating all maternity works against the differentiation that is supposed to be the main Oedipal achievement. Later, the male magically makes the world conform to his infantile wishes, and in this Oedipal universe the seductive succubus reigns supreme. Throughout life, his Oedipal rivalries will awaken his narcissism and the taste for omnipotence, those same maternal mergers fused by a wish for power which has been disguised by paternal identification. This is what leads a man to batter and abuse a woman.

Heroism is the frightening cost of matricide. In his state of solipsistic omnipotence, the male ends up symbolically castrating himself. The hero, it turns out, is the one who relinquishes the effort to know or recognize, and becomes an objectively knowing subject with a mother who remains a bundle of projections.

The projection of shame

Contained in the projection of shame is the need to keep mother's subjectivity, which carries with it a threat to his loss of self, from exploding; this becomes its own kind of enslavement. The denied feeling of smallness and dependency create Lilith the child killer, the quintessential symbiotic, omnipotent goddess of the unconscious. Not only does mother's goodness disappear, but the vengeful dimension of the Terrible Mother is catalyzed. Mother is destroyed, and then she retaliates in the intrapsychic form of destroyer, the succubus as child and mother killer. The fear that the maternal feminine can destroy a boy persists, and serves as a feeling which justifies his need to project. Ultimately, however, he is blind to his own destructiveness which is felt as the mother's terribleness. The psychic imbalance causes the tragic display of distortions and magical thinking to occur, described in the previous chapter.

An individual must integrate his projections in order to relinquish control and discover that it is not the mother who is the castrator, but nature herself. Winnicott (1992) put it this way:

> If there is no true recognition of the mother's part, then there must remain a vague fear of dependence. This fear will sometimes take the form of a fear of woman in general or fear of a particular woman, and at other times will take on less easily recognized forms, always including the fear of domination.

> Unfortunately the fear of domination does not lead groups of people to avoid being dominated; on the contrary it draws them towards a specific or chosen domination. Indeed, were the psychology of the dictator studied one would expect to find that, among other things, in his own personal struggle he is trying to control her by accommodating her, acting for her, and in turn demanding total subjection and "love."
>
> (1992: 10)

I would like to change a few of Winnicott's initial words. If there is no true recognition of the existence of the mother and the feminine, then there must remain an absolute form of shame. It can also be said that there is something really missing if a boy grows up and becomes in turn a father, but does not acknowledge just what his mother did for him from the start; remember Freud's "oceanic feeling" being attributed to a longing for the father?

Due to the need to both receive and provide recognition, the two fundamentals towards the creation of a subjective self, the separative ego cannot ultimately erase the feminine, maternal other. Whatever is so shaming in maternal feminine power, made dark and dangerous by virtue of denied dependency, can no longer be avoided. The expectation to completely dis-identify from the mother due to her gender causes her destruction, and she does not survive. The mother not surviving her destruction means that the creative aspect of destruction is not included. The repercussions from this fact are not simple matters.

Unresolved shame can arrest psychic development into transitional space or objects. The absence of maternal elements does not allow internalization and the transition into symbol formation, the function that reunites antagonistic tendencies through the development of the ability to abstract. Benjamin describes the capacity to symbolize this way: "the key to the symbolic function is the recuperation of identification with the 'missing half' of the complementarity" (Benjamin, 1988: 71). The absence of the symbolic function means that true creativity is lost. The child becomes the center of his own universe, and so must struggle to enhance the intensity of those feelings. He relies on instinctual gratification as opposed to reciprocity, and the creation of difference distorts rather than fosters. Disconnection from the feminine eliminates the elements that complete, complement, and inspire human wholeness. This creates a serious psychological problem for modern man, no different than what Victor White observed with regards to religious symbolism:

> Where the god is male and father only, and ... is associated with law, order, civilization, logos and superego, religion – and the pattern of life which it encourages – tends to become a matter of these only, to the neglect of nature, instinct, ... feeling, eros, and what Freud called the "id". Such a religion, so far from "binding together and integrating", may all too easily become an instrument of repression, and so of individual and social disintegration.
>
> (quoted in Engelsman, 1979: 40)

What is more, the man gives the projections the very psychic energy they need to overtake him, and then, just like Freud and Jung said, the situation will happen outside as fate, the "revenge of the unlived life."

Shame is the affect which sets the denial of dependence, hence recognition, in motion. Shame co-opts the need for recognition, submitting it to the powerful force of repudiation. When a man takes this route to establish his own power (his identification with maternal omnipotence), there is an absence where the feminine and maternal should be. This absence appears in images of seduction and child killing – the dual aspects of Lilith, Queen of the Succubi. The man's very self is threatened, and so he strives to maintain power over the other, a projection syndrome characteristic of patriarchal consciousness. A man projects his feelings about the mother who loomed so powerful in his early days and then had to be dismissed. Good mother becomes the bad mother when one is attempting to keep the bad object out. A vicious cycle ensues: the more he repudiates the feminine, the less he experiences his own humanity and the more aggression the ego must deploy against himself to maintain denial. A lack of recognition for the other has far reaching consequences for the individual as well as society. Masculine rationality sabotages maternal recognition; Oedipal repudiation of the mother splits her into the debased and the idealized object.

Shame consolidates its retreat from relatedness by embracing the insularity of pathological narcissism. A narcissistic structure creates the absence of any separate subject, a fantasized supremacy over sensed helplessness that must remain fanatically inhuman. No longer enjoying the symbiotic relationship he had with his mother long ago but still clinging to it, a man feels incomplete. He seeks what he has failed to outgrow, still yearning for it in his present relations without ever being able to find it.

In caring about nothing except himself, focusing on the balance sheet of his own profits and losses, and the pragmatic considerations which govern his actions, he has no stable centre from which to act. The dimensions in which he lives and has his being are narrow: he lacks growth, the fullness of self and inner depth, leaving an internal abyss that makes him even more vulnerable to feelings of diminishment.

The need to repress and kill creates the view that the other can annihilate the subject. The more a man denies his shame over dependency, the more it intensifies and dominates his own contact with the maternal feminine, which he then experiences as even more shaming in its power. Male identification with maternal omnipotence is a narcissistic fantasy of great power that can warp into a blind complicity with evil. Sight of one's shame does not lead to the development of conscience. Where the image of the succubus predominates, a preponderant denial of dependency has created a pathological infantile mother fixation that makes healthy life impossible. In absolute masculine shame, the psychotic core of phallic narcissism, the absence of the maternal feminine results in what basically amounts to an elimination of the entire outside world. The hold on reality in this psychic place is the creation of a personal world; he falsifies his real situation, which only separates him more from the standard level of cultural constructs. "One has so little personal 'ballast' ... that he has to suck in an entire human being to keep from disappearing or flying away" (Becker, 1975: 221).

The infantile narcissism contained in such feelings as arrogance, pride, envy, superiority, and self-importance – machoisms that dismiss or repudiate others – is really a defense against, or an attempt to ward off or undo, shame. His psychosis can become so consuming, so all-absorbing, that all he can do is serve his own personal idolatry. Shame is the affect masculinity unconsciously repels in visions of evil succubi that can become his future. Deep in the heart of man's matricidal impulses lurks a devil, a malevolent core possessed by the child-killing succubus, the shadow of a man's identification with omnipotence in defense against the shame of dependence.

Chapter 8

The evil female demon

> If there is any science man really needs it is the one I teach, of how to occupy properly that place in creation that is assigned to man, and how to learn from it what one must be in order to be a man.
>
> (Immanuel Kant)

> There is no doubt that healthy-mindedness is inadequate as a philosophical doctrine, because the evil facts which it positively refused to account for are a genuine portion of reality; and they may after all be the best key to life's significance, and possibly the only openers of our eyes to the deepest levels of truth.
>
> (William James, 1958: 137–138)

> I love those who do not first seek beyond the stars for reasons to go down and to be sacrifices: but who sacrifice themselves to the earth.
>
> (Nietzsche, 2007/1908: I, p. 4)

In the heroic world of display, a man has to maintain face and honor, or sink down to another role, that of the coward or ignoble churl. Heroic man is enslaved in a war with his shame. He will fight to the death in order to avoid the fate of the underdog, strike to avoid being in the submissive position. He experiences intolerable feelings of shame when backed into a subordinate position, and is willing to sacrifice anything to avoid them. He would rather die than feel shame, and in shame he wants to die.

For those men whose shame has been denied, frozen in their quest for masculinity, the psychic sensitivity to a "we" rather than an "I" is lost. He is addicted (whatever form that seduction takes) to proving a sense of invulnerability. The narcissism invested in the survival of the ego against shame occludes all empathic concerns for others, and evil lurks where this loss of humanity exists.

Masculine psychology limits a man's life to a restricted emotional space that makes him vulnerable to temptations present in the situations he meets. Enslavement to the requirement to prove to the world that he is masculine predisposes an individual to certain reactions that make him particularly vulnerable to evil. In not accepting his human limitations, a man becomes vulnerable to the demonic. He is ruled by his psychological needs and cravings; his only self-control is the outcome of the hold which these needs have on him. A man's engagements, sometimes frantic, do not involve giving, and what he gets out of his pursuits is consumed by the ego, leaving him craving for more. He identifies with an object, an extension of his ego in which he sees an admiring self-reflection. All of these efforts serve the denial of shame.

Evil and masculine shame

Evil and the repression of shame are intertwined in their need for invisibility. The invisibility of evil is the very reason it can take hold in the blindness of shame, and in the theater of illusion that follows the victim is lost. Evil grounded in the denial of shame is the kind of selfishness and greediness that makes a person prey on others; this means that the recipient of evil is a victim. Secrecy, concealment, denial, sightlessness, loss of hearing, loss of memory – it is through the victim made blind that evil consolidates its power.

Not knowing and not seeing are strategic to maintain the surface and avoid the depth of shame – the hiding place where evil eludes accountability. Shame wishes to hide from the penetrating gaze of the other, and demonic evil hides in complexity and confounds – it can twist the truth and make it unrecognizable so that decadence is perceived as heaven, or hide in love the greatest distortions of reality. Evil incites a man to harden his heart so that the self does not feel or know what he is doing, but this keeps him trapped in a toxic self-poisoning process in which shame is the most lethal pathogen. This poisoning process produces psychosis and the self-destructive loss of reality. "Demonized ego structures" grow out of blind spots (masculine shame) in the self, a selling out for power in some form or other, be it to triumph over the world or just to get by. Despite their lethal qualities, however, both shame and evil convey a grain of truth: shame contains the spark of conscience that makes self-awareness possible, and the presence of evil warns to be wary of glamorous, life enhancing illusions, and thereby tips its own hand by hinting at its reality.

Because it is so hard to see, an individual can all too easily fall prey to the demonic. There is the saying "see no evil, hear no evil, speak no evil." Thompson (1981) states that

> a flower cannot turns its head to see its stem; the human brain cannot turn to see what is outside its tiny frame of perception; and so angels and devils are always out of sight.
>
> (1981: 36)

Baudelaire says that "the Devil's cleverest guile is to convince us that he does not exist." In the psychological arena, evil has been described by Grotstein (1979) and Bollas (1995) as a diabolic arena of disorientation and confusion in which truth is gone, becoming unrecognizable even when seen. Hidden demonic aspects of patient and therapist slip past each other's gaze.

The ego

The ego is the percipient aspect of the mind, that portion which produces the assimilation to outer, on the surface realities. It lives by thinking incessantly of all sorts of things and is really no more than the thought of those things. Ego strives to maintain a continuity of integrated experience and mediates responses to stimuli. Through ego a man attempts to change his position from one of insignificance to one of absolute control and mastery of nature. In order to stand out as a hero, a man develops a craving for power to transcend the limitations of the human condition and achieve victory over impotence and finitude. He is drawn to images of power, the possibility of invincibility over his ultimate helplessness. Going beyond the realm of the limited entails an expansion of the ego, and it is this psychological element that lies at the root of all forms of evil. Temptation to evil is motivated by selfishness, greed, envy and power – forms of neediness grounded in the enlargement of the ego and the attempt to feel big, important and powerful. The masculine denial of shame is for the sake of the ego because only the affect of shame can be as intolerable and devastating as to bring about its complete collapse (the same reason for the creation of the image of the succubus as a repository for masculine shame).

In our patriarchal world, perverse mental operations are rewarded to maintain the ego in order to prove oneself a man. Repression splits the psyche. In a man's identification with cultural masculine gender ideas, the ego expands with his own idea of invincibility. This egocentricity is a puffed up ego that bars forgiveness, a kind of indifference to others to be people in their own right. It can deprive an individual of good feelings towards others: he may hate the other when they cross him, or stand in his way. He may feel like the other asked for it, deserves it, needs to be taught a lesson, and therefore his selfish actions are justified. He may think he is defending his honor, and yet what is really driving him is his inflated ego that pre-existed the insult that deflated him. Such inflation is what makes a person enjoy destroying another, from which he derives a distorted sense of power. Ego expansion is the root of the deepest distortion of mankind which says that it is a source of pride and honor to be the one who dispenses violence to others. This perception not only precludes the possibility of seeing the other as an object for compassion, but self disappears through atrophy, a mental division where humane response falls away.

When the ego dominates all aspects of his being, a man stops being a self. When his shame is petrified and self is lost, life becomes a script. A man begins to act, and the acting is a form of self-plagiarism, a staged drama of significance. Evil becomes a false means of self-affirmation. The individual does not know how to get himself out of his own way, trapped by the prop he has settled for in life. The more petrified a man is, the harder it is to get things moving. Also, the greater the difficulties he will have to face, and the more daunting the task of coming to terms with his shame.

When the destructive forces of evil intersect with the narcissism in developmental regression, history is re-written. The mind is evacuated of all humane thoughts. This serves to restrict feelings, which are remolded in accordance with evil. In this dissociated state, the person does not know what he is doing, "but returns contaminated and contaminating in a vicious self-poisoning process time and time again" (Grand, 2000). When the masculine ego takes the position of power over and presumes to heroically conquer the succubus, he rides sin proudly and is taken over by all he does not see. When weakness is repudiated, when a man avoids facing his humanity with its limitations and conditions of time and fragmentation, evil in some form is committed.

Enslavement of the ego

The person who has been consumed by evil ends up acting as its slave. Evil conditions are produced from a narrow perspective, a form of bondage or constriction that traps the self behind the ego. Always writing with Freud's ideas on the self, the ego and the fact of the Oedipal transition within his peripheral vision, Becker describes the prison this way:

> The enemy ... is the Oedipus complex. The child has built up strategies and techniques for keeping his self-esteem in the face of the terror of his situation. These techniques become armor that holds the person prisoner. The very defenses he needs in order to move about with self-confidence and self-esteem become his life-long trap ... like Lear, he must throw off his cultural lendings and stand naked in the storm of life ... Like many prisoners they are comfortable in their limited and protected routines, and the ideas of a parole into the wide world of change, accident and choice terrifies them.
>
> (1973: 86–87)

Men's souls are enslaved to cultural stereotypes and standards. In addition to being enslaved to the ego in order to repress shame, an individual is gripped by an illusion of freedom that is ignorant of selflessness or goodness. There is a succumbing in evil, for even if he pursues it with determination no one does evil voluntarily (Plato). What is more, once the person has succumbed, evil maintains its control. When evil becomes the main source of narcissism and egocentricity, one is unable to grow out of or escape them. This is linked to the fact that evil uses inflation as a compensation for the deprivation, insignificance, emptiness, and inner poverty an individual feels radiating from the absent self underneath. Forfeiting ego means descent into nothingness and shame.

A person who falls into evil inevitably fails to be himself. If he has built a secure identity, he will start to see it crumble under his feet. The evil that can take over a life erodes conscience, the moral glue that holds the self together. The self is now not only dissociated, but disintegrated. The missing self underneath is best described as the absence of humanitarian feelings that are lost in the retreat into early developmental modalities that lack the capacity for historicity and personal accountability (Grand, 2000), the "primordial arena of baby mind" where the "devil first sows his seeds" (Eigen, 1984: 93). Vulnerability to evil is fueled by the temptation in the infantile, omnipotent belief that he will receive the longed for recognition and affirmation for his being. But as we saw in the previous chapter, recognition has to be given in order to be received, and received in order to be given. Only through the process of interacting with other humans can a person develop a stable, integrated, differentiated identity and an equally important conscience. The self is delineated through progressive degrees of separation, and, ultimately in the natural world, the male is never really fully separated from the mother.

Since the evil that represses shame dissolves conscience, the individual who is steeped in it justifies, and in one way or another does not recognize, his evil acts. Evil is there to lie about the frightening reality of life's limitations, and embedded in this force is the temptation to destroy oneself. The self is forgotten as the unrestrained exercise of primary process omnipotence brings the individual the feeling that everything is possible. He loses touch with reality and his judgment deserts him. A man is self-deceived and lives a lie in which he cannot be himself. Evil is egocentric and alienates a person from the self that can only be found through the inclusion of the element of recognition. A narcissistic psychosis prevents him from knowing that what he is thinking is evil; vision simply cannot find a foothold in his perceptions. He may seek the kind of achievement and success that boosts the ego, that make him feel important. Nevertheless, the slightest failure will feel like a bombshell. His identity is external, not grounded in his self; to conceive of his own evil, he has to come down from the high position of his ego puffed up with power.

The evil female demon

The diabolizing of female eyes is the shamed man's cloak of invisibility. On an intrapsychic level, evil germinates in this fabric. When separation from the mother is accomplished through her repression, diabolical qualities are attributed to her and she becomes a demon. Maternal femininity combines with evil which are not separate for a man. However, since the male merges to maintain narcissistic omnipotence, and so identifies unconsciously with demonic aspects of the mother, evil gets in. The repression of the maternal feminine and her enantiodromia into distortions such as the child-killing and castrating succubus represents an extreme loss of human feeling that makes up what we mean when we speak of "humanity" itself.

Egohood dawned with civilization in the same way it emerges in the development of the infant in its frustrations and separations from mother. The Terrible Mother with the Evil Eyes is born of patriarchal distortions, not developed under its control. The evil eye has been described as a castrating gaze, threatening to make men impotent through the denial of vision. Even Perseus who killed Medusa in a primal act of violence was not afforded the right to look. The mighty hero gazed into his shield, echoing the magical image of narcissism and the curse to stare at one's own face.

The revengeful destroyer is created as a result of shameless thinking and attempts to have power over nature. The evil Lilith, Maid of Desolation "who dances in the ruins" resents the lack of recognition around her equality. This causes it to twist into "a pride born of envy;" with this her activities become wholly destructive. When the mother is repressed, she becomes succubus. Then her life-giving forces are turned towards annihilation, and we live in destruction and condemnation without end – manifestations of Lilith and her grandchildren, the seven deadly sins.

When shame is repressed to extinguish the maternal feminine, it becomes the core of a narcissistic psychosis. This is the moment the succubus seizes to climb on top of the male and co-opt the power of maternal absence to give birth to demons (evil). The memory of loss is transmuted into the perpetration of evil, an emotional ice jam maintained by shame and the fear of losing power over another. Alienated from the source of his conscience, he is ripe to fall into evil when a situation provides the temptation.

In order to control nature, man projects his shame into driving evil away and overcoming demonic succubi. According to Becker, "most of the evil that man has visited on his world is the result precisely of the greater passion of his denials ..." (1975: 90). He goes on to describe one of the great tragedies of human existence as mankind's need to "fetishize evil," a "shrinkage of vision" that attempts to

> locate the threat to life in some special places where it can be placated and controlled. It is tragic precisely because it is sometimes very arbitrary: men make fantasies about evil, see it in the wrong places, and destroy themselves and others by uselessly thrashing about.
>
> (p. 148)

The "shrinkage of vision" (depicted in Cezanne's *The Eternal Feminine*) is similar to Jung's concept of the shadow, the dark thing in one's own psyche, "an inferiority which nonetheless exists even though only dimly suspected"; the most direct way to avoid it is by "looking for everything dark, inferior and culpable in others" (1970: 203). Their formulation encapsulates in a nutshell the principle that fortifies the blinding power of the succubus as a repository for masculine shame. An evil lies hidden in the heart of mankind because the maternal feminine has been repressed. This, in turn, perpetuates a negative view of these qualities, visible over the course of history in a spiral that has been recurring, and intensifying increasingly, over the last seven thousand years. Not recognizing the mother and her goodness means being cut off from an important source of sustenance, pleasure and, most importantly, recognition. Worldly success or power does not provide any real fulfillment or enduring satisfaction.

When mankind does not give recognition to the maternal, he wants to dominate nature with culture, feeling with reason, and the whole psyche with the ego to create a world with magic power made real by a genie in a bottle. In addition to creating a dynamic of dominance and submission, power and the absence of recognition engages the aggressive, vengeful, evil side of the maternal image. The succubus is simply a reflection back to mankind of his own wild and primitive exercise of power, and if mankind resists her to hold onto his ego, then her manifestations will indeed be annihilating. This means that the hero may destroy whatever he has power over, but ultimately he destroys himself.

The integration of masculine shame requires a fuller awareness of the evil female demon within – that maternal feminine place in the back of a man's mind, hardened over and made coarse so that contact with shame is thwarted. And when there is a confrontation between the male self and the evil female demon, it is not the Oedipal hero, the one with immunity power, who confronts the succubus – it is the helpless infant (victim) self. As Riker puts it, "evil is not consciously and freely willed, but partly generated by unconscious compulsions arising out of profound childhood injuries and neglect. Until these experiences are exhumed and worked through, the tendency to create evil will remain" (1997: 103). Evil is the result of dark memories.

I would like to replace the words "profound childhood injuries and neglect" with "the repression of the maternal feminine," the more traumatic of the two. This is due to the fact that when the good mother and her containing function are internally absent, the mind evacuates and dissociates injurious feelings. Facing masculine shame is not about putting evil under control – that is a resolution centered on the ego: it is about seeing the shame that inevitably results from succumbing to it. This means that a resolution to shame lays in the victim self, the recipient of evil.

By facing shame in a process of restoring maternal feminine vision – the sight that was taken from all of us when the Great Mother was diabolized beginning in 5000 B.C. – mankind can redeem his shame and recapture his soul sucked away by the succubus. The succubus is not only a repository for shame, but of the forgotten, true self as well; it is for this reason that facing the child-killing and seductive female demon brings a man into the fullness of his creative life. It is just as the Sufi leader Pir Vilayat Khan questioned and taught his students to ask: "what is there in this that returns to me because it comes from me?" But the task is daunting – even God struggles to see His own shadow.

Lilith

Shame and evil share invisibility through Lilith since both have been banished from sight through projection onto the goddess diabolized as a repository for male shame. Shame and the evil activated by its denial lies in the deepest of fault lines in the human psyche created in the shift from matriarchy to patriarchy. It is this connection, therefore, that makes shame the affect which connects us most deeply to knowledge held within the collective unconscious.

Men are being introduced to a new level of feeling and emotion for which patriarchy has not prepared them. They are outgrowing stereotypes and the repression of their emotional and spiritual lives. An opening for Lilith and the recognition she requires is created, and is occurring now in the male psyche (Thompson, 1981). David Tacey (2007) describes a "New Man" in the making, a mixture of the best traditional masculinity with the addition of sensitivity and emotional expressiveness, dimensions required of masculinity today "if humanity is to be renewed." Modern man must commit to true masculinity. "Unless man in his individuality can differentiate himself from the collective patriarchal standards, both will go down together" (Wyly, 1989). Only as an individual, undivided, can man continue on his journey, meet the maternal feminine both within and without, as an equal opposite, and fulfill his creative destiny" (Wyly, 1989).

The image of Lilith is dissimilar to Jung's concept of the anima in a significant way: she is completely beyond the ego's command and conscious control. This difference can restore sight, and means that a man must realize that her blinding and diabolization is in fact his own shame. Individually and as a culture, mankind is re-confronting Lilith in order to learn how to distinguish the demonic from the spiritual, or, in psychological terms, an expanded ego from the true self, and power rooted in omnipotence and the denial of the maternal feminine from empowerment of self; such discrimination does not come easy.

So if Lilith, the archetypal repository for masculine shame, is rising up along with the evil that has historically been characteristic of turning points in human evolution, or what Thompson (1981) has called "catastrophic bifurcations," then perhaps we need to take a closer look at masculine shame and evil as a way of trying to feel our way through the darkness of our contemporary condition. "If a way to the better there be, it lies in taking a full look at the worst" as Thomas Hardy says.

Evil and destruction

Embedded in an individual's attraction to evil is the temptation to destroy his self, but this truth comes in the back door. For example, in seeking to destroy evil, man is responsible for bringing more evil into the world than any other organism on the planet. Becker (1975) describes the driving impetus for all forms of evil as "man's hunger for righteous self-expansion and perpetuation ... The paradox is that evil comes from man's urge to heroic victory over evil" (pp. 135–136). In other words, men work evil out of the impulse to do good deeds.

On both individual and collective levels, every step towards progress carries its own evil – its presence announces the next level of order. As Keen puts it,

> our desire for the best is cause of the worst. We want to clean up the world, make it perfect, keep it safe for democracy ... purify it of the enemies of god, eliminate evil, establish an alabaster city undimmed by human tears, or a thousand year Reich.
>
> (1997: xiii)

When looked at in this way, evil takes on a much wider meaning. There is a deep and tragic paradox about civilization. On the one hand, it has been up until now the most life-enhancing innovation mankind has ever created. But the paradox is that it has also increased human violence beyond anything pre-civilized culture could have envisioned. Due to the patriarchal repression of shame, civilization became the most potent force that created the succubus: the agricultural revolution of 9000 B.C. diabolized the Great Mother; the urban revolution of 4500 B.C. sealed the oppression of women; and the industrial revolution of the 1770s, a time when the power to overcome basic human helplessness simply got out of hand, has led to "the ruin of cities" wrought by the Lilith, "Maid of Desolation." In this "progressive" world, we try to have power over death and yet recreate it everywhere around us on a scale that staggers the imagination. Our attempt to turn from death and destruction has created an even larger form of it which confronts us now. In the past, the primary danger to humanity was nature; today, civilization is the greatest threat to nature (masculinity the greatest threat to femininity).

"Often cultural man kills his natural man and nature replies by making him impotent" (Johnson, 1989); this is our unfortunate reality today. According to Tacey (2007), many of the world's most serious problems and illnesses can be traced to the distortions of masculinity.

> The brutish spirit which rides roughshod over nature, women ... is largely a product of a heroic and conquistadorial style ... having little or no room for non-heroic or receptive dimensions of human experience. If humanity is to be renewed, if we are to be saved from the world-conquering aggressive ego and from the heroic complex that drives us to the brink of self-destruction, then clearly masculinity has to be altered in some way. If we are to be saved from the specter of ecological devastation, and from the push that would subdue the entire physical world in order to further the ego's short term needs, then clearly traditional masculinity has to be checked and restrained.
>
> (2007: 1)

The heroic in man does not find nourishment and growth, but war and fighting and violence. At this point, the male predilection for violence threatens world survival in countless ways.

Patriarchy speaks for separation, for loss of fusion and omnipotence, for the individuation world of the father that succeeds the symbiotic world of the maternal figure. This rupture creates an inherently negative relation to the concept of mother that requires a male, because of culture's patriarchal biases, to maintain separation and dominance. The patriarchal demand for a full identification with ego is inherently destructive, however, because masculinity can never really be separate from the maternal and the unconscious. The tension in this polarity will inevitably lead to the triggering of an apocalyptic, ego-shattering experience for a man as well as patriarchal civilization. On an individual level, a man may be plunged into depression unaccounted for by the externals of his life at face value, a depletion of the ego and a process of relinquishing outward trappings and love objects. The meaningful world somehow edges away, slipping out of one's grasp. The cozy self-justifications that blind a man to his own evil are no longer there. Collectively, we now live in an omnipresent catastrophic environment of terrorism and the real possibility of thermonuclear war, ecological catastrophe, economic disaster, and pathological disorders of containment that cut deeply into the very fabric of our cultural, social and moral lives.

And yet in this depression or catastrophe, a man or mankind is more in touch with himself and closer to the possibility of redemption. Hegel (1967) made the point that it is in blindness rather than self-knowledge that man serves the purpose of the Absolute Spirit. The cunning of this Spirit is that it exploits man's partial passions to serve cosmic ends. It is precisely in carrying the seeds of his own destruction that there can be transcendence, a concept presented over a century ago in Spielrein's paper *Destruction as a Cause of Coming into Being*, the direct repository of Freud and Jung's shame. Spielrein held that archaic vestiges, pieces in the soul's memory from an old cosmology, contained the seeds of death and rebirth, and both are discovered through the sexual instinct. This state of destruction is the nature of life itself, a state of tension between creation and destruction, good and evil. The seeds of destruction grow into creation and transcend into another form. The forces of limitation are necessary to balance the forces of dissolution and the return of the formless in unbridled creation. Life breeds death, and death feeds life; this process makes evolution and creation possible.

Her concepts amplify the meaning of destruction in the context of intersubjective theory, and its necessary role towards the creation of recognition. Here, destruction takes shape in an effort to differentiate subject from object, son from mother, in order to develop and balance a subject-to-subject relationship. When the heroic ego tries to stay on top and force the universal and maternal feminine to remain below, a man does not destroy the object, does not experience his insignificance. The psychic energy of the self cannot manifest when a man seeks to experience his feelings while maintaining control of his ego. In this dualistic tension recognition provides the necessary energy for the constant transformation of the toxic sting of shame. In confronting his erasure and absence of the maternal feminine, he reflects on his own presence and plunges into his ego opposite – absolute (feminine) shame, the annihilating, destructive force of nothingness (Ayers, 2003) that subjects human experience to a centripetal pull into a void.

The death of the ego and the transformation of evil into shame

> *While I thought that I was learning how to live*
> *I was learning how to die.*
>
> Da Vinci

> *Into every abyss I still bear the blessing of my affirmation.*
>
> (Nietzsche, 2007/1908, p. 108)

A man is doomed if he remains seeking the solution to his inevitable, all too human shame through the external world and projection onto something outside of himself. An individual who puts his energies into defending himself misses out on being himself. The resolution for conflicts with masculine shame and a hugely inflated ego to defend against it requires inner work and self-reflection. "Knowing thyself" is an act of the innermost self. This means that a man must lose his ego in order to find his self, let go of the outer world in order to discover his inner one. Coming into consciousness of shame is always a painful activity, bringing in its wake suffering, despair, and possibly even death – but there is no other way out.

When a man follows the cultural prescriptions of masculinity and represses his shame, he becomes self-forgetful and vulnerable to corruption. In order to be his true self, and extrapolate himself from the evil in which he has become entangled, a man needs shame. The sting of shame is the first step towards greater unity within the self. Letting go lays the potential for the development of a self that is grounded in humility, the development of conscience and the opposite of evil.

The nature of death

Shame is, in fact, inescapable. It confronts us all when in nature's grip in the face of death. Despite any patriarchal allusions to the contrary, we live in a world of limitation, a life with a beginning and an end. The edge of being is death, the irreducible common denominator for humankind. Near death, omnipotence is exposed as an illusion and the truth that ultimately mankind does not have power over anything is revealed. Perishing is inevitable. Once an individual is born he is vulnerable to death, a place where civilization's social distinctions are eliminated because the Mother of Death rules with an ultimate equality.

A man's mourning of his eventual death, and thus the extraction of it from the unconscious, entails a loss of ego. The true courageous hero, according to Becker, is the one who is able "to absorb into one's own being the maximum amount of non-being." It is only "his courage to face the anxiety of meaninglessness [blinding of the Eternal Feminine] that he becomes a true cosmic hero" (1973: 279).

In the context of facing masculine shame, death means an ending of oneself in a world simultaneous to recognition of the mother. Enduring this kind of massive trauma reacquaints the psyche with the nearness of extinction and organic dependence on the maternal feminine. Benjamin describes the process this way: "to find out that he exists, I must wish myself absolute and all alone – then, as it were, upon opening my eyes, I may discover that the other is still there" (1988: 38). When the ego dies (rather than slaying the mother) and recognition is achieved, the desire for mother and the feminine no longer provokes a complete loss of self just because "the other is still there." Many authors agree on the nature of this kind of death. Hegel describes the death of an ego this way:

> Death, as we may call that unreality, is the most terrible thing . . . But the life of Mind is not one that shuns death, and keeps clear of destruction; it endures

> death, and in death maintains its being. It only wins to its truth when it finds itself utterly torn asunder. It is this mighty power ... Spirit is this power only by looking the negative in the face, and dwelling in it .. the magic power that converts the negative into being...
>
> (1967: 93–94)

Pressfield offers a thought-provoking image of dying in his book on the Spartan Battle of Thermopylae, *The Gates of Fire* (1998). An infantryman who is part of an elite force willing to sacrifice his life dies and returns to life to tell the story of The Three Hundred:

> I had always wondered what it felt like to die...
>
> I had imagined that the dead would be detached. That they would look upon life with eyes of objective wisdom. But the experience proved the opposite. Emotion ruled. It seemed nothing remained but emotion. My heart ached and broke as never it could on earth. Loss encompassed me with a searing, all-mastering pain. I saw my wife and children, my dear cousin Diomache, she whom I loved. I saw Skamandridas, my father, and Eunike, my mother ... names ... which to me were dearer than life and now dying, dearer still ... That state which we call life was over.
>
> I was dead.
>
> (1998: 7–8)

Jung describes his experience in the land of the dead. He says of writing Septem Sermones: "From that time on, the dead have become ever more distinct for me as the voices of the Unanswered, Unresolved, and Unredeemed." He recognizes their need for him, and submits to the greater good:

> It was then that I ceased to belong to myself alone, ceased to have the right to do so. From then on, my life belonged to the generality. The knowledge I was concerned with, or was seeking, still could not be found in the science of those days. I myself had to undergo the original experience ... It was then that I dedicated myself to the service of the psyche ... My delivering myself over to it, as it were, was the only way by which I could endure my existence and live it as fully as possible.
>
> (1965: 191)

Thompson puts it this way:

> When you give up, God can give down. When you are totally defeated, you are totally open and receptive ... in defeat and the complete humiliation of the ego, the individual is completely open to receive grace.
>
> (1978: 37)

Everything about meeting the evil eyes of the succubus speaks of the intolerable condition of human shame that was projected outside of the hero system. Death of the ego means death of the omnipotent hero through an internalization of shame. In opening his eyes, the defenses used to protect a man from an awareness of his own demons breaks down. He is cast into utter darkness; the loss of ego boundaries brings with it the devastation of disintegration. In this moment, however, the now isolated ego will cry out in painful recognition of his complete alienation and weakness, fear of death, limitation, finality, helplessness, and hopelessness. He is staring into the eyes of Medusa, an embrace of deep pain associated with acknowledged patriarchal suffering.

He realizes his insignificance, his utter dependence on nature, his complete lack of control and power despite all of his attempts at it – just misguided devotion.

The phallus

The penis is an anatomical term referring to the male genital organ. It is an organ that serves biological functions, simply a tool of procreation. In patriarchal culture, however, men are preoccupied about the size, shape and erectile potential of their genitalia. Using the penis sexually marks the transition into manhood, an object used to judge the manliness of a man. Men with small penises become subject to mockery, while men with large penises are considered virile and powerful. Freud's mastery through the penis emphasizes the male's lack of commonality with the female, with the inadvertent result that he is given the right to violate femininity as a means of establishing his separateness. The core of narcissism for Freud, in fact, is that women do not have a penis.

The phallus, on the other hand, is an anthropological and theoretical term referring to an erect penis. The erect penis is venerated in various religions as a symbol of male fertility. Phallus is a key concept in psychoanalysis, and has had a tremendous effect on what we think about gender and sexuality. The phallus has been named by Lacan as the "signifier of signifiers," a symbol of power and privilege associated with patriarchal authority, control and dominance. In Lacanian terms, neither man nor woman ever fully embodies the power of the phallus. This means that no gender can claim supremacy over the other in relation to this image; phallus simply means power. In this exploration of masculine shame, I will be using the term phallus, which subsumes the penis in its meaning. Both body and metaphor, physical and psychological, the erect penis or ritual phallus, all are one and the same.

Loss of omnipotence and sacrifice

Traditional masculinity must be allowed to die, and a new masculinity brought to birth. Today, men are reaching for, and making an effort at retrieving or winning back the positive masculine attributes of the past. Phallic man – meaning authoritative, dominant and violent – must consciously sacrifice these qualities for the sake of the world. In this context, the act of facing masculine shame, the demystification of phallic omnipotence, becomes a veritable submission to castration. The sacrifice of the phallus, or castration, becomes an image that says a man recognizes his limitations, realizes and accepts that he cannot conquer death, cannot win over matter, and most of all, cannot accomplish matricide. He extinguishes his selfish, narcissistic ego, that part that only looks to save his own skin. Dragged out of sanity into madness as he enters a dark internal place of depletion behind the magical gratification of omnipotence – in death, a man confronts the cultural lie of the hero, the "Oedipal causa sui project" (Becker, 1975: 122).

De-mystification of the phallus

In the pre-history of matriarchal society, the phallus belonged to the mother as an organic part of nature. It enhanced the female with its mysterious life force, infusing the mother with the powers of fertility inherent in its column. This profound truth is embedded in the body of Great Mother figurines from that period; a phallus forms the backside of her body (see Figure 2.1 on page 14, Venus of Lespugue, 23000 B.C.). During this time the phallus was not the male's possession; it was, so to speak, on loan from the Mother.

In addition to the repression of shame and the demonization of the Great Mother, the story of civilization begins with the separation of the phallus from the body of the Great Mother. Rather than the phallus forming her backside, the carvings of the Great Mother began to depict facial features which reflected her connection to death, and eventually became the vehicle for her diabolization (Ayers, 2003: 99–145). Civilization evolves out of nature, and in this shift the phallus becomes an icon of patriarchy. The phallus as a symbol of civilization is carried in the transition into agriculture (the catalyst for civilization) through the image of the plough, as well as the sprouting stalk of wheat that sticks up, produces seeds, and then withers and dies to return to the soil and multiply.

Despite patriarchal civilization's efforts to claim the phallus as a symbol of enduring male power, however, there is no denying that the limiting and vanishing principle is inherent in an erect penis – nothing is more short-lived than an erection. Like the crocus in early Spring, the phallus blooms and then vanishes; in flourishing it is exhausted. One moment the penis is in a humble state, small, soft, shriveled up and insignificant. In an instant it can become hard, erect and exponentially larger than its previous tiny size (Thompson, 1998: 155). Symbolically, the phallus reflects the natural rhythms of rise and fall, galling limitations and disappearances emerging in climax, be it with the rise and fall of the stock market, the World Trade Center, or whole civilizations throughout history (Thompson, 1981: 128). Becker writes that psychiatrists in New York report complaints of impotency increase when the stock market is low, or during a "bear" market (a symbol of the mother) and, conversely, potency is vigorous when the market is high, or during a "bull" market, a very apt male symbol for such robustness (1975: 123).

The female, on the other hand, endures. She is nature, meaning the unlimited, eternal, and containing principle, of which the bleeding vulva is the perfect expression. Menstruation embodies the mystery of death followed by rebirth. At the beginning of the 28-day cycle she bleeds only to heal and begin the round all over again. This is the archetypal pattern of birth and death which are the Great Mother. That the female dies and is reborn, and the phallic male rises to greatness and then falls, is the unending pattern of nature. The feminine has long represented the core of being, the source out of which one is created and to which one returns. One is born, flourishes for a season, and death, the inevitable final destiny, is a peaceful return to the source of life. The first encounter with the feminine is the mother of infancy who conceives through the male and gives birth to the infant from her womb; second is the seductive mother, who calls the boy to her bed during the Oedipal period; and last is the other of death, who beckons a man to his tomb. Life as a cycle of death and eternal return, birth and rebirth, is the source of the maternal feminine's eternal aspects. These facts of nature reveal that the maternal principle is larger than life and more encompassing than the male.

Recognizing male dependency on the maternal feminine is an equivalent to sacrifice. There is no way to avoid paying the debt of dependency, and yielding to the larger meaning of the rest of nature and its demands; nor does there seem to be a way to accept having to make the payment, a demand from within. This tension creates the polarization of the opposites. In realizing his smallness, a man can no longer justify his own heroism. When a man gives up ego, new value is given to the individual. It is like Jesus who became the Christ, a man who struggled with the tests of life that we all face, and yet emerged into a wholeness of being without resorting to the temptations of power and evil. Themes connected to the story of Jesus are deeply embedded in the ancient culture of the Near East with its mythology of a dying Osiris, a male god who loses his phallus. Sacrifice of the phallus puts one into possession of the power not of this earth, but of eternity, soul and mother love, the things that are the same on both sides of death, in front of the curtain or behind, that which exists and endures beneath materialism and the world of the flesh. Castration restores good maternal functions, and, on an archetypal level, embraces the Eros of the Goddess. Pressfield describes the Goddess this way:

> Her face was beauty beyond beauty. The embodiment of truth as beauty. And it was human. So human it made the heart break with love and reverence and awe. I perceived without words that this alone was real which I beheld now, not the world we see beneath the sun. And more: that this beauty existed here, about us at every hour. Our eyes were just too blind to see it.
>
> (1998: 295)

Otto Rank taught us that when man is at his most submissive, he is giving expression to the agape urge in his nature. The outflow of submission is love, a unity with the rest of nature and completeness within oneself. The routine of the world forgets the whole; the sacred restores the awe-inspiring relationship of the self to the immensity of the universe. A sacred moment or place is thus one which connects things of immediate importance with the whole of creation and eternity. There can be no resurrection, however, without first enduring the horror and pain of the crucifixion, a principle which cuts across the life-instinct in all of us. And yet, as the image of Christ maintains, a man may not be crushed by what he is forced to admit. Beyond shame, there is a meaning that redeems and makes whatever has been suffered beneficial somehow. Atonement, apology and mourning become redemptive experiences if faced directly, honestly, and openly. The self can transcend (rather than deny) limits to realize powers beyond the ego and connect to the eternal aspects of the maternal feminine.

Dissolution of the ego

Through the sacrifice of castration, hence phallic disempowerment, the ego is destroyed, brought down to nothing. When the male gives up power, he does so unwillingly, but once begun, like the nine-month-old fetus in the womb, there is no turning back. The all encompassing elementary character of the maternal feminine tends to dissolve the ego and consciousness into the unconscious, back into the body, through infancy and beyond into birth through which the self originally emerged, back into the body of the mother, a source of creative expansion and regenerative power.

Heroic man avoids shame and castration in order to avoid a feeling worse than death, but the heroic in man faces it, the death of his ego and, hence, the loss of his phallic power. This aspect of the inner work on shame is fraught with danger, often with mortal peril, but necessary in the process of coming to terms with the fundamental aspects of one's basic humanity (from the womb to the tomb), without false consolations and the illusions of omnipotence. Facing shame is the apocalypse of an ego that no longer holds together, and so things become worse before getting better. A man is cast out of his patriarchal nature to an equivalent degree that he faces his shame as its fatal flaw – indeed, the greater the confidence in his ego image, the greater his shame and humiliation will be, an idea supported by the current upsurge of billionaire and CEO suicides in the wake of the economic crisis. These men had clearly become prisoners to the kind of success they wanted to obtain. Had they been able to face their shame, they may have become free to realize the real shame of their situations, which "breaks the spirit out of its conditioned prison" (Becker, 1973: 86).

The pain of shame means having the humility to take responsibility for what has been done, and acknowledging that he has transgressed or violated the values for which he cares. In Medusa's stare man brings that which is under consciousness into consciousness; he affirms what has been denied, raises up into living memory that which has been repressed, develops sight rather than staying blind, speaks the lie in the truth and the truth in the lie, negates the story of history as told by the patriarchy, and restores that which is primary and maternal to a privileged position. In this process a man sees past his distortions into reality, a full sight of the victimization of which he is capable – the blinding of the *The Eternal Feminine*. In grasping this negative moment, the projection is internalized; the terrifyingly demonic is recognized as an aspect of his self.

Emergence

The emergence of self involves giving up the ego's expansion needs that only lead to self-deception and defensiveness. A man becomes more realistic which involves toleration and patience, the courage to face the real difficulties of life, and to deal with them constructively and honestly. Living with a self and the way things really are requires shame and humility; in the world of masculine gender ideas, this change alone would be profound. In such a world, a man no longer needs to show off, to seek compensation for what he regards as inadequacies in himself or for the adversities he has been dealt with by fate. He is not big-headed; for instance, he doesn't think of these adversities as directed at him. He is not on the defensive, and does not need to justify himself. He can take a slight without over-reacting, a change in his fortunes for the worse without becoming petrified. He is self-contained, secure and on good terms with himself. He is not puffed up and blaming others for his failings. He is not afraid to face the difficulties of life and is prepared to accept responsibility for his actions. He can be spontaneous without being impulsive. He is forgiving and does not bear grudges. He admits his faults and has no problem apologizing. His relationships with others are not burdened by what he needs or what he projects. He is open with himself and in his relationships, and does not manipulate and carry secret agendas. He can stand by what he believes and there is no cost to doing so. He is loyal to his friends even when they fall down; he is self-reliant but not afraid to ask for help and admit his vulnerabilities. He is not afraid of acknowledging his indebtedness to others. What he does comes from inside of him instead of being forced upon him by his repressed needs and dependencies. What he comes to in finding his self and accepting it is not something given or taken, something ready-made: it comes through work and learning – a continuous process without end. In the course of things, an individual sheds desires and attitudes, grows out of needs, acquires new capacities and sentiments, and moves with temperament and affective dispositions natural to his being. A man can develop genuine interest and concern towards others, and be freed from the need to be above anyone else. Empathic concern for the human other awakens as mortal shame and its survival anxieties recede.

In this movement from heroism into shame, the individual's psychology leads him to real freedom, autonomy and authenticity. A man will start to obey an inner authority, to uphold conscience in all his words and dealings. If a man is able to do this, then self love starts to grow and he will begin to feel and achieve more wholesomeness in the world. A man will begin to know himself as a good man, develop warmth of character and be less defensive.

The ego is also the center of consciousness, so its dissolution through the process of destruction becomes a transcending of consciousness, an enlargement of being into the wholeness of self. In giving up a narcissistic, ego-absorbed part of himself that uses the world as his mirror, a man becomes a whole self. Becoming a self means, in fact, that he did not exist before he had a self – and non-existence is the nature of feminine shame (expressive of the nature of what femininity became under patriarchal authority). Becoming himself means owning the self that he is, a mode of being who he is without defending or apologizing for it. This is reflective of the trust now placed on inner knowledge, and reminiscent of one Zen Buddhist master who taught his pupils to find their inner mirror, and to make sure to keep it forever free of dust. This simple yet profound difference in how he goes about his life makes a huge impact on his own sense of uprightness and health in his being. If a man is ashamed, he must not hide in trickery or trivial excuses.

The self opens to recognition of the other and sharing. A man has risked being vulnerable, and emerges ordinary from behind ego inflation and the stage that props him up. Making a noble hearted effort to resolve his faults within himself and make clear reparation through recognition creates others who are separate and external from himself.

To live free is to not enslave one's self and soul to cultural stereotypes and standards. Self-acceptance calls for an inner coherence of self-knowledge, humility, and realism over one's limitations and capacities. Knowing and being are one with each other and so indistinguishable. His new psychology gives him the space in which to be himself, true to his convictions and considerate towards others. A man who goes through the anima experience in a self-aware manner, with a humble attitude, and thus wins his virility in a mature fashion, is capable of integrating the maternal as well as his feminine aspects.

And last but by far not least, when shame is acknowledged, the mother is left alive in the wake of her own destruction. Recognition of the mother means reconciliation with the mother. It means freedom from an annihilating mother and a return of her holding functions, the transformation of maternal reverie into the transcendent function. Recognition of the good holding mother, and, archetypally, these aspects of the Great Mother, supplies something vital to the self, a transitional place in which to emerge into something higher. Enduring the massive trauma of shame reacquaints the psyche with the nearness of extinction. And yet in this growth, annihilation anxieties recede and are replaced by an increasing sense of security.

Lilith and transcendence

When masculine shame is re-visioned, Lilith, even in her embodiment as death and destruction, becomes beneficent and releases a man from the definitions of his ego. Lilith becomes a cosmological principle of manifestation working for a subtler, higher purpose. The succubus is not only a repository for shame, but of the forgotten, true self as well; facing her brings a man into the fullness of his creative life. This, in effect, is the resolution to the myth of Adam and Lilith. Just as with Lilith's encounters with Elijah, all Lilith requires to withdraw her evil powers is recognition. In other words, the resolution for the battle between the sexes is quite the opposite of fighting – it takes destruction of the other, the absence of self, and therefore – recognition. When a man faces his shame, when he becomes nothing, he discovers the chthonic, spiritual aspects of Lilith. This means that submission is not simply a willing towards death, but rather a willingness towards eternal life – with Lilith as midwife to rebirth. To grow conscious of one's shadow is to develop a capacity to endure, prevail, live and create. By pushing life to its very extremes, to just the point where death becomes a true contingency – and in facing masculine shame it most certainly can – the submission to death and castration becomes in actuality a submission to love and to life. It is just as Joseph Campbell said, "We seek not the meaning of life, but the experience of being alive." In the most unimaginable of places (evil), the unthinkable can be thought, the unspeakable can be named, the invisible can be seen and the unhearable can be heard. The demonic becomes daimonic. When shame is metabolized, limitation and death is transformed into an oceanic moment of connection. Outer strength, the kind that identifies with power, becomes inner strength and reconciliation to his human lot. This feeling is described well by Pressfield in the words of a Spartan warrior: "I and every man there were never more free than when we gave freely obedience to those harsh laws which take life and give it back again" (1998: 361).

In the transformation of symbiosis into a unity with the mother, maternal reverie, the mindful reflection a mother gives her child, becomes the transcendent function, a term that Jung defined as a true labor, a natural "process of coming to terms with the unconscious" (1953: 80) that involves both action and suffering. The transcendent function bridges the yawning gulf between rational and irrational, thinking and feeling, conscious and unconscious. The ego begins to see through the higher consciousness of intuition. The ego stands on the ground of the self, and information passes between them. The individual is empowered by his own consciousness infused by the maternal feminine.

Man's first natural, instinctual self can be transformed into a spiritual self. Spirit can only be spirit when it is mediated through Mother Nature. The death of the ego is an attempt of spirit to know itself, the only true resolution of dependence on the mother. The self that gradually and painfully emerges from one's struggle with evil and instinct rises from the ashes of shame. Transcendent spirit wins its independence from every form of externality; otherness becomes a part of the totality of self, consciousness and freedom.

Man also moves towards participation in the created order as an equal, neither superior nor inferior. The emergence of weakness as a permitted masculine attribute depends upon a man's integrated awareness that he stands as one among a world of interdependent individuals. His shame is not to be feared, for it simply includes him in humanity's lot, which even God had to join if he were to reconcile himself to his failings towards humankind. Woman can be seen in a new light: rather than seeing the evil succubus, a woman becomes the mother who bears the mystery and misery of life through his seed, as well as providing for his pleasure. Recognition at both the infantile and Oedipal levels of the maternal feminine, described below, are restored:

> a simplicity and openness with regard to existence ... (an) attitude of a being who exists gladly, is unashamed of existing, stands upright in existence and for whom to be and to accept the natural limitations of existence are matters of equally simple assent. Trees and animals are like this.
>
> (Maritain, 1943: 17)

Then he can bond, share, emotionally relate, and reveal himself in full nakedness to a woman – as he is now fully human.

Archetypal images for the transformation of shame

Literature provides countless stories that depict an emergence from a death of the ego. For the sake of brevity, let's take a look only at images linked to the work of Freud and Jung. Emergence from the death of the ego can look like Perseus' experiences in Barth's re-telling of the story of Medusa's beheading. In *Perseid*, Perseus opens his closed eyes and meets those of Medusa (in order to cut off her head he was not allowed to look into her eyes). He discovers her beauty and realizes that there is no other true love. He returns to kiss her and gaze into her open eyes. Since then, the two lovers lay side by side as constellations in the skies. Medusa says that she is still tormented by the thought that perhaps Perseus' decision to look directly at her was "an act not of love but of suicide, or a desperate impulse to immortality-by-petrifaction." What she saw when she looked at her reflection in his eyes was a Gorgon, as Athena had foretold. Perseus assures her that he beheld in her eyes "two things in instantaneous succession." First, he saw himself as he was – no longer a hero but still vigorous and "grown too wise to wish his time turned back." Second "were the stars in her own eyes, reflected from his and re-reflected to infinity – stars of quite a miraculous, yes blinding love, which transfigured everything in view" (Barth, 1972: 133).

The ego dies when it is exposed to more shame than it can tolerate – and lives through it. Think of Oedipus who loses his kingdom, his position of power and wealth, and becomes the pollution of Thebes. Upon his realizations he gouges out his own eyes, and by doing so becomes a blind seer. In Sophocles' subsequent tragedy, *Oedipus at Colonus*, the old, blind Oedipus finds respite at last in the grove of the Erinyes, representatives of ancient maternal power. He returns to the maternal feminine, and so death crowns his tragic life with mystical solemnity. In the end, Oedipus the King, through the crash of his heroic fate, realizes the truth about himself: that he is an inferior, weak and small creature. And yet it is this knowledge that reconnects him to the earth. Blind and infirm, "the lightless depths of Earth bursting open in kindness to receive him" (Sophocles/Fagles, 1982: 364), the Great Mother takes her son back into herself. Only through her containment in the eternal round of existence can a man live with the truth of his existence.

> [Oedipus] is one of the great human figures whose agony and suffering lead to more gracious and civilized behavior, who, still embedded in the old order of which they are the products, stand there as its last great victims, and at the same time as founders of a new age.
>
> (Bachofen, 1948: 442)

In his *hubris*, Oedipus was possessed by a preconceived notion of who he was, and this prevented him from seeking or seeing otherwise. In other words, pride reigned supreme to the exclusion of other thoughts. Upon his own self-castration by plucking out his eyes, he overcomes his ego-inflated blindness and is strengthened by the tragic insight rather than succumbing helplessly to it.

Attis is another male who castrates himself. Remember the phallic rock carving of Attis from Jung's garden? He was a god eventually driven insane by his mother's mad love for him. He castrated himself, symbolic of a man's resistance to incest in protection of the mother of infancy. His auto-castration represents subservience to the Great Mother in an age where as yet there was no father to stand by the side of the son, a very different form of male sexuality that is so prized today.

The story of Jesus Christ

Special attention must be given to the biblical story of Jesus Christ, a story of reconciliation with shame (Miles, 2001). Jesus is the ultimate hero who provides a model for the transformation of shame for all of mankind: and this story is told through the idea of the Christ principle. God incarnates into Jesus through the Virgin Mary and is being crucified as the Christ so that everyone who believes in him may have eternal life. The Old Testament God is one of unquestioning invincibility, a wrathful warrior who through his mighty power torments His Chosen People. His shame and failure, however, is great: he has never fulfilled his promise to them. He simply protects the people of Israel by destroying their enemy, or curses and abandons them to their conquerors. The Israelites become either the winners or the losers.

The idea of Jesus, the very antithesis of a warrior, is conceived in God's realization of his failure. Just like any other man, God was blind to his weakness and had to discover his vulnerability by succumbing to it. Rather than projecting the blame blindly, the ultimate party finally accepts responsibility. When shame is included, the new creation somehow requires in turn the death of the creator. The "improbable and appalling conjunction of expiatory lamb and messianic warlord" is conceived; the disturbing power of Jesus as a character has everything to do with these two images (Miles, 2001: 27). "All mankind is forgiven, but the Lord must die ... This victim is God Incarnate, the Lord himself in human form" (pp. 3–4). "As God, the Lord cannot cease to exist; but as Jesus Christ, he can taste death [cease to exist] in the same way Adam and Eve were cursed to suffer their shame" (p. 4). God chose to undergo a human death in order to reveal to the world the full, mixed truth about Himself. The image of Christ on the cross depicts both the essence of His woundedness, His humanity, and yet these are visible signs of His powers of transcendence that triumph over shame, the sins inherited by all of humankind from the succubus.

When looked at through the eyes of shame, the story of Christ becomes a story of the warrior hero transformed into a resurrected victim. God, a messianic warlord who became human to cleanse the world of the sins brought on by the succubus Eve has revoked his ancient curse. The pacifist power of Christ is not power over, but the power of the victim against the victimizer – in other words, the power of that flicker of shame in the soul of the victimizer, the spark of conscience, activated by the empowerment that comes to the submitting shamed self through sacrifice. Miles (2001) provides a visceral image that amplifies the transformative power of shame and the face in such a process:

> What Jesus said, to quote the shocking line again and this time in Mathew's more revealing formulation, is "If someone strikes you on the right cheek, turn the other to him as well" (Matt. 5:39). Supposing a right-handed attacker, the blow should fall on the left cheek. That it falls on the right means that it is a backhanded slap, the kind delivered by a master to a slave or a ruler to a subject. If the victim then turns his left cheek towards his attacker, he places the features of his face where his right cheek had been when the first slap landed. He dares his master, his ruler, or whoever it is who has insulted him to insult him further by landing a second blow squarely on his nose and mouth. Thus does the victim shame the victimizer, forcing insolence into consciousness of itself and then, perhaps, into repentance.
>
> (2001: 126)

When conscience develops, shame has served its purpose. The death of John the Baptist, the man ultimately beheaded for speaking truth to Roman power and shaming Herod's wife (engaging the succubus), actually serves a much greater purpose: Herod, a man of great power without a conscience, begins to have one (Miles, 2001). Later, he does not sentence Jesus to death, but sends him on to Pontius Pilate to decide. With the restoration of Herod's conscience, the meaning of Salome is also transformed. Instead of remaining an evil and seductive succubus who beheads John the Baptist, she can be envisioned with the Prophet Elijah (of the Old Testament), who later returns as John the Baptist (of the New Testament) "for all eternity" (Jung, 1965).

Jesus "takes away the sins of the world" through his submission to shame. Through the resurrection of his victimized body, shame is transcended and the succubus in the form of Mary Magdalen is redeemed, the wronged and lost sacred feminine sought after by countless knights in what has been called the quest for the Holy Grail (Brown, 2003: 257). She is the first to discover his resurrected body in the tomb.

Sacrifice and depth psychology

And what might castration mean for the field of depth psychology? How can psychology facilitate a transformation of masculine gender ideas? We can begin by sacrificing some of our most cherished tenets, and the need for this is inevitable because we cannot ultimately "close the eyes" to the "revenge of the repressed."

The first tenet to sacrifice is the concept of matricide. The field of depth psychology must come into a full recognition of the maternal and realize the psychically violent and traumatic nature of the separation expectations of the male from his mother. Jung and Freud's "act of matricide" and the need to fit into heroism is fertile ground for the profound distortions of reality that result in evil and a denial of shame. It creates a miscarriage of the development of self in which a man has no life in which to be true to himself.

Secondly, we must recognize the primacy of the maternal feminine in the deepest levels of psychic reality. Depth psychology can facilitate a return of the maternal feminine and alternatives to masculinity by breaking the cycle of power, conquest and domination through the realization that masculine autonomy is, in fact, an illusion, and facilitates destruction rather than creation. This needs to occur without committing patricide, for that would only create a situation for the son to end up in an Oedipal marriage with the mother. Indeed, we must not forget that Freud and Jung were right: if the father is killed an unconscious return to the mother and infantilism, satiety and self-destruction is precipitated in the false paradise of maternal source. This constitutes a loss of self through an identification with the maternal, archeyptal world – masculinity falling into the unconscious. This results in the same dynamics as matricide; compensatory eruptions and explosions of narcissistic masculinity.

Our notions about masculinity and femininity are not so much the contents of knowledge that come to us through history and science as the structures of consciousness that come to us from myth. This is why, for example, the particulars of myths were changed to manipulate the image of the witch as Abusch (2002) identified through ancient Babylonian texts. This is where maternal images of dependency for the necessities of life, the woman who lies at the heart of human and humane existence, need to be discovered and differentiated in order to properly serve the feminine archetypes. Deep impulses in the collective unconscious must be allowed to enter our contemporary thought – cavernous shame whose avoidance is built into humankind's societal and psychological foundation. To effect the psychic transformation of gender ideas, we need to turn towards myth, not science. And since patriarchy is notoriously resistant to change, the myths should not lull us back into illusion, but in their boldness be truly generative (see Epilogue).

And last but not least, depth psychology must sacrifice the scientific position adopted by both Freud and Jung. The transformation of masculine shame requires a unification of the scientific and spiritual perspectives. In other words, the scientific perspective of the human condition coincides with a religious understanding of human nature. In thinking it was just as good in addressing the needs of humanity, psychoanalysis sought to replace religion, and so became an intricate symbolic system that is covertly spiritual. Depth psychology, however, will never replace religion, and the spiritual will never be reduced to the psychological. Both may seek self-knowledge and liberation of the self (soul), but in a deep process of self-confrontation that entails vision of one's shame, one inevitably arrives at faith, the ultimate fulcrum for creative, psychic change. Kierkegaard/Lowrie describes faith this way: "not that [faith] annihilates dread, but remaining ever young, it is continually developing itself out of the death throes of dread" (1844/1957: 140). Faith naturally emerges as a way of finding coherence, meaning and purpose in the darkness of chaotic, maternal forces.

Due to an individual as well as a collective need to face our shame, the time is ripe for a synthesis that covers the best in both depth psychology and religion. Consider the words of Hogart Mauer, past President of the American Psychological Association and secular thinker who committed suicide several years ago:

> For several decades we psychologists have looked upon the whole problem of sin and moral accountability as a great incubus and we have acclaimed our liberation from sin epic making. But at length we have discovered that to be free in this sense, that is to be sick rather than sinful, is to court the danger of also becoming lost. In becoming amoral, ethically neutral and free, we have cut the very roots of our being, lost our deepest sense of self hood and identity, and with neurotics now find ourselves asking, who am I, what is my deepest destiny, what does living really mean.
>
> (Zacharias, 1999)

Shame and the human evil that results from its denial need to be understood in conjunction with spirituality. At the edge of shame, one transcends the world into some spiritual dimension which contains tremendously purposeful, creative energy. When a man feels his shame in his utter dependence and vulnerability, and hands over his life to its meaning and value, he submits to forces beyond his control and is led to faith. How could this not be the case when a man realizes that he cannot omnipotently make the world into something that it cannot be – free of pain, suffering, and most of all, shame.

Shame and depth psychology

The study of the unconscious is about probing human experience, the inner work of stripping an individual down to his real self. An obstacle to this pursuit, however, is masculine shame – both the fact that man is ashamed, as well as the fact that he is even ashamed because he has not faced his shame. Shame can be used in the unpacking and disassembling of patriarchy, and the development of new meanings and metaphors for masculinity. Through it we may find a way forward, toward a respectful, unified, interdisciplinary integration of knowledge which does not simply steamroll over distinction and difference. Perhaps the recognition of this kind of shame can lead to a unification of Freud and Jung's ideas on the basic problems of life, the synthesis of animal instinct and transcendence, body and spirit – the duality of Lilith that reconciles us to our human lot. And in this pursuit we can begin with what both Freud and Jung knew without a doubt: that the "return of the repressed" comes back with a vengeance, so the best we can hope for is to lessen the quantity of evil we spawn.

Thompson (1981) describes what he calls *Seraph*, a transcendent form of the Eternal Feminine created by the vibrations of music and mathematics. Her being manifests in a thousand eyes that glisten like facets of a diamond. Thompson's being is an angelic one whose "consciousness is not polarized between crotch and crown, genitals and brain" [the masculine places shame has been repressed], but is "completely holographic." This image evokes very different feelings than Cezanne's *Eternal Feminine*, painted by the artist as a stripped female body with bloody eye sockets. By envisioning the inevitable shame of humanity in order to make it visible, mankind may be able to turn destructive energies to a creative use – diabolized eyes transfigured into diamond eyes. Besides, the enormity of our crises cannot afford the politics of masculine conquest and the garnering of power that has created them in the first place. We've been repeating the same societal plot of domination, power over, sadism, masochism, oppression and victimization – the projection of masculine shame and the denial of the maternal feminine – for many thousands of years. In this turn of the spiral of history masculine heroics of ego and materialism are self-destructive. Is it presumptuous to imagine that depth psychology might claim to be able to address a problem of this magnitude?

Epilogue

Envisioning a return of the eternal feminine

> The darkening of the sky above man has always prevailed in proportion to how the shame of man in front of man has increased.
>
> (Nietzsche, *The Genealogy of Mortals*)

> When you know the male yet hold onto the female,
> You'll be the ravine of the country.
> When you are the ravine of the country,
> Your constant virtue will never leave.
> And when your constant virtue doesn't leave
> You return to the state of the infant.
>
> (Lao Tze)

> I proposed to do good (with her),
> And I was not put to shame, for I found her.
> My soul was attached to her,
> And I turned not away my face from her;
> I spread forth my hands to the heavens above,
> And for ever I will not go astray from her.
>
> (Sirach 51: 18–20)

> To Earth, Mother of All
> Earth who is mother of all shall I sing on your noble foundation.
> Eldest are you and you feed everything that exists in the world, all
> Those that inhabit the glorious surface of the earth and the deep sea,
> Plus those that fly in the air – they are fed, every one from your bounty!
> By you are excellent children and fruitfulness brought to perfection,
> Lady, there lie in your hands both the giving of life and the taking,
> Where mortal men are concerned. He is happy whom you in your humor
> Willingly honor, for everything then will be his abundance…
>
> (Homeric Hymn, Greece, sometime before 700 B.C.)

Today, many leading figures in human thought claim that we are at the end of a planetary age. This is a time of shifting from one mentality to another, when the insides of nature erupt into another form of being, a new chapter being written in our own time as civilization prepares to receive the conception of a new one. Matriarchal culture lived at the edge of a vanishing world in 5000 B.C., just as patriarchal culture does now in 2000 A.D. We are past the point of no return on a lot of the established masculine ways of doing things, and the necessity to explore and evaluate the new gestalt which seems to be emerging lies with the domain of depth psychology. It is my belief that shame has been studied intensively over the last 30 years not only because it had formerly been neglected as a core problem of the self, but also due to its necessary role in our shifting planetary needs at this time.

Masculine shame entered world history as the tragic flaw of patriarchy. It laid concealed in the chasm that opened up between heart and mind, intuition and reason, soul and body, woman and man. Its denial led to human evil, which is, in turn, creating an inhuman environment in which we are attempting to be human beings. The enormous increase in technological power and military might that civilization has brought with it joins with the enormous increase in aggressiveness and violent impulses that develop to repress shame. The stage is now set for the apocalyptic tragedies that the history of civilization, mythology and science suggest can indeed happen.

Seen or unseen, visible or invisible, recognized or unrecognized – there is an immense challenge for mankind in the transformation going on outside the frame of ordinary human perception. In other words, there is a completely different drama going on in the world than the one we think we see. Massive collective repression grows in negativity as the maternal feminine is banished from consciousness, and the content of patriarchal repressions has been intensifying over the past seven thousand years. Lilith is the repository for masculine shame and evil, two strands that fell between the cracks in the transition from matriarchy to patriarchy synthesized into her being. The "return of the repressed," therefore, means that Lilith will lead the way in raising consciousness to a new level if humanity is to survive as our patriarchal world comes apart. Thompson describes "the archangel of evolution" inevitably created out of this deep repression, and her eruption out of the collective unconscious into culture:

> But if the feminine is totally repressed and blood, nature, and the esoteric dimension of the heavens totally wiped out, then a terrible situation is created which will necessitate the appearance of another avatar of evolution, a Lilith of transformation through destruction.
>
> (1981: 241)

Where patriarchal civilization developed, the affect of shame began to be repressed and split-off into the deepest recesses of our being. This constellated shame's most petrifying feature – the absence of humanity. This calloused force, grown demonic due to its denials, may now be dominating and oppressing a world that can no longer master the disruption. We are so advanced in a state of entropy that, archetypally speaking, Lilith forces us into this fix so that our evolution can keep moving. This is the portentous power of negativity, the creative energy contained in evil discussed earlier, the meaning of Lilith's desolation, her "place of repose" in the Great Mother's round of eternal return. Envisioned imaginally through the eyes of shame, the current entropy and manmade evils of our world is an epiphany of the Great and Terrible Mother Goddess, the black hole lit by the light of stars.

Mankind's attempts at heroic conquering, a position that justifies his plunder of the earth's resources, has resulted in our destruction of the natural order. Opening our eyes to contemporary conditions reveals that we are inundated with archetypal manifestations of Lilith's decimation: we live menaced by terrorism and an invisible ocean of electromagnetic and chemical pollution; unprecedented numbers of animal species are going extinct; millions of human beings suffer humiliating poverty; there is a fertility crisis, and medical technology has taken over the creation of children in petri dishes; on the other hand, human social life is an almost uninterrupted, escalating series of mass slaughters and genocidal wars; autoimmune diseases and cancers proliferate, while pandemics and environmental destruction threaten humanity's future on the planet; the global economy has been exposed as the ultimate sleight of hand illusion right on Wall Street, the financial capital of industrial civilization. And rising temperatures and the meltdown of the ice caps are a threat to the continuation not only of civilization but more importantly of the human species – those for whose sake civilization was invented in the first place. All in all, our omnipresent catastrophic environment reflects the hubris of our omnipotence and omniscience.

Under Lilith's evil spell, conscience has been lost. Our value systems have disintegrated into utter shamelessness. Many people have lost their roots and feel alienated in the world, which devalues the invisible in favor of the more concrete, visible markers for success. People mistake this for reality, and so narcissism constitutes our world of individual and private property, our ego ownership of objects that become containers for identity. The fall out of civilization is selfishness, shameless greed that denies death, destruction, craving for power, and a maternal deprivation that creates deeply pathological disorders of containment. In the heart of this narcissism and its varied manifestations, the succubus is very much alive – and all too evident in the places where the forces of nature are hidden. Evil wrought through mankind derives its powers of temptation from shame sensitivity. And so it is that for mankind, the sting of shame is the antidote for the disease of power and infantile narcissism which is destroying civilization.

The succubus is returning from repression in her form as the "Maid of Desolation," and in order to effect reconciliation with her, mankind can no longer keep her down under him.

> If he seeks to continue his domination of nature through … the repression of the spiritual, he will ensure that the only release from his delusions can come from destruction. Lilith will then dance in the ruin of Western civilization. But if man can accept initiation to see that Lilith is his long-lost primordial wife, then the energies of destruction can be transmuted and taken up into the

> creative destructuring of the old civilization, the industrial civilization that humanity has already outgrown.
>
> (Thompson, 1981: 251)

Lilith rising up through the air to flee Adam is the rising up from "below," the place of the maternal feminine, of all that would be denied by "the above," the place of the masculine. The shadow cast by our civilization, which has made a single polluted city of our entire world, is that of Lilith "who dances in the ruins of cities." Power thinks that man's ingenuity is stronger than Mother Nature's, but we're living and "looking through the glass darkly" to imagine that wielding any amount of force, whatever form it takes, will prevent the world as we know it from vanishing in one glance from her Evil Eyes.

A culture that creates the succubus is a culture of limitation and death. The revolt of Lilith expresses the explosion of all that would be denied by patriarchal consciousness. The intensity of repressed contents only intensifies her terribleness, and it is for this reason that today we deal with forms of death that are unequivocally annihilating and from which there may be no return. What September 11 should teach us is that what is familiar to our sight, like the Twin Towers of the World Trade Center, can be incinerated in "six seconds," to quote a National Geographic program.

Some of the greatest thinkers of our time have seen the backlash for repression coming for some time. Becker (1975) has this to say about mankind's psychology and the Earth:

> Today we are living the grotesque spectacle of the poisoning of the earth by the nineteenth century hero system of unrestrained material production. This is perhaps the greatest and most pervasive evil to have emerged in all of history, and it may even eventually defeat all of mankind.
>
> (1975: 156)

Jung (1954) would probably agree. He believed that repression is not only bad for women, but for the whole human race. A cornerstone of Analytical Psychology is the feminine, which Jung felt if not restored to its archetypal place might be catastrophic for mankind. Although the repression of the feminine creates especially poignant problems for women, its restoration may be necessary for the psychic health of all people.

> It is a task that today faces not only individuals but whole civilizations. What else is the meaning of the frightful regressions of our time? The tempo of the development of consciousness through science and technology was too rapid and left the unconscious, which could no longer keep up with it, far behind, thereby forcing it into a defensive position which expresses itself in a universal will to destruction.
>
> (1954: 349)

At the end of his life, Freud seemed to share Jung's point of view. He had the foresight to see that the human species would come to extinction through its uncontrolled destructiveness. He spoke very little about the basic human drive towards destruction until after the age 60. Yet over time, it became clearer and clearer to him just how pervasive the human inclination towards destruction is – and that's when Freud began to talk about love. He wrote that it was neither reason, nor intelligence, nor science, nor the superego that would contain aggression (1964e: 122). Only Eros could serve mankind in the struggle with the psychic forces of destruction:

> But no one is under the illusion that nature has already been vanquished ... There are the elements, which seem to mock at all human control: the earth, which quakes and is torn apart and buries all human life and its works; water, which deluges and drowns everything in a turmoil; storms, which blow everything before them; there are diseases, which we have only recently recognized as attacks by other organisms; and finally there is the painful riddle of death, against which no medicine has yet been found, nor probably will be. With these forces nature is up against us, majestic, cruel and inexorable; she brings to our mind once more our weakness and helplessness, which we thought to escape through the work of civilization.
>
> (p. 15)

> Men have brought their powers of subduing the forces of nature to such a pitch that by using them they could now very easily exterminate one another to the last man. They know this – hence arises a great party of their current unrest, their dejection, their mood of apprehension. And now it may be expected that the other of the two "heavenly forces," eternal Eros, will put forth his strength so as to maintain himself alongside of his equally immortal adversary.
>
> (p. 144)

Thompson would agree with Freud on the importance of Eros – and adds an essential ingredient he missed:

> In the world epoch about to begin it is a sacrament of Eros, a physical sexuality in which lovers of eternity give birth to the world on the physical plane. The avatars of the New Age, as the Irish mystic A.E. realized in a vision fifty years ago, will not be the solitary male, but the male and the female together.
>
> (1981: 254)

One way or another – call it what you will – the maternal feminine must be re-visioned in order to avoid our own foreseen destruction. Her destructiveness seems to be the price mankind pays for individuation – and at this point she has him by the balls. Lilith has arrived, and through the sun, a symbol for masculine, ascendant, solar power, she is sucking the planet dry.

The Revenge of Gaia (Lovelock, 2000, 2006)

When a way of living is in the process of vanishing, people strive to hold on to it. What is disappearing finds more intense expression, like the supernova of a star in its last gasp of light. Examination of the shifting mentalities from a depth psychological perspective brings the core of narcissism (absolute masculine shame) created by the absence of the maternal feminine clearly into focus; and when one sees this, one can't miss the fact that it is being psychotically enacted collectively. In Thompson's (1981) words, "catastrophism is crystallizing" (p. 46).

Global warming

Nature in the form of weather and the reversal of the Earth's magnetic field are, at least at this point, beyond the management of science. Critical transformations of civilization are associated with profound climatic instability, and so it is an area where the invisible transfiguration of human culture is also taking place. Culture takes nature for granted, but when the weather changes, humankind is forced to change. We are forced into another ecological niche – and we are outgrowing the present one very quickly.

Such a difficult time is facing us now. During this period of transition, we deal with what scientists have named global warming, a phenomenon which is producing unprecedented climatic changes. I would be reaching far beyond my competence to discuss cellular evolution and atmospheric chemistry, but there is a new scientific imagination that provides a bridge to discuss these planetary changes in psychological terms. This is a necessity due to the collective psychic fact that great ages of transition, and their attendant climate changes, are psychologically difficult times; chaos erupts from the upsurges in the collective unconscious and can occupy the entire psychic energy of the people.

All planetary awakenings are invisible; yet the story of this kind of transformation is accessible through the patterns contained in myths – and the imagery of the collective unconscious is enduring. Mythological themes associated with the Maid of Desolation's catastrophic revenge run parallel to the ideas in the award-winning "visionary scientist" James Lovelock's (2000, 2006) narratives on global warming and its role in humanity's future. Lovelock has linked the evolution of the planet with human evolution through the myth of Lilith. His theory is called the Gaia Hypothesis, named after the ancient Greek mother goddess of the earth (also known as *Ge*, the root word of geology and geography). Lovelock explains:

> Unfortunately for me, the way forward splits at a cruel bifurcation. To establish Gaia as a fact I must take the first path, that of science. As a guide on the

> best way to live with the Earth, it will only be believed if it comes with the majority support from the scientific community – politicians and governmental agencies dare not act on myth – and demand scientific approval. To keep Gaia as something we all can understand I must take the second path, the one that goes to the postmodern world. Here science itself is questioned, but the Gaia of this book is acceptable even to statesmen and stateswomen.
>
> (2000: p. xi)

His evolutionary theory of advanced science invokes the ancient Goddess of the Earth to explain the processes of global warming. Lovelock (2000) proposes that the Earth has been shaped by life, defined as one of those processes which are found whenever there is an abundant flow of energy. As I understand it, life is characterized by a tendency to shape or form itself as it consumes, but to do so it must always excrete low-grade products to the surroundings. Rather than viewing the Earth as a big rock that circles the sun and happens to host a thin, slim encrusted layer of life on the surface, the Earth is considered to be a living, self-regulating entity much like the human body: it can control the salinity of the seas, the temperature of the surface, and the level of oxygen in the atmosphere. Life began to "take charge" of the planet to regulate itself. Thompson (1989) summarizes the concept clearly, "the largest living thing on earth is the planet itself" (pp. 48–49). In this holistic vision of the planet, the entire range of living matter on Earth, from whales to plagues, from redwoods to algae, all is regarded as constituting a single living entity capable of manipulating the Earth's atmosphere to suit the balance of its needs overall. In the same way that a group of individuals becomes more than the mere sum of its parts, the Earth is endowed with faculties and powers far beyond those of its constituent parts.

Gaia, however, is out for revenge. The Earth's atmosphere, the metabolism of a complex organism, has been poisoned. Air is a gaseous fluid into which toxic substances have been dumped. Cities pull in huge amounts of water, goods, timber, metal and people, and export large amounts of toxins in the form of household and industrial waste, wastewater and gases that are linked to global warming. The fact that no one seems to have been noticing has transformed Gaia from the Great Mother of Life to a killing succubus out for revenge. Only as the results of pollution and ecological destruction become severe enough to threaten even urban humanity's omnipotent powers of adaptability (a concept that reaches its pinnacle in the creation of Dubai from the desert) have we come to recognize the importance of ecological balance and the interdependence of the whole of life on our planet. And now our debt to life needs to be paid somehow.

The United Nations (UN) recently published a new environmental book of before and after satellite pictures illustrating the unmistakable disfigurement wrought by human hands of our once beautiful planet. The UN made the pictures available to the public "to serve as an early warning." If there is any message in the book that comes across loud and clear, it is that we are all of part of the Earth's destruction which will ultimately, if we continue the way we are going, render the planet unfit for life. The photos dramatically depict a world that is being taken over by cities – explosive urban sprawl, major deforestation and the sucking dry of inland seas over less than three decades – clear evidence of the devastating impact of our so-called civilization upon the Earth. We must transcend the patriarchal thinking that says it is only the good of civilization that matters, and realize that Gaia is alive. She has not been conquered by the matricidal hero, and she is not under mankind's control. In the intersubjective terms of psychology, she is an autonomous subject, and her subjectivity and how mankind is impacting her must be recognized.

Lovelock has discovered that the mythopoetic has its role to play in opening our eyes to the effects of global warming, which he feels is crucial, and thereby creates a link between atmospheric science and depth psychology. He uses the ancient ways of seeing imaginally, and writes in a simple form of arcane language, to reach the masses. The Gaia Hypothesis is a fine example of scientific data transformed as it is linked up to the imagination, a synthesis of the masculine and the feminine, thinking and feeling, science and mythology. It is not unlike the way depth psychologists turn to myths for answers to their questions. Lovelock returns the Earth to the Great Mother, for contained in his hypothesis is the survival of the old goddess religion, an esoteric mystery school right in the midst of the new exoteric society of heroes.

In order to restore our health physically and mentally, symbiosis needs to be transfigured into a unity with the mother on both intrapsychic and collective levels. In Havel's (1995) words

> according to the Gaia hypothesis, we are parts of a greater whole. Our destiny is not dependent merely on what we do for ourselves, but also on what we do for Gaia as a whole. If we endanger her, she will dispense with us in the interests of a higher value – life itself.

If science proves that Gaia is a living entity the relationship between her and humankind, a dominant animal species in a complex living system, and the shifting balance of power between them, becomes a concern of obvious importance that falls within the domain of depth psychology. Conceptually, the relationship between the Earth and humankind is no different than the relationship that exists between mother and child.

Displaced from her position of equality, Lilith seeks revenge upon the children of humanity. In repressing her, mankind is acting with complicity towards our own extinction. On a collective level, this occurs when we take from, plunder, rape, dominate and act without conscience towards the natural world in which we live. The repression of shame can be a powerful corruption that warps things up to the point that now our collective relationship to the very Earth from which we derive our life is threatened. Global warming is a clear manifestation of mankind being subject to destructive forces it does not understand, cannot control and thinks to master (as is the collapse of our global economy).

A world in transition

The Gaia Hypothesis is a new way of looking at the whole as the worlds of myth and science move closer together – exactly what both Freud and Jung were attempting to achieve. Lovelock's work clearly demonstrates a shifting mentality; science is transcending its own limits by straddling myth, the stories that contain the history of soul and create the preconditions of consciousness out of which science arises. In other words, soul and science spring from the same root structure of consciousness. As Thompson puts it,

> it is as valid to say that science is a dim intuition of a truth which the mystic experiences, as it is to say that myth is a dim intuition which only a scientist can prove. Myth and science seem to be like continents which are oceans apart, but if one dives into the depths of the sea, one discovers that the oceans cover that which is, in reality, the single crust of the planet.
>
> (1981: 48)

And so, while science studies climate change, psychology, the study of the soul, can look at bringing masculine shame and the loss of omnipotence into consciousness. In this endeavor, an understanding of the potential for transcendence in the reverie and recognition between mother and child, man and woman, Earth and humanity, can be a focus. Religious stories, a repository for the myths of humankind, provide the images. In ancient Egypt during the decline of the matriarchal age and rise of patrilinear succession, the story of Isis and Osiris was the prevailing, transitional myth. Isis is the Mother Goddess who fashions a wooden phallus to replace the castrated one from the dismembered Osiris, the man of the transition from matriarchal village to patriarchal civilization, and who is in the process transformed into the Lord of the Dead. From the union of Isis and Osiris, Horus is born, the son of the lame Father who demotes his mother, Isis – a movement which presages the patriarchal age.

Today, as patriarchy breaks up in the human psyche, it is releasing all the old unconscious programs. As mankind's shame presses to the surface, we encounter an epiphany of the Great Goddess with her male companion, in one form or another a dying male who becomes a castrated victim. God, Mary and Jesus – father, mother and son – pick up the problems of humanity where Isis, Osiris, and Horus left off. Isis rises in the form of the Virgin Mary who gives birth to the divine child, Jesus Christ, an incarnation of God on the physical plane. Jesus is the living embodiment of the mystery of a conscious death and rising from the dead on the material plane. Through the story of Jesus, which is a story of shame, consciousness descends into matter through the maternal feminine. In transcending shame through victimhood, Jesus is resurrected in the body. The sting of shame is the antidote for the blindness of power and narcissism (shamelessness) which is destroying civilization.

Developmentally and psychologically, the mother is our first object of love and therefore our first object in search for wholeness. Today, it is not the bonding between men that is required to kill which rose to power in 5000 B.C. that is needed: it is the empathic bonding between mothers and sons, between Mother Earth and humankind, between the Virgin Mary and Jesus, that is required if our species is to survive. Most of all, we must recognize that the Great Mother, in her embodiment as Earth, needs our recognition to avoid our own ultimate extinction. As Lovelock says, "we need to love and respect the Earth with the same intensity that we give to our families and our tribe" (Lovelock, 2000). This is a living, organic truth – the rest is culturally constructed.

Lovelock sees humans as part of a community of living things that keep the Earth a comfortable home. We are presently overdeveloping our niche – an expansion that, if continued, will produce catastrophically unthinkable results. Another contribution depth psychology can make towards facilitating a "return of the repressed" is a continued exploration of shame in order for the "release of the true perceptions of empirical reality in place of wishful cultural and private fantasies we put there [manifestations of omnipotence]" (Becker, 1975: 163). Psychology can also facilitate the harmonization of human beings and a changing culture that possesses a deeper recognition of the symbiotic ecology of people with the Earth. What global warming forces us to realize is that each of us is inextricably bound to others in relationship. All human action, even the act of a single individual, is relational and requires the presence of recognition – the opposite and cure for the blindness of projected shame.

We cannot exist without the Great Mother. In the words of Lovelock, "the well being of Gaia must always come before that of ourselves: we cannot exist without Gaia" (1991: 39). Like a flame that requires an atmosphere to burn, we require Gaia. In revenge driven by her search for recognition, the Terrible Mother with the Evil Eyes is on a mission to reveal the truth of things. The image of the succubus holds men's fears of humiliation and shame, the source of the energy from which she draws her powers of destruction. She will annihilate again and again in order to effect shame's revelation and restore sight of her beneficence.

Mine has been a small attempt to unsettle the ancient diabolization of Lilith in order to expose masculine shame in light of the modern world. Through this study, I have come to believe that a contribution depth psychology can make to our current human condition is to facilitate recognition of the maternal feminine. Accomplished through a confrontation with masculine shame, her recognition contains the potential to move us out of our current state of destruction, our petrifaction in shame, into whatever form may be our future. The succubus reveals the tragic flaw of civilization in order to create a different way of being at this point in our planetary development, a new mentality in the world that is guided by nature – hence the need for humankind's recognition of the Earth. The study of the soul can lead the way through ever deeper explorations into the "forest of shame" in order to understand the whole arrangement of psychological meaning in this affect. "Midway along the journey of life" when "I woke to find myself in a dark woods," I was led to just a glimpse of shame's deepest mysteries (Dante, *Inferno*, Canto 1).

Bibliography

Abusch, T. (2002). *Mesopotamian Witchcraft: Toward a History and Understanding of Babylonian Witchcraft Beliefs and Literature*. Leiden: Brill.

Aeschylus (1969). *Oresteia*, trans. Richmond Lattimore. Chicago: University of Chicago Press.

Alphabeta de'ben Sira. (1858). M. Seeinschneider (ed). Berlin.

Anzieu, D. (1986). *Freud's Self-Analysis*, trans. Peter Graham. Connecticut: Intl. Univ. Press.

Apuleius, L. (1639). *The Golden Asse of Lucius Apuleius*, trans. William Adlington. Great Britain: The Abbey Library.

Ayers, M. (2003). *Mother-Infant Attachment and Psychoanalysis: The Eyes of Shame*. Hove: Routledge.

Bachofen, J. (1948). *Das Muterrecht*. Basel.

Barth, J. (1972). *Chimera*. New York: Random House.

Becker, E. (1973). *The Denial of Death*. New York: Simon and Schuster.

—— (1975). *Escape from Evil*. New York: The Free Press.

Benjamin, J. (1988). *The Bonds of Love: Psychoanalysis, Feminism and the Problem of Domination*. New York: Pantheon.

Bennett, S. (1971). "Infant-caretaker interactions," *Journal of the American Academy of Child Psychiatry* 10: 321–355.

Bernstein, R. (2005). "Fall of the House of Von Kloberg," *The Washington Post*, July 31, D1–7.

Bollas, C. (1995). "The structure of evil" in *Cracking Up: The Work of Unconscious Experience*. New York: Hill and Wang.

Booth, W. (2005). "The undercover lawman who went hogwild," *The Washington Post*, October 18, C9.

Breuer, J. and Freud, S. (1893–1895). *Studies on hysteria*. Standard Edition, Vol. 2, trans. James Strachey. (Original work published 1922.)

Brown, D. (2003). *The DaVinci Code*. New York: Doubleday.

Broyles, W. (1984). Why Men Love War. *Esquire Magazine*.

Campbell, J. (1969). *Flight of the Wild Gander: Explorations in the Mythological Dimension*. New York: Viking Press.

Carotenuto, A. (1983). *A Secret Symmetry: Sabina Spielrein between Freud and Jung*. New York: Pantheon.

Coomaraswamy, A. (1973). "The Christian and Oriental or true philosophy of art" in *Why Exhibit Works of Art?* London: Luzec and Co.

Dickey, N. (2005). *Newsweek*. December 12, 32–35.

Dinnerstein, D. (1977). *The Maid and the Minotaur: Sexual Arrangements and Human Malaise*. New York: Harper Perennial.
Eigen, M. (1984). *Evil and Self*. New York: Human Science Press.
Eisler, R. (1987). *The Chalice and the Blade: Our History, Our Future*. San Francisco: Harper & Row.
Elworthy, F. (1958). *The Evil Eye: The Origins and Practices of Superstition*. New York: Macmillan.
El Saffar, R. (1994). *Rapture Encaged: the Suppression of the Feminine in Western Culture*. New York: Routledge.
Engelsman, J. (1979). *The Feminine Dimension of the Divine*. Pennsylvania: Westerminster Press.
Erikson, E. (1950/1985). *Childhood and Society*. New York: Norton.
Feldman, B. (1992). "Jung's infancy and childhood and its influence upon the development of analytical psychology," *Journal of Analytical Psychology* 37: 255–274.
Freud, E. (1960). *Letters of Sigmund Freud (1873–1939)*. London: The Hogarth Press.
Freud, H. (1956). "My uncle, Sigmund Freud" in H.M. Ruitenbeck (ed.) *Freud As We Knew Him*. Detroit: Wayne State University Press.
—— (1964a). "On the sexual theories of children" in James Strachey (trans.) *The Complete Psychological Works of Sigmund Freud*, Vol. IX, pp. 207–226. London: The Hogarth Press. (Original work published 1908.)
—— (1964b). "The future prospects of psychoanalytic psychotherapy" in James Strachey (trans.) *The Complete Psychological Works of Sigmund Freud*, Vol. XI. London: The Hogarth Press. (Original work published 1910.)
—— (1964c). "An infantile neurosis" in James Strachey (trans.) *The Complete Psychological Works of Sigmund Freud*, Vol. XVII. London: The Hogarth Press. (Original work published 1917.)
—— (1964d). "The dissolution of the Oedipus Complex" in James Strachey (trans.) *The Complete Psychological Works of Sigmund Freud*, Vol. XVIIII. London: The Hogarth Press. (Original work published 1924.)
—— (1964e). "Civilization and its discontents," in James Strachey (trans.) *The Complete Psychological Works of Sigmund Freud*, Vol. XXI. London: The Hogarth Press. (Original work published 1930.)
—— (1964f). "Female sexuality" in James Strachey (trans.) *The Complete Psychological Works of Sigmund Freud*, Vol. XXI, pp. 221–231. London: The Hogarth Press. (Original work published 1931.)
—— (1964g) "Medusa's head" in James Strachey (trans.) *The Complete Psychological Works of Sigmund Freud*, Vol. XXI. London: The Hogarth Press. (Original work published 1940.)
—— (1974). *The Freud/Jung Letters: The Correspondence Between Sigmund Freud and C.G. Jung*, William McGuire (ed.), trans. R. Manheim and R.F.C. Hull. Princeton, New Jersey: Princeton University Press.
Fromm, E. (1959). *Sigmund Freud's Mission: An Analysis of his Personality and Influence*. New York: Harper.
Frymer-Kensky, T. (1992). *In the Wake of the Goddess: Women, Culture and the Biblical Transformation of Pagan Myth*. New York: Fawcett Columbine.
Fuss, D. and Sanders, J. (1996). "Bergasse 19: Inside Freud's Office" in M. Garber and N. Vickers (eds) *The Medusa Reader* (2003), pp. 262–266. London: Routledge.
Gilligan, J. (1992). *Violence: Our Deadly Epidemic and its Causes*. New York: GP Putnam's Sons.

Gold, S. (1998). "Divine mornings" in E. Dame, L. Rivlin and H. Wenkart (eds) *Which Lilith? Feminist Writers Re-create the World's First Woman*. New Jersey: Jason Aronson.

Goldberg, H. (1976). *The Hazards of Being Male: Surviving the Myth of Masculine Privilege*. New York: Penguin Books.

Goux, J.J. (1993). *Oedipus Philosopher*, trans. Catherine Porters. California: Stanford University Press.

Grand, S. (2000). *The Reproduction of Evil: A Clinical and Cultural Perspective*. Hillsdale, NJ: Analytic Press.

Graves, R. (1955). *The Greek Myths*, 2 vols. Oedipus, Vol. 1, no. 85, Narcissus, Vol. 2. Harmondsworth: Penguin.

—— (1966). *The White Goddess: a Historical Grammar of Poetic Myth*. New York: Farrar, Straus & Giroux.

Grimm, J. and Grimm, W. (1944). *The Complete Grimm's Fairy Tales*. New York: Pantheon Books. (Original work published 1886.)

Grotstein, J. (1979). "Demonical possession: Splitting and the torment of joy," *Contemporary Psychoanalysis* 3: 407–445.

Grunberger, B. (1979). *Narcissism*, trans. J. Diamanti. New York: International Universities Press.

Havel, V. (1995). The need for transcendence in the postmodern world. *The Futurist*, Vol. 29, No. 4 / July/August.

Haviland, J. and Malatesta, C. (1981). "The development of sex differences in nonverbal signals: fallacies, facts and fantasies" in C. Mayo and N.M. Henly (eds) *Gender and Non-verbal Behavior*. New York: Springer-Verlag.

Hegel, G.W.F. (1967). *The Phenomenology of Mind*, trans. J.B. Baille. New York: Harper. (Original work published 1807).

Heinemann, E. (2000). *Witches: A Psychoanalytical Exploration of the Killing of Women*, trans. Donald Kiraly. London: Free Association Books.

Hurwitz, S. (1999). *Lilith: The First Eve*, trans. Gela Jacobson. Switzerland: Daimon Verlag.

Husain, S. (2003). *The Goddess: Power, Sexuality and the Feminine Divine*. Ann Arbor: University of Michigan Press.

Huxley, F. (1990). *The Eye: The Seer and the Seen*. London: Thames and Hudson.

Huxley, J. (1966). *From an Antique Land: Ancient and Modern in the Middle East*. New York: Harper & Row.

James, W. (1958). *The Varieties of Religious Experience*. New York: Mentor.

Johnson, R. A. (1989). *He: Understanding Masculine Psychology*. New York: HarperCollins.

Jones, E. (1953). *The Life and Work of Sigmund Freud*. New York: Basic Books.

Jung, C.G. (1925). "Marriage as a psychological relationship" in R.F.C. Hull (trans.) *The Collected Works of C.G. Jung*, Vol. 17. Princeton, NJ: Princeton University Press. (Original work published 1951.)

—— (1951). "The syzygy: anima and animus" in R.F.C. Hull (trans.) *The Collected Works of C.G. Jung*, Vol. 9, Part II. Princeton, NJ: Princeton University Press. (Original work published 1951.)

—— (1953). "Alchemy" in R.F.C. Hull (trans.) *The Collected Works of C.G. Jung*, Vol. 12. Princeton, NJ: Princeton University Press. (Original work published 1944.)

—— (1954). "Psychological aspects of the mother archetype" in R.F.C. Hull (trans.) *The Collected Works of C.G. Jung*, Vol. 9, Part I. Princeton, NJ: Princeton University Press. (Original work published 1938.)

—— (1955). "Symbols of transformation" in R.F.C. Hull (trans.) *The Collected Works of C.G. Jung*, Vol. 5. Princeton, NJ: Princeton University Press. (Original work published 1951.)

—— (1956). "Symbols of transformation". In H. Read (Ed.) *The collected works* (R.F.C. Hull, trans.) (Vol. 5). Princeton, NJ: Princeton University Press.

—— (1965). *Memories, Dreams and Reflections*, trans. Richard and Clara Winston. New York: Vintage Books. (Original work published 1961).

—— (1970). "After the catastrophe" in R.F.C. Hull (trans.) *The Collected Works of C.G. Jung*, Vol. 10. Princeton, NJ: Princeton University Press. (Original work published 1945.)

—— (1975). *C.G. Jung Letters*, Vol. 2, R.F.C. Hull (trans.). New Jersey: Princeton University Press (Original published 1953.)

—— (1989). *Analytical Psychology. Notes of the seminar given in 1925 by C.G. Jung*, William McGuire (ed.). New Jersey: Princeton University Press.

Keen, S. (1997). Foreword to *The Denial of Death*. New York: The Free Press.

Kerr, J. (1993). *A Most Dangerous Method*. New York: Random House.

Kierkegaard, S. (1957). *The Concept of Dread*, trans. Walter Lowrie. New Jersey: Princeton University Press. (Original work published 1844.)

Kramer, H. and Sprenger, J. (1971). *The Malleus Malefircarum of Heinrich Kramer and James Sprenger* trans. Montague Summers. New York: Dover Publications. (Original work published 1486.)

Lacan, J. (1993). *The Psychoses 1955–56*, trans. Russell Griggs. London: Routledge.

Lansky, M. (1995). "Shame and the scope of analytic understanding," *American Behavioral Scientist* 38, 8: 1076–1090.

Lerman, H. (1986). *Mote in Freud's Eye. From Psychoanalysis to the Psychology of Women*. New York: Spring Publishing Co.

Leroi-Gourhan, A. (1967). *Treasures of Prehistoric Art*. New York: Abrams.

Levy, G.R. (1948). *Gate of Horn: A Study of the Religious Conceptions of the Stone Age and their Influence upon European Thought*. London: Faber and Faber.

Lichtenburg, J. (1991). *Psychoanalysis and Infant Research*. Hillsdale, NJ: The Analytic Press.

Lovelock, J. E. (1991). *Healing Gaia*. New York: Harmony Books.

Lovelock, J. (2000). *Gaia*. Oxford, England: Oxford University Press.

—— (2006). *The Revenge of Gaia: Earth's Climate Crisis & the Fate of Humanity*. New York: Basic Books.

Mahler, M. (1975). *Psychological Birth of the Human Infant. Symbiosis and Individuation*. New York: Basic Books.

Maritain J. (1943). *Education at the Crossroads*. New Haven: Yale University Press.

Masson, J. (1985a). *The Assault on Truth: Freud's Suppression of the Seduction Theory*. New York: Penguin Books.

—— (1985b). *The Complete Letters of Sigmund Freud to Wilhelm Fliess 1887–1904*. Massachusetts: Harvard University Press.

Miles, J. (1996). *God: A Biography*. New York: Vintage Books.

—— (2001). *Christ: A Crisis in the Life of God*. New York: Vintage Books.

Neumann, E. (1974). *The Great Mother: An Analysis of an Archetype*, trans. R. Mannheim. Princeton, New Jersey: Princeton University Press. (Original work published 1955.)

Nietzsche, F. (1872/1956). *The Birth of Tragedy and the Genealogy of Mortals*. New York: Anchor Books.

—— F. (2007). *Ecce Homo: How To Become What You Are*, trans. Duncan Large. Oxford, UK: Oxford University Press. (Original work published 1908.)

Ovid. (1955) *The Metamorphoses, Book III, Echo and Narcissus*, trans. M. M. Innes. Harmondsworth: Penguin.

Pagels, E. (1979). "What became of God the Mother?" in C. Christ and J. Plaskow (eds) *Womanspirit Rising: A Femininist Reader in Religion*. San Francisco: Harper.

Pines, M. (1987). "Shame – what psychoanalysis does and does not say," *Group Analysis* 20: 16–31.

Pollack, W. (1998). *Real Boys*. New York: Henry Holt and Company.

Pressfield, S. (1998). *Gates of Fire*. New York: Bantam Dell.

Riker, J. (1997). *Ethics and the Discovery of the Unconscious*. New York: SUNY Press.

Robson, K. (1967). "The role of eye-to-eye contact in maternal-infant attachment," *Journal of Child Psychiatry* 8: 13–25.

Russell, J. (1984). *Lucifer: The Devil in the Middle Ages*. New York: Cornell University Press.

Sagan, Eli. (1988). *Freud, Women, and Morality: The Psychology of Good and Evil*. New York: Basic Books.

Salyard, A. (1988). "Freud as Pegasus yoked to the plough," *Psychoanalytic Psychology* 5: 403–429.

Sartre, J.P. (1956). *Being and Nothingness*, trans. H. Barnes. New York: Simon and Schuster. (Original work published 1953.)

Schiller, F. (1861). "Pegasus in harness," in C. Hempel (ed. and trans.) *Schiller's Complete Works*, Vol. I. Philadelphia: Kohler. (Original work published 1796.)

Schur, M. (1972). *Freud: Living and Dying*. New York: International University Press.

Seal, M. (2003). "Gianni Versace: from 'The Versace moment' by Mark Seal (1996)" in M. Garber and N. Vickers (eds) *The Medusa Reader*. UK: Routledge.

Shakespeare, W. (1936). "King Richard II" in W. Wright (ed.) *The Complete Works of William Shakespeare*. New York: Garden City Publishing.

Sophocles (1951). *Oedipus Rex*, trans. Dudley Fitts and Robert Fitzgerald. London: Faber and Faber.

—— (1982). *The Three Theban Plays: Antigone, Oedipus the King, Oedipus at Colonus*, trans. Robert Fagles. New York: Viking Penguin Inc.

Spielrein, S. (1994). "Destruction as the cause of coming into being," *Journal of Analytical Psychology* 39: 151–154.

Starhawk. (1979). *The Spiral Dance: A Rebirth of the Ancient Religion of the Great Goddess*. San Francisco: Harper & Row.

Stern, D. (1977). *The First Relationship*. Cambridge, MA: Harvard University Press.

—— (1985). *The Interpersonal World of the Infant: A View from Psychoanalysis and Developmental Psychology*. New York: Basic Books.

Stone, M. (1976). *When God was a Woman*. New York: Dial Press.

—— (ed.) (1984). "The Literature of the Jewish People in the Period of the Second Temple". *Compendia Rerum Iudaicarum ad Novum Testamentum*, Section II, vol. 2. Assen: Van Gorcum/Philadelphia: Fortress.

Tacey, D. (2007). "Remaking men: Jungian thought and the post-patriarchal psyche: reflections on psychology, culture and life," *The Jung Page*, January 31.

Thompson, W.I. (1978). *Darkness and Scattered Light*. New York: Anchor Press.

—— (1981). *The Time Falling Bodies Take to Light: Mythology, Sexuality, and the Origins of Culture*. New York: St. Martin's Press.

—— (1989). *Imaginary Landscape: Making Worlds of Myth and Science*. New York: St. Martin's Press.

—— (1998). *Coming Into Being: Artifacts and Texts in the Evolution of Consciousness*. New York: St. Martin's Griffin.

Von, Schubert, G. H. (1808). *Views of the Night Side of Natural Science*.

Walker, B. (2000). *Restoring the Goddess: Equal Rites for Modern Women*. New York: Prometheus Books.

Warshaw, R. (1994). *I Never Called It Rape: The MS Report on Recognizing, Fighting, and Surviving Date and Acquaintance Rape*. New York: Harper.

Wehr, G. (1987). *Jung: A Biography*, trans. David Weeks. Boston: Shambhala.

Weininger, O. (1907). *Sex and Character*. New York: Putnam.

Williams, S. and Williams, P. (1978). *Riding the Nightmare: Women & Witchcraft*. New York: Atheneum.

Winnicott, D.W. (1960). "The theory of the parent–infant relationship (1960)". In D.W. Winnicott, *The Maturational Processes and the Facilitating Environment* (pp. 37–55), London: Karnac. 1990.

—— (1964). *The Child, the Family and the Outside World*. Reading, MA: Addison-Wesley Publishing Co.

—— (1965). "Ego integration in child development" in *Maturational Processes and the Facilitating Environment*. New York: International Universities Press.

—— (1971). "Mirror role of mother and family in child development" in *Playing and Reality*. London: Tavistock.

—— (1992). "Metapsychological and clinical aspects of regression within the psycho-analytical set-up" in *Through Pediatrics to Psychoanalysis: Collected Papers*. New York: Brunner/Mazel.

Wright, W.A. (ed.) (1940). *The Complete Works of William Shakespeare. Cambridge Edition*. New York: Garden City Publishing.

Wyly, J. (1989). The perversions in analysis. *Journal of Analytical Psychology* 34: 319–337.

Zacharias, R. (1999). *Do Evil and Suffering Have Meaning?* CD.

Index